ENGAGING THE THOUGHT OF BERNARD LONERGAN

Engaging the Thought of Bernard Lonergan

LOUIS ROY

McGill-Queen's University Press
Montreal & Kingston · London · Chicago

ISBN 978-0-7735-4706-3 (cloth)
ISBN 978-0-7735-4707-0 (paper)
ISBN 978-0-7735-9887-4 (ePDF)
ISBN 978-0-7735-9888-1 (ePUB)

Legal deposit first quarter 2016
Bibliothèque nationale du Québec

Printed in Canada on acid-free paper that is 100% ancient forest free (100% post-consumer recycled), processed chlorine free

McGill-Queen's University Press acknowledges the support of the Canada Council for the Arts for our publishing program. We also acknowledge the financial support of the Government of Canada through the Canada Book Fund for our publishing activities.

Library and Archives Canada Cataloguing in Publication

Roy, Louis, 1942-, author
Engaging the thought of Bernard Lonergan / Louis Roy.

Includes bibliographical references and index.
Issued in print and electronic formats.
ISBN 978-0-7735-4706-3 (bound). – ISBN 978-0-7735-4707-0 (paperback). – ISBN 978-0-7735-9887-4 (PDF). – ISBN 978-0-7735-9888-1 (ePUB)

1. Lonergan, Bernard J. F. (Bernard Joseph Francis), 1904-1984. – Criticism and interpretation.
I. Title.

BX4705.L75R69 2016 230'.2092 C2015-907126-7
C2015-907127-5

Typeset by New Leaf Publication Design in 10.5/13 Sabon

Contents

Acknowledgments

Since the essays collected here were generally praised in classes or at congresses as clarifying Lonergan's thought, McGill-Queen's University Press and I wanted to make them accessible to a wider audience. I want to thank the Jackman Foundation in Toronto for their generous funding that helped bring this endeavour to completion.

I wish to express my gratitude to professors and students who attended my lectures on Bernard Lonergan at several universities or conferences: Boston College, Concordia University (Montreal), Dominican University College (Ottawa), Loyola Marymount University (Los Angeles), Oscott College (Birmingham, England), Saint Anselm College (Manchester, New Hampshire), Saint Paul University (Ottawa), Universidad Santo Tomás (Bogotá), Wonkwang University (Korea), the Lonergan Philosophical Society (USA), the Lonergan Research Institute at Regis College (University of Toronto), the Thomas More Institute (Montreal), and Lonergan workshops given in Boston, Rome, Toronto, and Seoul.

Some of the essays included in this book were previously published; all have been revised and a few have been expanded. I am grateful to Robert E. Czerny who translated Studies 1, 2, and 6 from French with a grant from the Jackman Foundation in Toronto. Moreover, he kindly offered numerous suggestions to enhance the clarity and style of the whole manuscript. I thank Pierre LaViolette and Anne Louise Mahoney, who translated Study 9, and Rev. Adam Bonaventure Chapman, Prof. Thomas Ewens, Dr Philippe Fluri, Prof. Charles C. Hefling, Prof. Kenneth Melchin, Prof. Giovanni Sala, the anonymous reviewers of the manuscript, and Kyla Madden and Kaarla Sundstrom of McGill-Queen's University Press, all of whom made clarifying and/or stylistic remarks. I also want to show my appreciation to Miriam Westen for compiling the index (done with monetary support from the Dominican University College in Ottawa).

I thank the following periodicals and publishers for permission to include reworked versions of previous studies:

"Rahner's Epistemology and its Implications for Theology," in *Lonergan Workshop*, ed. Fred Lawrence, vol. 22, 421–39 (Chestnut Hill, MA: Boston College, 2011) (Study 8).

"Grace, Mediation, and Liturgical Orientations," in *Lonergan Workshop*, ed. Fred Lawrence, vol. 9, 209–24 (Chestnut Hill, MA: Boston College, 1993) (Study 10).

"Lonergan on Catholic Education: A Few Suggestions," in *Faith Seeking Understanding: Learning and the Catholic Tradition*, ed. George C. Berthold, 155–63 (Manchester, NH: Saint Anselm College Press, 1991) (Study 11).

"Gandhi and Lonergan: The Issue of Human Authenticity," *Toronto Journal of Theology* 15 (1999): 127–38 (Study 13).

"Bernard Lonergan's Foundations for Human Rights," *Science et Esprit* 62 (2010): 313–22 (Study 14).

In all quotations, unless otherwise indicated, italization is by the authors themselves. Texts from Scripture come from *The New Oxford Annotated Bible* (*The New Revised Standard Version*). Since Lonergan wrote before inclusive language became normative, we have not reformed his English. Lastly, insofar as his two major books are concerned, namely *Insight*, first published in 1957,[1] and *Method in Theology*, first published in 1972,[2] references are given not in endnotes but in brackets within the main text.[3]

NOTES

1 Bernard Lonergan, *Insight: A Study of Human Understanding*, ed. Frederick E. Crowe and Robert M. Doran, volume 3 of *Collected Works of Bernard Lonergan* (Toronto: University of Toronto Press, 1992).

2 Bernard Lonergan, *Method in Theology* (Toronto: University of Toronto Press, 2003).

3 For another discussion of Lonergan, readers may be interested in Louis Roy, *Coherent Christianity* (Ottawa: Novalis, 2005), chapter 13, entitled "Bernard Lonergan: A Theologian in Dialogue."

ENGAGING THE THOUGHT OF BERNARD LONERGAN

Introduction

The Canadian philosopher-theologian Bernard Lonergan was born in 1904 to Irish-Canadian parents in Buckingham, now a part of Gatineau, Quebec. His secondary education took place at Loyola College's High School in Montreal, where he learned Latin and Greek and was steeped in English literature. At the university level, he studied mathematics, philosophy, and theology in England and in Italy. The last year of his long Jesuit formation took place in Amiens, France. Capable of speaking both English and French fluently, he was a model of Canadian bilingualism at a time when our bilingual citizens numbered far fewer than today. He could also read Italian and German. He taught in Montreal, Toronto, Rome, and Boston and he gave workshops at Jesuit universities, mainly in Canada and in the US. He was a member of the Order of Canada and received several honorary doctorates before his passing in Pickering, Ontario in 1984. The critical edition of his *Collected Works* (25 volumes) is being put together by University of Toronto Press.[1]

Since 1966 I have benefited greatly from my exposure to his outstanding creative works in philosophy and theology. From early adulthood on, after being led in class through his masterpiece, *Insight: A Study of Human Understanding*, I have remained convinced that he was far ahead of his time. Although I was not an intimate of Lonergan, I enjoyed several conversations with him as chief translator of *Method in Theology* into French. After – and some would say because of – this venture, I became a professor for twenty years at Boston College, one of the centres of Lonergan scholarship and a place where he himself taught during the last years of his career. I now live and teach in Ottawa, approximately thirty-five kilometres away from Buckingham, the town where he grew up.

Lonergan was taught philosophy in the context of modern scholasticism, a conceptualist, anti-historical, closed, and deceptively safe worldview from which he very soon distanced himself. One of the main influences upon his thinking was the thorough revision of Western perspectives on history and politics by brilliant German and British historians and philosophers. He was particularly impacted by these new perspectives in two waves: first in the 1930s, while still in the shock of the First World War and in the midst of a dire economic crisis with the social turmoil it entailed; and second in the 1950s, following the shock of the Second World War and during both the clash between Communism and the democracies and the stimulating confrontation between phenomenologists and existentialists. What is typical of him is the depth of his response to such challenges, namely a radical epistemology and methodology, thanks to which he came to grips with the basic problems raised by modern thinkers.

Lonergan is definitely a thinker for our twenty-first century, indeed for the third millennium. At least four reasons can be advanced for this assertion.

First, to an incomparable degree among modern philosophers, Lonergan understood how the human mind operates, both in its theoretical and in its practical activities. Indeed, his principal contribution was to gradually guide his readers towards intellectual self-knowledge. He was able to make that contribution because he had assiduously read Plato, Augustine, Aquinas, and Newman, along with experts in mathematics and the scientific method.[2] The American Protestant theologian Langdon Gilkey, formerly Professor of Theology at the University of Chicago, captures this point very well with his facetious remark: "Lonergan is one of the greatest minds of Christendom. I used to read Jacques Maritain or Etienne Gilson to find out what Roman Catholic intellectuals were thinking. Now I read Lonergan to find out what *I* am thinking."[3]

Second, Lonergan grasped the historicity of cultures. He detailed a balanced and nuanced account of the complementarity between universality and particularity in the humanities and in religious studies. One of his two principal works, *Method in Theology*, deals not with the contents of Roman Catholic theology but, as the title indicates, with a method, which purports to be transcendental, that is, universal. Since it is extendable to several forms of non-Christian experiences of God, this approach to religious phenomena warrants an ecumenical theology that recognizes a moderate pluralism.

Third, Lonergan's vision of a contemporary method places religious experience at the centre of theology. Thus much of what he presents in his corpus can equally count as philosophy of religion. Consequently, the Studies included here introduce and assess a good number of key philosophical and theological notions.

Fourth, Lonergan's influence has been and still is extensive. Since the 1950s, researchers inspired by him have advanced along new avenues of academic development. Throughout the book, I will refer to many of those advances.

Lonergan has much to offer to those who have engaged in a cognitive and affective journey and who enjoy sharing questions and discoveries with friends and colleagues. Most of the time, I have compared him favourably with other thinkers. I have frequently freely clarified his insights and drawn inferences for, and made applications to, various fields of human activity. In fact, he was keen on objectifying the functioning of the human mind not only in science and in history (as mentioned above) but also in religion, art, interpersonal relationships, and the everyday-life events prompting common sense decision making. Such significant implications reveal the richness of his thought, which sheds light on an amazingly great variety of issues. What he termed "generalized empirical method" is so encompassing that, in this relatively short book of mine, I have chosen not to cover all the topics into which he ventured. Nonetheless, I will broach a broad swath of subjects.

So this is not an introduction to all the facets of Lonergan's philosophy and theology but, as the title indicates, my project here consists in "engaging" his thought. My intention is simply to open up pathways for explorers of his ideas, that is, for those who want to walk – at times meditatively and at times argumentatively – along the manifold pathways in which his convictions can be actualized and expanded.

Accordingly, my aims are as follows: to represent his thinking faithfully, to further it (while at times changing the vocabulary for the sake of clarity), to compare it with other stimulating thinkers, and to demonstrate how seminal his works are for diverse areas. The objective of my book is to discuss Lonergan's ideas, not topics in themselves; the latter course would have required a comprehensive review of the bibliography on each topic, as we must do in a monograph or in an independent article on a particular topic.

These chapters should appeal to interested Canadians and Americans as well as to Anglophones and English speakers worldwide who have heard of and are intrigued by Lonergan's originality. Several of these Studies found in these pages bear on aspects of his thought that are seldom treated. Other Studies, which have become inaccessible or quasi inaccessible, are reprinted here after having been diligently reworked. And with due and sincere respect for most books and articles on Lonergan, these essays of mine are less for insiders but for a larger, more novice readership. The targeted audience consists of three groups: knowledgeable readers and pastors who entertain questions and have concerns about the place of wisdom, humanism, and critical thinking in our troubled twenty-first century; theologians and philosophers of religion; and present or former students, advanced or graduate, in theology or in religious studies. So in all probability my contribution will reach more than specialists of Lonergan because its content is both introductory and actualizing. Thus Part One introduces newcomers to his method and Parts Two, Three, and Four, which I think are creative and inspiring for our times, put his ideas in interaction with current issues.

Part One of this book presents a bird's-eye view of Lonergan's contribution to methodology, philosophy, and theology. Study 1 characterizes his method as empirical, in the sense that it starts with data about which one asks questions and advances towards verification and evaluation. In a biographical manner, his method refers to problems and thinkers that influenced him and reveals "what was going forward" (*Method*, 178) on his intellectual journey. Prompted by the reflections of natural scientists, practitioners in the human sciences, and historians, he proposed a self-knowledge and a self-appropriation that can serve the agenda of all such people, far from being confined to the domain of philosophers and theologians. This first Study also stresses the role of meaning as constituting the human world and it explains how, for Lonergan, the methodical mind can control meaning. It ends with comments on attempts to make use of this method and on criticisms that have been voiced regarding his overall program.

Study 2 adds that his method is integrative because it places philosophy and theology within the broad panorama of knowledge; to pinpoint this location, Lonergan compares the various realms of meaning and wonders where philosophy and theology fit. Given that Lonergan underlines the importance of human subjectivity, this Study compares the various realms of meaning and speculates where philosophy and theology fit. Given that Lonergan underlines the importance of human subjectivity, this Study also enquires into the relation of objectivity to subjectivity. Moreover, since he grants a considerable significance to what he calls "historical-mindedness," this Study weighs the impact of historicity upon philosophy and theology; it does so by specifying his eight functional specialties in theology. Finally, it promotes an intellectual engagement marked by an intent to be responsible and authentic in a world nonetheless torn by aberrations and inadequate policies.

Part Two discusses various elements of religious experience. Study 3 shows Lonergan's innovative (I am tempted to say: unique) understanding of religious experience – an understanding that is neither premodern nor typically modern. He situates religious experience within the global working of the human mind, as one of the manifold realms of meaning, and describes two movements: an ascending movement towards religious experience, and a descending movement from religious experience. In the end, I argue that Lonergan affords us a fine elucidation of the interaction between reason and faith.

Study 4 depicts what goes on at each level of human intentionality, that is, in our built-in fourfold tendency to intend reality. It highlights the two sides – intellectual and affective – of religious experience and then proceeds to find out how the process of coming to believe unfolds on each of the four levels of intentionality. Subsequently, it illustrates the continuity of Lonergan's thought with respect to past masters and uses the Thomist distinction between metaphorical and literal language as an example of this continuity. It then revisits Augustine's famous maxim "Believe in order to understand," and offers reflections on belief and the deepening of it – a deepening that is effectuated thanks to love and symbolism. Furthermore, since the exercise of human intentionality is marred by biases and stands in need of conversion, it spells out how each level of intentionality is touched by grace. As a final point, by drawing attention to human relatedness as the richest aspect of faith, it probes the complementarity between interiority and relatedness as the two components of intentionality.

Study 5 asks whether Lonergan sides with Schleiermacher and Wilfred Cantwell Smith against Thomas Aquinas concerning the pair faith/belief. It begins with Aquinas's three categories of believing: to believe God (= the formal aspect); to believe this or that (= the material object); and to believe in God (= the affective aspect). It observes that in Schleiermacher and Smith the formal aspect (to believe God) is absent and that, as a consequence, the material aspect (to believe this or that) and the affective aspect (to believe in God) cannot be normative. The last section of that Study resumes pursuing the question of whether Lonergan's position corresponds to that of Aquinas, or to that of Schleiermacher or Smith, or whether it should be equated with a third, distinctive position.

Study 6 highlights the paramount import of Lonergan's distinction between meaning and truth in regard to divine revelation. It contrasts two unilateral stances, one that accentuates meaning at the expense of truth, and the other that accentuates truth at the expense of meaning. It details how meaning and truth are intertwined in the functioning of the human spirit, not only in religion but in all domains. It then transfers the collaboration between meaning and truth to the twofold nature of the Christian experience: an interior inspiration operating in conjunction with an exterior revelation. It finishes off by stressing the role of affectivity in the passage from meaning to truth.

Study 7 explicates the shortcomings of both classicism and relativism. It presents the way Lonergan defines them and it contrasts the classicist notion of culture with the empirical notion of culture. Thereafter, it highlights all-important considerations in his writings, which are keys to overcoming the confinements of classicism and relativism: method as supplanting theory; human intentionality as self-transcending; subjectivity in search of objectivity; the progression from a perspective towards a universal viewpoint; and the compatibility between historicity and permanence concerning religious truth.

Part Three draws out implications of Lonergan's cognitional theory in four quite different areas: theology, mysticism, liturgy, and education. Study 8 uses Lonerganian tools as it demonstrates that Rahner misread Aquinas. It exposes the consequences of the German theologian's conceptualism in his own systematic theology, that is, on the doctrine of God, the beatific vision, and the Trinity. Lastly, it mentions his opinion about theological pluralism and finds it very close to relativism.

Study 9 applies Lonergan's understanding of consciousness to an accurate representation of the specific nature of mysticism. It differentiates three kinds of consciousness – mystical consciousness being one of them. It denounces a common misunderstanding of mysticism, which construes it as an experience of objects. It shows how mystical consciousness can be simultaneous with ordinary consciousness. It closes with emphasizing the mutual influence between the cognitive and the affective factors in mysticism.

Study 10 utilizes the assets of Lonergan's cognitional theory to gauge what is going on in liturgical experience. It characterizes four positions: naïve realism, extrinsicism, immanentism, and critical realism. It lays open the weaknesses of the first three and it asserts that solely the fourth one justifies the required, double appraisal of vertical as well as horizontal relationships in liturgy.

Study 11 has recourse to Lonergan's epistemology, ethics, and theology in order to shed light on issues of education. It sketches out the components of learning in secular fields. It tackles the problem of moral development as distinct from and yet connected with religious experience. It concludes with listing the aspects of education that are needed if faith is to be renewed in university campuses.

Part Four is entitled "Ethics." Study 12 moves into the field of social ethics, comparing John Macmurray's and Lonergan's concerns about modern societies. It delineates their respective philosophy of the person. It scrutinizes Macmurray's tenets regarding the primacy of action and of the personal, the individual's modes of apperception, and the task of religion. Thereafter, it contrasts Macmurray's and Lonergan's views on intersubjectivity. It ends up by restating Lonergan's stance that intentionality is at the service of relatedness.

Study 13 reports Gandhi's and Lonergan's critique of Western civilization. It carefully portrays the diagnosis and the prescription that we find in each of those thinkers. Gandhi's principle of healing is "satyagraha," which literally means "firmness in truth"; Lonergan's principle of healing consists in a "being-in-love in an unrestricted fashion," which can be self-sacrificing. Focusing on the challenge of human authenticity, this Study maintains that their models of human excellence are similar, with a few diverging accents.

Study 14 stays in the field of social ethics. With a citation of Aquinas and a brief contrast with Kant, it grounds human rights in human nature seen as self-motivated. It proceeds to indicate how the *basic* rights emerge from the four levels of intentionality, and how the countless *secondary* rights can be prioritized according to a transcendental scale of values. Four types of bias – dramatic, individual, group, and general – engender an ignorance of or a disrespect for the true hierarchy of values. This brings us to Lonergan's complex solution: a certain communitarianism (as opposed to manipulative technocracy); three conversions (to which Robert Doran's "psychic conversion" must be added); several resources such as education, psychotherapy, humour, irony, and satire; and the creation of a "cosmopolis," namely an interdisciplinary, global-scale cooperation with a view to scrutinize and revise existing political projects.

Finally, Study 15 proposes a perspective on divine providence based on Aquinas and Lonergan. This vision can help people be confident and ethical in the face of evil while not falling into the providentialism of naïve religiosity. It steers away from two erroneous pictures: a universe misconstrued as pure chance or as inflexible necessity. Defined as putting all agents in relation to each other, providence is envisioned as including three kinds of intelligibility: the classical laws, the statistical frequencies, and the raison d'être of each concrete event. The first two kinds can be explained by the sciences, whereas the third category belongs to the existential construal of what happens to particular individuals and concrete societies. Men and women are confronted with evil every time there is a disturbance in dynamic cycles – physical, chemical, biological, etc. Divine power, which does not do away with contingency and human freedom, is interpreted as countering evil while operating within an overall providential frame of reference.

NOTES

1 For documentation on Lonergan and on Lonergan studies, see lonergan-lri.ca, lonerganresource.com, bernardlonergan.com, and francais.lonergan.org.

2 For two intellectual biographies of Lonergan, see Pierrot Lambert, *Bernard Lonergan: Introduction à sa vie et à son œuvre* (Montréal: Guérin, 2008), and Pierrot Lambert, "The Life: Patterns Lifting Towards a Philosophic Living," Part 1 of Pierrot Lambert and Philip McShane's *Bernard Lonergan: His Life and Leading Ideas* (Vancouver: Axial Publishing, 2010).

3 Cited in *Current Biography* 33/1 (January 1972), 27, under "Lonergan, Bernard J.F."

Part One

Method

Study 1

An Empirical Method

The present scholarly world regards Bernard Lonergan as an innovative philosopher, a profound theologian, and a daring methodologist. And yet, most philosophers, theologians, and specialists in religious studies who have tried to read *Insight* or *Method in Theology* without guidance from Lonergan himself or from his disciples are left wondering what precisely the importance is of these two works for their fields. Moreover, it is difficult to assess the impact of Lonergan's oeuvre. This is why in this study I wish to answer questions concerning his real contribution to method while presenting a list of books on Lonergan that would allow readers to look further into what might interest them about this thinker and to ascertain for themselves what he offers to philosophy, theology, and religious studies.

I will begin by recounting four interpretations of Lonergan's work. These interpretations will introduce us to the heart of our subject because they all point in the same direction in spite of their differences. Then I will highlight some problems and some authors who attracted Lonergan's attention in the course of his evolution. Next, we will focus on what he calls the generalized empirical method, his great contribution to philosophy and theology. I also highlight the role of meaning as constituting the human world and I will explain how, for Lonergan, the methodical mind can control meaning. I will end with comments on attempts to make use of this method and on criticisms that have been made of Lonergan's program.

FOUR INTERPRETATIONS

We begin then with a look at four authorized interpretations of Lonergan's oeuvre as a way to survey the terrain to be explored. The four authors are Tracy, O'Callaghan, Crowe, and Miller.

In a 1970 publication that remains a good introduction to Lonergan's thought, David Tracy situates him in a dual context: twentieth-century Catholic and Protestant theology and intentionality as explored by such authors as Husserl, Heidegger, Merleau-Ponty, de Waelhens, Ricoeur, Coreth, and Rahner.[1] Like these philosophers, Lonergan believes it is necessary to analyze intentionality – that is, to elucidate what the inquiring subject can achieve. The key notion for Tracy is *horizon*, understood as the totality of the knowledge and interests that delimit the scope of a person's intentions, affirmations, and actions. He shows how Lonergan constantly expanded his horizon in the course of his intellectual development. Tracy highlights Lonergan's activities, his "achievement," and his progression between 1935 and 1970.

In the opinion of Michael O'Callaghan,[2] one of Lonergan's greatest preoccupations concerns the problem of pluralism and the unity of theology.[3] Using a classification borrowed from Kasper, O'Callaghan contrasts three approaches: the historical approach of Pannenberg with its scientific character (*Wissenschaftlichkeit*), Rahner's experiential approach with its ecclesial focus (*Kirchlichkeit*), and the political approach of Metz with its engagement in contemporary reality (*Zeitoffenheit*). He tries to show that turning to Lonergan's methodology can assist in revealing the complementary aspects of these three theological enterprises. Thus, O'Callaghan puts the accent on the integrative force of the method. In contrast with Tracy's emphasis on Lonergan's evolution, O'Callaghan demonstrates how Lonergan explains the transformations of theology across the ages, the foundations on which he intends to base philosophy and theology, how his method is articulated, and what it offers to the Church and to society.

In a small book dating from 1980,[4] Frederick Crowe provides his take on Lonergan's input. He sees it as an intellectual tool destined to be adopted by thinkers who wish to thoroughly know how their own conscious activities are structured and who wish to apply their talents in a sustained undertaking of understanding and scientific production. Crowe insists upon the programmatic and practical character of what he also calls an intellectual *organon*. Using the term *organon* underlines the fact that this organon has to be part of the very person of the thinker. Thus Crowe rejects an interpretation of the Lonergan method that would take it as a set of rules that guide research from the outside. He focuses his attention on the practical support that the Lonergan method is able to provide to future theology. In two complementary articles,[5] he distinguishes this methodological program from what Lonergan himself managed to carry out, whether as a theologian in a particular field (for example, Trinitarian theology) or as a thinker striving to elevate his knowledge to the level of the twentieth century.

The final interpretation belongs to Mark Miller, whose recent contribution focuses on Lonergan's anthropology.[6] He divides up his subject matter into three fundamental situations concerning the human person as well as society. So Part One is entitled "Progress: Nature as Good," Part Two "Decline: Nature as Fallen," and Part Three "Redemption: Nature Raised into Supernature." He states: "These three general categories account for human achievement, human failure, and divine assistance. They constitute Lonergan's translation of the traditional categories of nature, sin, and grace into a broader, historical context that better accounts for changes over time."[7] And he explains:

> Lonergan's philosophy of history is comprised of three vectors or differentials: progress, decline, and redemption. Each differential is an abstraction of a particular aspect of the complex reality that is human history. Taken individually none of them provides an accurate account of human history in its entirety, because human history is never in a pure state of nature, a pure state of sin, or a pure state of grace. But taken together as a dynamic whole, progress, decline, and redemption provide a full and highly verifiable framework for understanding and explaining human history – in other words, for a theological anthropology that accounts for changes over time.[8]

Within this broad framework, Miller develops many important themes in Lonergan's writings, for instance the classical versus the historical view of human nature, emergent probability as world order, various kinds of insight, intentionality, cooperation in human community, the forms of bias, grace, the conversions, and the collective aspect of salvation.[9]

However their preoccupations differ – the development of Lonergan's thought (Tracy), the way his work supports the integration of various theological enterprises (O'Callaghan), the richness of the intellectual tools that he invites thinkers to appropriate (Crowe), or Lonergan's threefold assessment of the human person (Miller) – these four interpreters of Lonergan nevertheless agree that the role he played is not to be found principally in the theological specialties on which he worked, but rather, and overwhelmingly, in the area of a methodology that opened the way to the future.[10]

PROBLEMS AND THINKERS: WHAT WAS GOING FORWARD

As we have seen, there is universal agreement on the great importance of methodology for Lonergan. Now I would like to turn to the problems that he encountered and the thinkers who influenced him, in order to retrace "what was going forward" (see *Method*, 178–9, 186–7, 203, 230) in his thinking during his long years of work.[11]

Lonergan encountered a first epistemological difficulty towards the end of the 1920s when he was reading philosophy at Heythrop College, located at that time near Oxford, England. Reacting against the dominant role given to universal concepts in scholastic philosophy, he considered himself to be a nominalist[12] until one day he came upon a book by J.A. Stewart titled *Plato's Doctrine of Ideas*. From Stewart he learned that Plato was interested in the process that led to scientific or philosophical discoveries and that this process consisted of an interplay of questions and responses. This was the guiding thread for his reading of dialogues by Plato and Augustine in the early 1930s in Montreal; thanks to the latter, he grasped the difference between the two mental operations called insight and judgment. A few years later, studying theology in Rome, one of his companions, another Jesuit who had been a student of Maréchal, helped Lonergan to recognize that human knowledge is not intuitive (in the sense of an exterior or interior looking) but discursive, with judgment as its decisive element. Further, Lonergan developed a deeper appreciation of the reflective role of judgment in the course of extensive probing into Newman's great work, *A Grammar of Assent*.

No doubt readers of *Insight* have already detected, in the preceding paragraph, some of the ideas that led to the birth of that book. In the same period, however, Lonergan devoted a decade to the study of Thomas Aquinas. The Thomas Aquinas he discovered was not the "conceptualist" rendering of scholasticism. This was an "intellectualist" Thomas Aquinas, one who, rather than enclosing himself within a conceptual logic, devoted all his strength to understanding the realities that he encountered. Thanks to the historical method applied to medieval studies in the 1930s and thanks to his interest in the intellectual vitality manifest in insight and judgment, Lonergan was able to see in Thomas Aquinas the astonishing dynamism and subtlety of reflective intelligence in search of the systematic, conscious coherence of its cognitive interiority. His studies of the research done by Thomas Aquinas into grace[13] and into the inner word[14] allowed him to go far beyond the Thomistic interpretations of the day and to adopt a style of thinking and a cognitional theory that he would eventually present with originality in *Insight*.

He also felt the need to explore the fields of mathematics and the natural sciences. Starting in the 1940s, his friendship with his Jesuit colleague Eric O'Connor stimulated Lonergan's thinking about the sciences enormously. (O'Connor's specialties were mathematics and physics, which he taught at Loyola College in Montreal.) It was with the help of this friend that he managed to formulate the philosophy of science found in *Insight*. Lonergan certainly ranks among the theologians of the twentieth century who are closest to the world of science. This aspect of his thought has doubtless helped more than a few to understand the scientific realm better – so important to our culture – and to connect it to other spheres of human experience.[15]

Lonergan was profoundly interested in one other sphere of human experience, that of action and history. By reading historians like Dawson, Toynbee, and Collingwood, reflecting on philosophers of history such as Dilthey and Gadamer, delving into existentialist writings, learning about the input of psychoanalysts and about various schools of psychology, he reached a new level that both integrated and surpassed the intellectualism of the *Insight* period[16] by giving priority to responsibility and to love, which he set at the fourth level of intentionality. We may speak of "the later Lonergan" to designate the Lonergan of the post-*Insight* period, namely the one who grants priority to value and action.

Theologians and religious studies specialists also taught Lonergan a good deal regarding methodology. Doing research and teaching about grace, the Incarnation, Christology, and the Trinity, he came up against what were really very complex problems: interpretation and connections among very diverse Christian sources presented by the historical method; and reformulation of ecclesial doctrines in the light both of the past and of contemporary mental categories. These two series of problems (around receiving the Christian heritage and expressing its meaning for today) underlie Lonergan's proposal to divide the eight functions of theology into two large groups, the mediating phase and the mediated phase (see *Method*, 133–45). His explanation of these theological functions is the fruit of many years of slow, cautious exploration in his teaching of theology as well as in his own methodological reflections. In addition, in the field of religious studies, Lonergan was reading such authors as Eliade, Smith, Whitson, and Panikkar. The mystical aspect of religion thus found its place within his theological method. He shares with Karl Rahner a familiarity with the mysticism of St Ignatius (see *Method*, 106, including note 4) and he is indebted to a study on *The Cloud of Unknowing* by a fellow Jesuit, William Johnston (see *Method*, 342, note 7).

As a final point, it is noteworthy that Lonergan's first and last intellectual passions had to do with economics. From 1930 to 1944, he focused intensely on understanding the workings of markets and produced two manuscripts on the subject.[17] He showed the second of them to several economists. They found nothing especially pertinent and so Lonergan abandoned this research. However, after *Method in Theology* appeared in 1972, a remark by a Latin-American theologian inspired him to return to the topic. During an international meeting of the review *Concilium*, Gustavo Gutierrez proclaimed in effect that the weakness of liberation theologians was their ignorance of economics.[18] While at Boston College (1975 to 1982), Lonergan returned to economics and he produced several revised versions of *An Essay in Circulation Analysis*.[19] Although I am unable to provide even a hint concerning this final intellectual achievement of Lonergan's, I want to bring it to the reader's attention simply as an illustration of his intellectual daring.[20]

GENERALIZED EMPIRICAL METHOD

Lonergan's "generalized empirical method" is a *method*, albeit not in the sense of endlessly repeating the same material operations.[21] Rather, it is a method in the formal sense of four broad types of operations that recur in differentiated ways in a huge variety of situations. These four broad types of operations – attention to data, understanding, judgment of reality, and decision – are found at the four levels of intentionality: empirical, intellectual, rational, and existential. Their *empirical* character arises from the condition that everything is based on data, both sense data and data of consciousness, which attain the status of facts when they are understood, judged to be true, and, within the realm of action, judged worthy of being actualized.[22]

The method is *generalized* to the extent that it rises above specialized methods, which, for good reason, focus their attention on certain types of data. The natural sciences, for example, limit themselves to data of the senses, while hermeneutics and historical studies concentrate on data associated with human meaning. The Lonergan method further generalizes the notion of data to include the data of consciousness (see *Insight*, 95–6 and 268). Far from being restricted to particular domains, this method applies to all fields of knowledge, with the transpositions required by each special method.

Moreover, perceiving, interpreting, judging, and ratifying are a quite costly affair in terms of intellectual and moral effort. After summarizing the movement and essential components of intentionality in the first chapter of *Method in Theology*, Lonergan warns his readers: "the process of self-realization occurs only slowly, and, usually, only through a struggle with some such book as *Insight*" (*Method*, 7). The importance of this invitation, to appropriate an instrument or a method rooted within the human spirit itself, must be emphasized. Occurring as it does in dialogue with practitioners of the natural and human sciences and of history, this appropriation constitutes a philosophical achievement that makes it possible to elucidate the foundations of various types of knowledge.

In this project, Lonergan takes account of the radical changes that marked the self-understanding of the natural sciences in the early decades of the twentieth century.[23] These changes resulted (among those who were knowledgeable) in the jettisoning of mechanistic and deterministic pretensions that had encumbered so many interpretations in the human sciences, history, philosophy, and theology.

One of the mistakes that had gained many adherents in the Western Enlightenment was the belief that mathematical rigour and an empiricism that discounted all data except data of the senses would give rise to human emancipation and progress. By demonstrating the role of meaning in the human sciences and in history and in showing that intentionality is open to religion, the generalized empirical method verifies the validity of all data that may become objects of knowledge. Thus it allows the human sciences and history to escape all forms of reductionism (positivism, behaviourism, relativism, etc.) and it finds a proper object for religious studies and theology that is neither an illusion nor a simple projection. Accordingly, it rejects the totalitarian pretensions of a scientism that is not based on scientific discoveries but on a bad philosophy. It releases the human sciences and other sorts of knowledge from their inferiority complex in relation to natural sciences. It clears a space for ethical and religious inquiry that is neither legalistic nor narrowly confessional, but rather one where it is possible that people who wish to behave responsibly with regard to the grave problems of our planet can express their deepest concerns.

THE ROLE OF MEANING

In addition to the foundational and critical function that I have just presented, the generalized empirical method can assist researchers by drawing their attention to two aspects of meaning. On the one hand, meaning mediates and constitutes the human world. On the other, the control of meaning is different when moving from common sense to the systematic mind, and then from the systematic mind to the methodical mind. Let us examine each of these two roles played by the method that Lonergan proposes.

Lonergan often compares the world of immediacy with the world mediated by meaning.[24] The former is the world of the infant, limited to what it can see, touch, and experience in the here-and-now. The latter begins to take shape for the child when it discovers "not only what is present but also what is absent, not only what is near but also what is far, not only the past but also the future, not only the factual but also the possible, the ideal, the ought-to-be."[25] So we come to know this world via the meanings or interpretations of those who are close to us and, more broadly, from our culture. This world evolves when our actions, which we consider meaningful, add new features to it. Such features may be external due to the many acts by means of which we transform nature into a humanized universe; they may be interior via the actions through which we transform our own selves as human beings. Through education, the arts, economic and political decisions, and daily routines, we receive and constitute our world mediated by meaning. It is fortunate that we can return occasionally to the world of immediacy, for instance in physical play. For adults, however, the immediate is surrounded and located by the world that is mediated and constituted by meaning.

One of the dangers that the generalized empirical method must confront is confusion of the differing criteria of these two worlds with regard to how reality is apprehended. Many philosophers, for example, have tended to consider as real that which can be seen or touched (the empiricists) or that which ought to but cannot be seen or touched (the idealists). In the face of the complex problems explored by these philosophers, the transcendental precepts of Lonergan's method appear overly simple at first blush: be attentive, be intelligent, be reasonable, be responsible, be in love. In fact, they only appear banal to readers of Lonergan who have failed to notice that the precepts are in constant tension with opposed orientations that exist due to a lack of self-knowledge.[26] What proves very difficult, in effect, is to imagine all of the epistemological and ontological consequences of the fact that we belong not just to the immediate world but also to the mediated world. These consequences concern the possibility of moving beyond a subjectivist manner of living with one's own feelings and interpretations towards an engagement in cognitive or ethical judgments through which one verifies the meaning of realities and reaches out to them in a more objective manner.

Accordingly, simply knowing the proper intellectual functioning of the generalized empirical method is not sufficient for its appropriation, as if this functioning were perfect among its practitioners. There must also be a self-awareness that triggers self-correction in order to ensure that the method is functioning properly. With respect to notions of being and objectivity, of the existence and actions of God, of the supernatural character of Christian life, this self-correction in the functioning of the method privileges positions that respect all of the data of experience and of tradition. A growth in subjective authenticity corresponds to enlargement of the horizon of the believer involved in exegesis, history, or other theological functions.[27]

The second facet of meaning to which Lonergan draws the attention of theologians has to do with the control of meaning.[28] This control varies greatly when one moves from common sense to the systematic mind, then from there to the methodical mind. The contrast between common sense and the systematic mind is exemplified by the perplexity of Socrates' interlocutors when he asked them to define virtues such as courage or justice. Those Athenians knew what they wanted to say when they spoke of a courageous action or of a just decision. Nevertheless, they remained unable to reach the level of precision in technical meaning that would soon be found in Aristotle and eventually in medieval thought or in modern science. For Lonergan, the systematic mind does not displace common sense from its practical role in everyday life. However, the systematic mind has the great advantage of achieving a finer control of meaning by highlighting coherence, by detecting and eliminating incompatibilities, by following the antecedents and consequences of an idea or a hypothesis – in brief, by raising and applying the principles of logic. Thus, this mind promotes clarity and precision with regard to truth and it allows us to distinguish what is real from what arises from myth and magic.

The systematic mind gave rise to classical culture. This culture believed wholeheartedly in its inheritance and achievements. As much with Aristotle as in the French seventeenth century of Louis XIV, for instance, the accent was on what was thought to be permanent, immutable, eternal. Later, reacting against views of life that accented change and progress, the nostalgic Catholicism of modern times turned in large part towards the social and religious ideals of the Middle Ages, judged to be valid for all time. During those long years when Catholicism retreated within a sort of cultural ghetto, scientific method and historical method made inroads in various fields of knowledge. The result within the Catholic Church has been an intellectual crisis that erupted many times since the dawn of modernism.[29]

Lonergan interprets this crisis as the difficulty of passing from a classicist conception to an empirical conception of culture. The latter allows for the pluralistic character of culture and recognizes the legitimacy of Christianity being embodied in different contexts. Lonergan takes a very clear position in this most pressing debate. Judging on the one hand that "the classical mediation of meaning has broken down,"[30] he does not accept the traditional solutions that are regaining strength nowadays in ecclesiastical circles. On the other hand, he also does not agree with relativism in regard to Christian revelation, as he believes in the capacity that the human spirit has, when aided by the Holy Spirit, to discern continuity among highly varied modes of expressing truth.

For Lonergan, the solution to this crisis requires moving from the classicist mind to the methodical mind.[31] In effect, the methodical mind proposes a different control of meaning, exemplified by what one sees in modern empirical sciences, where original and pertinent questions allow data to be seen in a new way and allow fresh hypotheses to arise. Unlike the systematic mind, which tends to perfect and refine a static content, this new experimental mind accepts the imperfect, incomplete, and provisional character of knowledge. When this mind is applied to the history of religious ideas, it delves into the particular characteristics of texts, authors, and epochs. It is attentive as much to differences of contexts as to the unity of an evolving dogma.

While many learned Catholics and Protestants isolate themselves in their specialized research, Lonergan advocates the launch of an integrating effort. The unity that his method invites researchers to discover within the diversity of their historical and exegetical studies is not a unity formulated in a classical, logical manner. Rather it invites them to discover continuities – as well as oppositions – expressed and interpreted in a genetic and dialectical manner. The genetic method studies the continuities, while the dialectical method tackles the oppositions (see *Insight*, chapter 4, §2, chapter 7, §5, chapter 14, §4, chapter 15, §6–8, and chapter 17).

To take an instance in theology, Lonergan goes beyond the Roman Catholic understanding of the development of dogma, which flourished in the first half of the twentieth century and was linked to different universes of discourses according to the schema of implicit/explicit, where explicit doctrine was seen as implicitly present in a previous one and therefore justified thanks to a logical inference. Instead, he suggests that attention be applied to the phases of meaning in which these universes of discourses might belong, to analyzing the alterations of context that arose, and to devising transpositions for today (see *Method*, chapter 11, §2, chapter 12, §5–10).[32]

It is worth noting that, beginning with his Latin corpus in theology, Lonergan worked more and more in this historically sensitive fashion in order to attack head-on the problem whether, in the succession of Christian formulations, the new versions truly retained the essential elements of what was asserted by the ancients, while adding the clarity that is needed in view of the questions being posed.

CONCLUSION

Since the 1970s, philosophers and theologians have been reading Lonergan, producing many commentaries on his works and comparing them with the writings of other thinkers.[33] A process of assimilation of his thought has taken place, as well as an effort to situate it in relation to other trends. Several other studies give an idea of the many fields opened by researchers inspired by Lonergan, including philosophy, exegesis, religious experience, systematic theology, political theology, and economics. At the same time, numerous critiques have addressed his philosophy, his theology, and his methodology. Those who long for solidity in Catholic identity worry about what appear to them to be his subjectivism, relativism, and non-Christian philosophy of religion; those who belong to the liberal wing fear his systematic mind or his conservatism; others who reject a firm distinction between religion and theology prefer a more symbolic or more catechetical approach and dislike what seems to them to be intellectualism; still others, of a Barthian bent perhaps, reject the idea of a generalized empirical method in favour of a theology that from the start is situated epistemologically in faith alone.

Finally, there are those who ask what kind of results this method can generate in practice. To that end, I would like to draw attention to an experience of putting the eight functions of theology into practice as outlined in the edited volume *Papal Infallibility*.[34] In its Epilogue, the authors faithfully recounted the problems they had in their collaborative effort. Moreover, they brought together theologians of different backgrounds who, over three days, examined their work and offered commentaries and criticisms. There have been other attempts too, dealing with one or another theological function. To my knowledge, the most impressive are that of Frederick Crowe in his application of the functional specialty "history" to the theme of the Word of God,[35] that of Ben Meyer in his use of Lonergan's epistemology in exegesis,[36] and that of Robert Doran in his expansion of the functional specialties "dialectic" and "systematics."[37]

Since Lonergan's death in 1984, discussion continues on his contribution to philosophy and theology. No doubt, further attempts to put his method into practice are helping to clarify the importance of this contribution.

NOTES

1 David Tracy, *The Achievement of Bernard Lonergan* (New York: Herder and Herder, 1970).

2 Michael O'Callaghan, *Unity in Theology: Lonergan's Framework for Theology in its New Context* (Lanham, MD: University Press of America, 1981).

3 See Louis Roy's review of O'Callaghan's book in *Science et Esprit* 33 (1981): 273–4; James R. Pambrun, "Through O'Callaghan to Lonergan," *Église et Théologie* 12 (1981): 389–411.

4 Frederick E. Crowe, *The Lonergan Enterprise* (Cambridge, MA: Cowley Publications, 1980).

5 Crowe, "The Present State of the Lonergan Movement," *Lonergan Studies Newsletter* 3 (1982); Crowe, "Creativity and Method: Index to a Movement. A Review-Article," *Science et Esprit* 34 (1982): 107–13. The latter text is a commentary stimulated by reading Matthew L. Lamb (ed.), *Creativity and Method: Essays in Honor of Bernard Lonergan, S.J.* (Milwaukee: Marquette University Press, 1981), a collection of thirty-four articles that discuss or apply various aspects of Lonergan's thought.

6 Mark T. Miller, *The Quest for God & the Good Life: Lonergan's Theological Anthropology* (Washington, DC: The Catholic University of America Press, 2013).

7 Ibid., xii.

8 Ibid., xiv.

9 For a longer presentation of Miller's book, see the review by Brian J. Braman in *Method: Journal of Lonergan Studies*, New Series, 3 (2012): 89–94.

10 Among the indications that Lonergan saw himself as a methodologist in the epistemological sense of the term, we may note that a considerable time after *Insight* appeared, placing what had been his first book in proper perspective, Lonergan affirmed that it set out a general methodology that was intended to provide the foundations for another work that would deal with method in theology. See his "Foreword" to Tracy's study, *The Achievement*, xi; see also "An Interview with Fr. Bernard Lonergan, S.J," and "*Insight* Revisited," in *A Second Collection: Papers by Bernard J.F. Lonergan, S.J.*, ed. William F.J. Ryan and Bernard J. Tyrrell (Toronto: University of Toronto Press, 1996, reprint), 213 and 268.

11 My information is from "*Insight* Revisited," in *A Second Collection*, 263–78; and from *Caring about Meaning: Patterns in the Life of Bernard Lonergan*, ed. Pierrot Lambert, Charlotte Tansey, and Cathleen Going

(Montreal: Thomas More Institute Papers, 1982), six interviews with Lonergan.

12 Nominalism is the doctrine that general names are merely logical tools used to classify and compare things; only individual things exist. By contrast, for Aristotle, Aquinas, and Lonergan, universal forms are really found in individual things. See Richard M. Liddy, *Transforming Light: Intellectual Conversion in the Early Lonergan* (Collegeville, MN: The Liturgical Press, 1993), 33–7. On Lonergan's philosophy, I have also profited from Richard M. Liddy, *Startling Strangeness: Reading Lonergan's* Insight (Lanham, MD: University Press of America, 2007).

13 *Grace and Freedom: Operative Grace in the Thought of St Thomas Aquinas*, ed. Frederick E. Crowe and Robert M. Doran, volume 1 of *Collected Works of Bernard Lonergan* (Toronto: University of Toronto Press, 2000).

14 Bernard Lonergan, *Verbum: Word and Idea in Aquinas*, ed. Frederick E. Crowe and Robert M. Doran, volume 2 of *Collected Works of Bernard Lonergan*, (Toronto: University of Toronto Press, 1997).

15 See for example this remark by the English bishop and theologian Christopher Butler, in *An Approach to Christianity* (London: Collins, Fount Paperbacks, 1981), 7: "Through Father Lonergan's great book, *Insight*, I escaped from the kind of intellectual schizophrenia that had resulted from a classical and classical-philosophical education, set against a layman's contact with the world of modern science."

16 See Lonergan, "The Subject," in *A Second Collection*, 69–86.

17 Lonergan, *For a New Political Economy*, ed. Philip J. McShane, volume 21 of *Collected Works of Bernard Lonergan* (Toronto: University of Toronto Press, 1998). This volume includes "For a New Political Economy," "Fragments," and the first version of "Circulation Analysis."

18 This information is from Fred Lawrence, "A Lonergan Tribute," *Lonergan Studies Newsletter*, Special Commemorative Issue (February 1985), 7–15, especially 8–9.

19 Lonergan, *Macroeconomic Dynamics: An Essay in Circulation Analysis*, ed. Frederick G. Lawrence, Patrick H. Byrne, and Charles C. Hefling, Jr., volume 15 of *Collected Works of Bernard Lonergan* (Toronto: University of Toronto Press, 1999).

20 See also Philip McShane, *Lonergan's Challenge to the University and the Economy* (Washington, DC: University Press of America, 1980), chapters 6–7, and William Mathews, "Lonergan's Economics," *Method: Journal of Lonergan Studies* 3 (1985): 9–30.

21 See "Religious Knowledge," in *A Third Collection: Papers by Bernard J.F. Lonergan, S.J.*, ed. Frederick E. Crowe (New York: Paulist Press, 1985), 129–45, at 140–4. In *Method in Theology* he spoke of a "transcendental method." See 13–20 in Lonergan's *Method*.

22 See Charles C. Hefling, Jr., "Consciousness," in *The New Dictionary of Catholic Spirituality* (Collegeville, MN: The Liturgical Press, 1993), 202–7.

23 Note what Lonergan writes in his "Foreword" to Matthew L. Lamb, *History, Method, and Theology: A Dialectical Comparison of Wilhelm Dilthey's Critique of Historical Reason and Bernard Lonergan's Meta-Methodology* (Missoula, MT: Scholars Press, 1978), ix–xii.

24 See Lonergan's "The World Mediated by Meaning," in *Philosophical and Theological Papers 1965–1980*, ed. Robert C. Croken and Robert M. Doran, volume 17 of *Collected Works of Bernard Lonergan* (Toronto: University of Toronto Press, 2004).

25 Lonergan, "Dimensions of Meaning," in *Collection*, ed. Frederick E. Crowe and Robert M. Doran, volume 4 of *Collected Works of Bernard Lonergan* (Toronto: University of Toronto Press, 1988), 232–3.

26 As an exercise, one might compare Lonergan's criteria with those that he attributes to John Dewey: see "An Interview with Fr. Bernard Lonergan, S.J.," *A Second Collection*, 218–19. Concerning Dewey, see Robert O. Johann, "Lonergan and Dewey on Judgement," in *Language, Truth, and Meaning*, ed. Philip McShane (Notre Dame, IN: University of Notre Dame Press, 1972), 79–92 and 310.

27 In *The Question as Commitment: A Symposium*, ed. Elaine Cahn and Cathleen Going (Montreal: Thomas More Institute Papers, 1977), 20–2, Lonergan recounts what Carl Becker said about what a thinker takes to be possible or impossible: "Becker argues: 'If the historian is convinced that what the witnesses are affirming is impossible, they are clearly self-deceived.' He holds that even if there were two hundred witnesses attesting to the same fact, with no evidence whatsoever of poor memory or emotional disturbance, one would yet have to say they were self-deceived if all were affirming the impossible."

28 On this topic, see his lengthy exposition in *Method*, 81–99; for a shorter presentation, see Lonergan, "Dimensions of Meaning," 232–45.

29 For example, at the end of the 1930s, the conflict between Marie-Dominique Chenu and Roman representatives of neo-scholastic theology. See the studies of Giuseppe Alberigo and others in the re-issue of Marie-Dominique Chenu, *Une école de théologie: le Saulchoir* (Paris: Cerf, 1985).

30 Lonergan, "Dimensions of Meaning," 244.

31 In a manner that does not do away with the logical requirements of the systematic mind, but rather subsumes them in locating them within the larger context formed by methodological requirements.

32 See also his answers to "Questionnaire on Philosophy," *Method: Journal of Lonergan Studies* 2 (1984): 1–35, esp. 23–5.

33 In addition to the texts that I have already cited in this chapter, numerous articles on Lonergan, and hundreds of doctoral theses on his thought, I would like to mention *Foundations of Theology*, ed. Philip McShane (Notre Dame, IN: University of Notre Dame Press, 1972); *Looking at Lonergan's Method*, ed. Patrick Corcoran (Dublin: Talbot Press, 1975); *Lonergan Workshop*, ed. Fred Lawrence (25 vols. so far; Chestnut Hill, MA: Boston College, 1978–), as well as supplementary volumes. Other collective works on his thought will be mentioned as this book of mine unfolds. The Lonergan Research Institute of Regis College, University of Toronto houses the Lonergan archives: all his published works, recordings of his lectures and courses, articles, books, and theses devoted to the study of his thought, and indices. There are numerous other Lonergan centres around the world.

34 *Papal Infallibility: An Application of Lonergan's Theological Method*, ed. Terry J. Tekippe (Washington, DC: University Press of America, 1983).

35 Frederick E. Crowe, *Theology of the Christian Word: A Study in History* (New York: Paulist Press, 1978).

36 Ben F. Meyer, *The Aims of Jesus* (London: SCM Press, 1979) and several other books on interpreting the New Testament.

37 Robert M. Doran, *Theology and the Dialectics of History, What Is Systematic Theology?* and *The Trinity in History: A Theology of the Divine Missions*, vol. 1, Missions and Processions (all three are published by the University of Toronto Press in 1990, 2005, and 2012, respectively).

Study 2

An Integrative Method

Bernard Lonergan devoted his life to clarifying the intellectual requirements that flow from the fact that Christians live in a world marked by transformation. In the opinion of this thinker, the fundamental problem of the Church both before and after the Second Vatican Council does not stem from questions of structure or of power, nor is it about a crisis in the experience of faith. The current challenge for Catholics is rather to renew their self-understanding in the face of the profound scientific, social, and cultural changes that have taken place since the beginning of the modern era.[1]

This adjustment with regard to the expression of their beliefs is certainly not a new phenomenon in the history of Christianity. Nevertheless, what makes the present situation distinctive are such factors as the rise of scientific method, the emphasis of modern philosophies on subjectivity, the emergence of a consciousness that is both historical and international, and the pressing urgency of responsible involvement in a world to be remade. These factors, which will be taken up in the four sections of this Study, have already had profound influence on the increasingly varied and complex labour of theologians. At the same time, for there to be fruitful and rigorous interaction among their diverse fields of interest, practitioners of theology need a global methodology that allows them to situate their contributions and demarcate their particular boundaries with precision. This is what Lonergan offers them in *Method in Theology*. In addition to the methodological aspects introduced in the preceding Study, let me try to present other key points of the method he puts forward, with links to the topics enumerated above.

PHILOSOPHY AND THEOLOGY WITHIN THE PANORAMA OF KNOWLEDGE

What is striking in any reading of Lonergan, no matter how brief, is the attention he accords to the knowing subject.[2] This is more than a personal interest consistent with the Socratic adage "Know thyself." Rather, for our author, if theology hopes to grapple seriously with the most pressing epistemological questions of our times, it has no choice but to follow the shift to interiority that is a singular characteristic of modern philosophy.

What stimulated this turn is the rise of scientific method. Scientific method has allowed many disciplines to mark out their territory within the panorama of human knowing, and it challenges philosophy and theology to do likewise and redefine how they accede to their respective objects of knowing. In effect, the natural and human sciences, having established procedures for handling all data of the senses and of culture, force philosophy and theology to explore more rigorously the interior domain of human existence where they encounter their own particular data. It follows that the specific role of philosophy is to provide us with an account of what Lonergan terms "interiority," that is, the inner events that constitute knowledge, action, and love (see *Method*, 257–62, 290). Theology in turn must take on the task of situating, in relation to other domains, what our author calls "transcendence," "religion," or "religious experience": that aspect of experience that consists of being open to transcendence by welcoming otherworldly love and ultimate meaning (see *Method*, 84, 257, 265–6, 290). Since he calls the domain of transcendence "the other interiority" (266, twice) or "religious interiority" (290), it might be helpful to speak of a first interiority (philosophical self-knowledge) and of a second interiority (religious experience). Moreover, this more profound, second interiority should not be construed as purely inner-directed but as, in John Dadosky's words, a "vertical alterity" in relation with God and a "horizontal alterity" in relation with others.[3]

The Lonergan methodology starts off with philosophy performing the invaluable service of differentiating the various domains of human endeavour, called "realms of meaning." The first of these domains is common sense: the practical, concrete knowledge that a collectivity develops in the course of everyday activities. The second domain is theory, which arises from the desire to understand the many aspects of reality systematically. Lonergan regards the works of Aristotle and of Thomas Aquinas as supreme theoretical achievements prior to the formal distinction between science and philosophy. Nevertheless, from the seventeenth century onwards, those theoretical achievements were confronted by a scientific method that sought to explain all observable sensible data. Thus it came about that philosophers in modern times have found themselves constantly challenged to deal with the apparent contradiction between the sort of vision of things that is typical of common sense on the one hand and scientific explanations of the same perceived phenomena on the other; they are then challenged to establish the legitimacy of these two domains by showing that each of them constitutes a useful and intelligent approach to reality.

To do this, it is necessary to go deeper into the multi-faceted functioning of the human mind, that is, to explore a third domain, namely the first interiority, by distilling from it a structured understanding of the self. Thematizing such an understanding not only allows cognitive consciousness to be differentiated in distinct domains – common sense, theory, first interiority, second interiority (also called "transcendence" or "religion"), scholarship, and art (see *Method*, 81–5 and 271–6)[4] – but also to establish the foundations of a universally applicable "transcendental method" that pertains to every enterprise of knowledge. Lonergan defined this method as "a normative pattern of recurrent and related operations yielding cumulative and progressive results" (*Method*, 13–14).

This transcendental method is nevertheless just one part of theological method, to which it provides its anthropological but not its religious element. The latter emerges from religious conversion, which will be discussed in the next section. It is sufficient for the moment to point out that discoveries that are truly religious, even if they remain ineffable as long as we abide in that "cloud of unknowing" that conceals God from us, nevertheless become communicable once they are formulated.[5] This communication consists of providing meanings by embodying them in tangible data (persons, events, words, works of art, etc.).

The fact that these data are carriers of human meanings distinguishes them from the data collected by the natural sciences. It follows that theology is very close to the human sciences, which deal with meanings, and must use their tools. With religious studies it shares an interest in symbols that relate to ultimate meaning. While the religious studies coincide to some extent with theology when the latter examines the documents of traditional religions, what specifies theology from religious studies is that it takes a stand on the truth of the meanings that have been interpreted. As Lonergan metaphorically submits, "Theologians endeavor to discern whether there is any real fire behind the smoke of symbols employed in this or that religion."[6]

Lonergan's support for Rahner's anthropological turn can be understood in the light of this methodological redefinition of theology – even though their philosophical contexts are different, as we shall see in Study 8. This anthropological consideration does not require that all discourse about God be eliminated. Rather, it proposes that this discourse be paired and compared with another parallel discourse in terms of human realities.[7] The anthropological character of the theological enterprise is more than a question of knowledge of divine realities by means of analogical reference to finite beings, for it aims to go beyond this epistemological position that was already recognized by the great Christian thinkers of the past. It focuses rather on talking about God while simultaneously pointing to his relations with humanity, by approaching him via the effects of his grace on human consciousness. That is, the angle of vision in the elaboration of such a theology is no longer that of a cosmological framework and a descriptive narrative, but will focus on the religious meanings that are offered to human minds. The symbolic language in which revelation occurs will of course be respected, but, thanks to the reinterpretation carried out, the logic proper to such language will cease to dominate. This enterprise will require a methodical control of meaning based on differentiation of the various modes of expression.[8]

So, as Thomas Aquinas had situated the theology of his time in relation to faith and to the varied modes of knowledge explored by Aristotle, in a similar way Lonergan resituates theology in the range of contemporary knowledge: common sense, theory (including the natural and human sciences), philosophy (centred on the first interiority), religion (second interiority or transcendence), scholarship (comprising history and the religious studies), and art.

A SUBJECTIVITY IN SEARCH OF OBJECTIVITY

Once the anchoring of religion in the second interiority is recognized (in a quite Augustinian manner), two questions can be asked. The first concerns doctrinal objectivity. Does this priority given to inner religious experience lead us to discount the truths which come to us through the mediation of persons, words, and events external to ourselves? The second question expresses a problem of discernment and of verification: what are the conditions of the authenticity of the personal as well as communal experience of theologians?

Should we be surprised to see a thinker of the quality of Lonergan having recourse to subjectivity, and should we wonder whether this point of departure will lead inevitably to his being constrained by a stronger or weaker subjectivism? In fact, everything depends upon how this subjectivity is practised. If the subjectivity of theologians focuses only on what has meaning and value for themselves – or again, if this subjectivity limits itself to the accepted mentality of its milieu (notwithstanding that it could be a movement of high intellectual quality) – then it is unlikely to fully admit the authority of revealed truth. By contrast, whenever subjectivity obeys its fundamental tendency, which consists in a drive towards objective knowledge,[9] we have an intentionality capable of attending to data that differ from its own lived experience, of recognizing the value of religious beliefs, and thanks to those beliefs, of assimilating truths handed down by tradition (see *Insight*, 725–40, and *Method*, chapter 2, §5).

As Lonergan forcefully puts it, "genuine objectivity is the fruit of authentic subjectivity" (*Method*, 292; see 265).[10] One progressively avoids the traps of subjectivism by vigorously obeying the transcendental precepts: be attentive, be intelligent, be reasonable, be responsible, be in love. Moreover, this same obedience to the innate demands of the spirit allows us to unmask the illusion of objectivism – what Lonergan calls "naïve realism" – which imagines itself able to receive revealed truth with no critical regard for the manner in which it appropriates such truth and without seriously confronting religious questions and perceptions that belong to different approaches from its own.[11]

Thus, while objectivism amounts in fact to a disguised subjectivism in which the theological options are governed by insufficiently clarified personal and collective convictions, full objectivity is only acquired gradually, by means of long reflection and laborious study. Elsewhere in *Insight* (366–71) Lonergan refutes a speculative form of relativism, whose fundamental mistake is to accept a view of the universe as an explanatory system which we must grasp as a whole before anything particular can be received as true.

It practises what this author labels a "generalized empirical method," the openness and rigour of which might be able to restore the credibility that theology once had in medieval universities. This empirical method encourages a multidisciplinary effort that pushes constantly towards greater objectivity via attention to any evidence that is apt to clarify the phenomenon of religion, effort to understand their meaning, dedication to verifying hypotheses of understanding, and dialogue that is likely to elucidate the values and positions that underlie the ways in which researchers react to data, to meanings, and to verifications. Objectivity is thus a result towards which we move thanks to working as a team and thanks to a set of personal and collective dispositions.[12]

The second question raised by the fact that subjectivity is the point of departure of Lonergan's enterprise, has to do with issues about the personal and collective dispositions that have just been alluded to. Under what circumstances are they authentic? If the sincere desire to appropriate as objectively as possible the religious data that come from tradition is not a sufficient guarantee of truth, then one must find means to remedy the personal and collective distortions that affect the workings of appropriation. Lonergan describes the tough medicine required as a triple conversion: intellectual, moral, and religious. Conversion profoundly affects the person. According to Lonergan, it is more than a development; whereas the latter operates horizontally, within the same horizon, the former operates vertically. It involves an ascent, a change of horizons, thanks to which people become very different from what they were before.

The most important condition for doing good theology is to have entered into a process of religious conversion. The key phrase from Scripture that refers to this grace is: "God's love has been poured out into our hearts through the Holy Spirit that has been given to us" (Rom 5:5). Lonergan cites this verse repeatedly when he evokes the highly radical state that consists in "total and permanent self-surrender without conditions, qualifications, reservations" (*Method*, 240) to an otherworldly love capable of entirely changing the ultimate meaning of one's existence and of providing eyes of faith that can discern the inestimable value of what revelation has to offer.

Religious conversion has a big impact on the way people read the Bible or, for that matter, any classic. Lonergan affirms, "The major texts, the classics, in religion, letters, philosophy, theology, not only are beyond the initial horizon of their interpreters but also may demand an intellectual, moral, religious conversion of the interpreter over and above the broadening of his horizon ... This is the existential dimension of the problem of hermeneutics. It lies at the very root of the perennial divisions of mankind in their views on reality, morality, and religion" (*Method*, 161).

Another Canadian philosopher, Donald Evans, says the same thing: "There is a personal or existential prerequisite for *understanding* biblical language correctly. One must have a *rapport* or affinity with the divine if one is to understand talk about the divine."[13] Both Lonergan and Evans clearly underline the relation between the readers' existential transformation and their adequate interpretation of religious texts.

Once set in motion, religious conversion supports and propels the second kind of conversion: moral conversion. "Moral conversion changes the criterion of one's decisions and choices from satisfactions to value ... [It] consists in opting for the truly good, even for value against satisfaction when value and satisfaction conflict" (240). It takes place when people decide to be fully responsible and to accept the existential fact that willy-nilly they become what they freely make of themselves. A deep respect and a steadfast resolve to promote the values that are needed in all circumstances, take root gradually within the person who grows in ethical quality through successes and failures. These dispositions lead towards heightened solidarity and clear-sightedness in the face of both individual and social circumstances.

The third kind of conversion, intellectual conversion, depends on overcoming false construals of knowledge, objectivity, and reality. Human knowing is not the equivalent of merely seeing what is out there now to be looked at; this account would reduce knowing to the first level of intentionality. Objectivity requires more than observing the data with exactitude; it encompasses insight and judgment. And reality comprehends infinitely more than the world of immediacy in which infants move; it must be defined as the world mediated by meaning, in which adults think, love, and decide. "Knowing, accordingly, is not just seeing; it is experiencing, understanding, judging, and believing. The criteria of objectivity are not just the criteria of ocular vision; they are the compounded criteria of experiencing, of understanding, of judging, and of believing. The reality known is not just looked at; it is given in experience, organized and extrapolated by understanding, posited by judgment and belief" (*Method*, 238).

Religious conversion promotes intellectual conversion through the revealed beliefs to which it opens a person. In effect, these beliefs orient intelligence towards a critical-realist vision of humanity, the world, history, and God, and help it to escape from the erroneous epistemological and metaphysical positions, whether reductionist or idealist, that truncate the realities of faith. Lonergan does not conceal the fact that this last sort of conversion is the rarest of the three. It must come to grips with, and reverse, counterpositions, namely philosophical doctrines that contradict the basic position on the real, on knowing, and on objectivity (See *Insight*, 413–14).[14] Nevertheless, he holds that intellectual conversion can exist either as a latent intellectual attitude in the believer, or as the theologian's explicit appropriation of his or her cognitive faculties (*Method*, 238–40 and 243).[15]

Lastly, basing himself on passages of Lonergan's *Insight*, which deal with the psychological dimension of the human person, the American Jesuit Robert Doran submitted that there exists a fourth conversion, which he called "psychic conversion."[16] John Dadosky would rather call it "psychological conversion" in order to integrate Bernard Tyrrell's analysis of that conversion, which belongs to a larger psychological scope than pure depth psychology.[17] Lonergan concurred with the fact of that fourth conversion. It refers to the role played by the human psyche, with its affects and images, in the overall process of conversion. The life of the psyche can either block or facilitate conversion in all its facets – religious, moral, and intellectual. For the psychological conversion to aid the other conversions, it must overcome a particular bias, which Lonergan terms "the dramatic bias," a phenomenon that will be explicated, along with the others biases, in Study 15.

Thus, this fourfold conversion exercises its influence throughout the theological enterprise, guiding practitioners and giving them clear vision within the maze of ideas and contexts through which they seek the truth. Indeed, Lonergan even foresees that a specific function of theology – he calls it "foundations" – will make it possible to elucidate the results of conversion before undertaking detailed doctrinal and systematic work. As we see, conditions that are both precise and complex govern the access of subjectivity to true theological objectivity.

HISTORICAL CONSCIOUSNESS

Christians live today in a world of contradictory opinions about every aspect of human experience. The enormous quantity of information from experiments, surveys, and scientific hypotheses, and the massive volume of historical evidence pouring out of universities, schools, and mass media, overwhelm our mental universe. They promote arbitrary choices, random accents, and intellectual fashions in the realm of ideas, and so they give rise to options of a relativistic bent. More radically, they appear to justify the ambiguous thesis that the human relation to the real is culturally constructed. In the face of this grave problem, a healthy theological method can help us to regain a doctrinal communion that is both supple and solid.

As to the suppleness of this doctrinal communion, Lonergan acknowledges that variety in religious thinking across the ages is well-founded. He even asks us to give up a classicist, normative conception of a universal and permanent culture and of changes as mere accidents against the backdrop of an unvarying human culture. He urges us to take an empirical look at cultures, defined as connections of meanings and values that inform styles of living (see *Method*, xi, 28–9, 123–4, 300–2, and 362–3). Human nature, he explains, comprises two fundamental components: the one a variable historicity which explains the multiplicity of cultures; the other a constant, natural right, made up of the transcultural dynamisms of the person.[18] Throughout their diverse levels of questioning, these dynamisms open the person to the reality of the world as well as to the mystery of God.

Coupled with this transcendental self-knowledge as a human being to which the author invites his readers in the first four chapters of *Method*, a historical mentality will put into play the procedures of research, interpretation, and history – the first three functional specialties of theology that arise from scholarship – in order to allow us to receive with open minds what is taught by the religious texts of the diverse epochs we are studying (see the eightfold division, in *Method*, 127–33). *Research* tells us where the available information is located and gives us the means to acquire it. *Interpretation* assumes that we penetrate into the genuine common sense of a milieu – which may differ substantially from our own – and into the spirit of an author in order to understand the texts and documents that have been produced. *History* that is specifically theological in character compares the diverse writings and the factors respecting a writer and an epoch in order to bring to light "what was going forward," what was advancing in the thinking of the times. This kind of historical investigation, which Lonergan himself carried out,[19] allows us to discover intelligible sequences in the evolution of dogma by identifying the new and pertinent questions that appear successively, in parallel with changing circumstances, among the Christian thinkers and in the Churches.

Conversely, we also observe tensions and points of divergence in the answers that are submitted. *Dialectic*, the fourth specialty of theology, endeavours therefore to align the diverging answers on a particular subject – whether the topic is grace, Christ, the Trinity, or any other subject that concerns faith. It brings these intellectual conflicts back – exercising caution and applying scholarship – to common denominators and distinguishes differences merely of perspective or of origin from the disagreements of a fundamental nature. Needless to say, at the same time, theologians identify within themselves a dialectic that is similar to the dialectic that is being analyzed through the historical studies. As the reader might have surmised, these very detailed confrontations guide theologians progressively towards a solid doctrinal communion by helping them to overcome the relativism inherent in isolated evidence-based studies. Hence the all-important task of dialectic, which consists in grouping the fruits of research in terms of religious, moral, and intellectual similarities and differences.

In the fifth specialty of theology (called *foundations*), one undertakes to explicate, with reference to the living tradition, the processes – both personal and communal – of religious, moral, and intellectual conversion, and to clarify the horizons that have been opened up thanks to such radical transformations. In the sixth specialty, called *doctrines*, practitioners of theology probe the ecclesial dogmas in light of the horizons within which they can be adequately apprehended. They thus attempt to determine which of the positions under debate in the dialectic correspond to the truth and are thus worthy of being taken as doctrines, namely as judgments of fact and judgments of value. Let us note that for Lonergan, this does not mean challenging the Church's magisterium but exercising a specifically theological role, that of identifying by means of historical, philosophical, and religious criteria that which appears to belong to faith in a particular field.

This is not the place to explore the details of Lonergan's historical and dogmatic hermeneutics. *Method in Theology* presents enlightening distinctions in the problem of hermeneutics and lays out a well-balanced proposal concerning the permanence and historicity of dogma and the unity of faith and pluralism (153–5 and 320–30). Furthermore, following a grounding of doctrines that has respected their historicity as well as their truth, one can proceed to *systematics* and to *communications* – the seventh and eighth functional specialties. Systematics undertakes to propose a modest understanding of various aspects of religious belief and practice within the framework of the contemporary world with its questions and its challenges; communications subsequently expresses that understanding in the images and ideas of a particular culture.

The eight functional specialties of theology divide into two broad phases: a mediating phase, which serves as an intermediary between the past and ourselves, and a mediated phase, which reformulates the information received from the past for the sake of the present. The assimilation of the past is achieved through research, interpretation, history, and dialectic, and the problems of the present and the future are addressed in foundations, doctrines, systematics, and communications. Clearly these two broad phases must be interdependent; a lack of articulation between them impoverishes the thinking of the Church and a unilateral emphasis either on historical studies or on dogmas induces theologians either to neglect the intelligible unification of doctrines or else to oppose historical consciousness (see *Method*, 145).

Let us end this section by noting the striking absence of reference to Jesus Christ as a norm, as much in the situating of theology within the body of all knowledge as with respect to the problems of authenticity, objectivity, or historical consciousness with which we have dealt so far.[20] In fact, if Jesus Christ does not constitute a *methodological* norm, it is because the methodology is supported by a historical and ecumenical consciousness that includes non-Christian religions. It is clear that the Lonergan methodology is conceived initially with reference to *Christian* theology, more precisely from the perspective of grace, translated as the subjective (not subjectivist!) concept of "inner word." However, his methodology welcomes questions that present themselves in the study of world religions, questions that can be clarified over time by means of a conscientious application of a method tailored to the complexity of the data. We shall return to this issue in Study 6.

INTELLECTUAL ENGAGEMENT IN A WORLD SEEKING SALVATION

The intellectual commitment of Christian theologians in the world comprises two important tasks according to Lonergan. In the first place, it involves applying the eight functional specialties to studying and presenting the message of revelation. At the point of the eighth functional specialty, communications, the offer of salvation remains to be linked up with the contemporary search for salvation. In many of his articles we find Lonergan inquiring into the role of religion in the world.[21] According to appearances, God seems to be absent as much from the spheres of the natural and human sciences as from everyday life. And yet, beneath the current desire to reinterpret the human being and to reorganize society so as to render it more just, there lurks a sense of responsibility in the search for foundations. For Lonergan, this personal and collective embracing of human responsibilities depends upon a reaching beyond the self that is based on a love which is religious in origin. The triple conversion – religious, moral, and intellectual – allows for a threefold self-transcendence that girds us for the long and difficult battle to become authentic human beings. Based on unconditional love, welcoming the perspectives of faith and hope, this self-transcending fights actively for progress and commits itself to set aside the effects of decline by practising forgiveness and the sacrifice of personal interests. In other words, it engages in a dual process: creativity in applying intellectual and moral energy to planning and carrying out worthwhile projects; and healing by shouldering the consequences of sin and evil.[22]

The first principal task of theologians is then to prepare (in the first phase of theology) or to carry out (in the second phase) the actualization of the Christian message in a world marked by responsibility in search of religious foundations. The second principal task consists in encouraging – whether by contributing to it directly or through dialogue – an evaluation of the cultural heritage that shapes our praxis. Praxis is far more than material action as such; it consists of action that obeys interior conditions of authenticity or of inauthenticity. An assessment of our culture and of its praxis will lead us then to elucidate the religious, ethical, and philosophical options that make the procedures and uses of science and technology so ambiguous.

This brings us to the role that Lonergan assigns to the communications specialty in theology, not just that of straightforward transmission and application of Christian thought, but also the much more demanding and concrete one of simultaneously providing a critique and a deepening of societal policies in light of the Gospel (*Method*, chapter 14). In effect, this means submitting the presuppositions of human praxis to a rigorous critical examination which is itself clarified by an explanation of the religious, moral, and intellectual foundations of contemporary social agents in order to contribute to improving current policies.

CONCLUSION

My goal has been to present four distinctive elements of Lonergan's theological method in relation to cultural factors that have developed in the West over several centuries. These four contributions are: situating philosophy and theology within the panorama of knowledge; construing authentic subjectivity as a search for objectivity; demonstrating the vital role of historical consciousness in theology; and highlighting the challenge of an intellectual engagement in a world seeking salvation.

The complexity of this methodology, which aims at nothing less than restructuring all of knowledge, makes it promising for long-term results. Although its influence can already be detected here and there in the theological world, it is still notably difficult to master this instrument of scientific labour personally and to put it into collective practice. Nevertheless, being enlightened by Lonergan does not require being a professional theologian. I hope that this sketch, with its quotations and references, will entice many readers to know more about it.

NOTES

1 See Lonergan's "Belief: Today's Issue" in *A Second Collection: Papers by Bernard J.F. Lonergan, S.J.*, ed. William F.J. Ryan and Bernard J. Tyrrell (Toronto: University of Toronto Press, 1996, reprint), 87–99.

2 Lonergan explains the importance of this attention in his paper "The Subject" in *A Second Collection*, 69–86. Let us keep in mind that the knowing subject is seen as part of the subject that acts.

3 John D. Dadosky, "Is There a Fourth Stage of Meaning?" *The Heythrop Journal* 51 (2010): 768–80, at 772–5.

4 I shall return to scholarship in the third section of this chapter. Insofar as art is concerned, Lonergan considers it an irreplaceable mode of approaching and expressing reality, including religious reality; see *Method*, 61–4, 72–3, 112, and 273. Moreover, from what he says about symbolic apprehension and expression, we may note that symbolism has much to do with art; see *Method*, 64–9, as well as 305–7.

5 According to *Method*, 112–15, first interiority allows us to situate the religious word at the intersection of the sphere of transcendence and the other domains of meaning.

6 Lonergan, "The Ongoing Genesis of Methods," in *A Third Collection: Papers by Bernard J.F. Lonergan, S.J.*, ed. Frederick E. Crowe (New York: Paulist Press, 1985), 146–65, at 131.

7 See Lonergan's "Theology and Man's Future" and "The Future of Christianity," in *A Second Collection*, 147–8 and 161.

8 On myth, especially cosmological myth, and on primitive language, see *Method*, 89–93; on the methodical control of theological categories, see 292–3; on the various modes of religious expression, see 271–81.

9 Chapter 13 of Lonergan's *Insight*, which presents the notion of objectivity, is decisive in this regard. See also the "Objectivity" references in the index to *Method*.

10 Lonergan recognized that thanks to discussions he had with a Belgian seminarian, Maréchal had indirectly influenced his thought by making him appreciate the discursive character of the process culminating in human judging. See Lonergan, "*Insight* Revisited," in *A Second Collection*, 263–78, at 265. Had he read Maréchal's writings, undoubtedly he would have agreed with the latter's brilliant argument in favour of the priority of objectivity over subjectivity. For that lengthy and nuanced analysis, which never sets objectivity against subjectivity, see Joseph Maréchal, *Études sur la psychologie des mystiques* (Paris: Desclée de Brouwer, vol. 1, 2nd ed., 1937), 69–131; English translation: *Studies in the Psychology of the Mystics*, trans. Algar Thorold (Albany, NY: Magi Books, 1964), 55–101.

11 On human subjectivity in quest of meaning and as reaching objectivity, see Louis Roy, *Coherent Christianity* (Ottawa, Novalis, 2005), chap. 13, "Bernard Lonergan: A Theologian in Dialogue." There is a later, slightly expanded French version of this book: *La foi en dialogue* (Ottawa: Novalis, 2006).

12 Let us notice that the focus here is theological objectivity, which is subordinate to religious objectivity. In my opinion, the latter, which springs from religious conversion, constitutes the first condition of theological objectivity.

13 Donald Evans, *Faith, Authenticity, and Morality* (Toronto: University of Toronto Press, 1980), 249; his italics.

14 See also "Positions, vs. counterpositions" in the Index of Lonergan's *Insight* and his lecture "Method in Catholic Theology," in *Philosophical and Theological Papers 1958–1964*, ed. Robert C. Croken, Frederick E. Crowe, and Robert M. Doran, volume 6 of *Collected Works of Bernard Lonergan* (Toronto: University of Toronto Press, 1996), 29–53.

15 See also Lonergan's lecture "The Origins of Christian Realism (1961)," in *Collected Works*, volume 6, 80–93 and the 1972 version of "The Origins of Christian Realism" in *A Second Collection*, 239–61.

16 See Robert M. Doran, *Psychic Conversion and Theological Foundations: Toward a Reorientation of the Human Sciences* (Chico, CA: Scholars Press, 1981).

17 See John D. Dadosky, "Healing the Psychological Subject: Towards a Fourfold Notion of Conversion?" *Theoforum* 35 (2004): 73–91, esp. 80–3.

18 See Lonergan's "Natural Right and Historical Mindedness," in *A Third Collection*, 169–83.

19 See Lonergan's *Grace and Freedom: Operative Grace in the Thought of St Thomas Aquinas*, ed. Frederick E. Crowe and Robert M. Doran, volume 1 of Collected Works of Bernard Lonergan (Toronto: University of Toronto Press, 2000); *Verbum: Word and Idea in Aquinas*, ed. Frederick E. Crowe and Robert M. Doran, volume 2 of *Collected Works of Bernard Lonergan* (Toronto: University of Toronto Press, 1997); *The Way to Nicea: The Dialectical Development of Trinitarian Theology*, trans. Conn O'Donovan (London: Darton, Longman & Todd, 1976).

20 Karl Rahner raised this objection in 1970 at a congress in Florida before the publication of *Method.* See P. McShane ed., *Foundations of Theology* (Notre Dame, IN: University of Notre Dame Press, 1972), 194–6 and 233 (Lonergan's response).

21 For example Lonergan's, "*Existenz* and *Aggiornamento*," in *Collection*, ed. Frederick E. Crowe and Robert M. Doran, volume 4 of *Collected Works of Bernard Lonergan* (Toronto: University of Toronto Press, 1988), 222–31, and "The Absence of God in Modern Culture," in *A Second Collection*, 106–16.

22 See Lonergan's "Healing and Creating in History," in *A Third Collection*, 100–9.

Part Two

Religious Experience, Faith, and Belief

Study 3

An Original Understanding of Religious Experience

This Study is an introduction to Bernard Lonergan's understanding of religious experience. It is divided into six sections. First, it will signal the emphasis placed on doctrine rather than on experience by ancient Christian doctors during premodern times, which cover the long period lasting from the first to the fifteenth century. This premodern prominence of doctrine will then be contrasted with the typically modern way of highlighting religious experience. Second, I will show how Lonergan locates religious experience within the broad functioning of the human mind. Third, since he characterizes religious experience as a realm of meaning, I will briefly return to the realms of meaning, which were compendiously introduced in Study 2. In the fourth and fifth sections, I will report Lonergan's description of the ascending and descending movements towards and from religious experience; this will be an opportunity to explicate the interrelations between the several components that he carefully sets within religious experience. Lastly, I will suggest an interpretation of his project as an integration of faith and reason.

PREMODERN TIMES CONTRASTED WITH MODERN TIMES

Prior to modern times, the significance of religious experience lay in its content not in the form or characteristics of the experience as such. The conceptualization of religious experience is a modern phenomenon.

In biblical concordances we learn that the few Hebrew and Greek words for "experience" are used to describe aspects of *non-religious* experience instead of aspects of *religious* experience. Nevertheless, the idea of religious experience was nascent in biblical revelation, with the accent that this revelation increasingly placed upon the individual conscience. This is clear for example in Ezekiel, chapter 18, and throughout the New Testament, particularly in the free decision to believe in Jesus and be baptized. Moreover, equivalent words were employed that clearly point to a religious experience, for instance when God says "a new heart I will give you, and a new spirit I will put within you, and I will remove from your body the heart of stone and give you a heart of flesh" (Ezek 36:26), or when Paul points to the spiritual state of having "the eyes of your heart enlightened" (Eph 1:18), or when John and his disciples proclaim "what we have heard, what we have seen with our eyes, what we have looked at and touched with our hands, concerning the word of life" (1 Jn 1:1).

Over the first fifteen centuries of Christianity, the initial proclamation of the Gospel, almost constantly meditated upon, led to the standard patristic-medieval presentation of the Christian message. Clearly the biblical texts as well as the writings of the Church Fathers include depictions of religious experience, but they are not composed from the perspective of religious experience. Instead, their authors locate it in the broad context of a history of salvation, because their goal is kerygmatic: to announce what God has done for his people, to proclaim the good news of the great gift that the Father has granted us in Jesus and in the Holy Spirit.

In addition to the kerygmatic concern of the patristic writers, their other principal interest can be said to be dogmatic. Their doctrinal teaching is central. They tell the great story of humankind's redemption and they draw out its implications in terms of beliefs and of principles of conduct. So far as I know, the reflections of the Desert Fathers, typically expressed in short maxims, were the only exception to the standard dogmatic ensemble. Commenting on their "very practical and unassuming wisdom," Thomas Merton stated: "Our time is in desperate need of this kind of simplicity. It needs to recapture something of the experience reflected in these lines. The word to emphasize is *experience*."[1]

Nonetheless, during that extended period between the time of the New Testament and the Renaissance, the general non-experiential preoccupation of the premodern Christians never reduced their ability to convey a deep religious experience. One finds that rich experiential substratum not only in Paul's letters and in John's epistle, as we have just observed, but also in the profound doctors Gregory of Nyssa, Augustine, Pope Gregory the Great, Bernard, and

Bonaventure, to mention but a few. As evidence, Gregory of Nyssa praises "the experience (*peira*) of those who have been judged worthy of enjoying what is beyond conception."[2] In addition, Dom Pierre Miquel refers to the widespread vocabulary of *experientia* in the Middle Ages.[3]

Even in objective thinkers such as Dionysius the pseudo-Areopagite and Thomas Aquinas we notice the expression "experiencing the divine realities" (*pathōn ta theia* in Greek, *pati divina* in Latin).[4] Undoubtedly Dionysius and Thomas teach that there is an experience of the divine realities. Thomas states that besides speculative knowledge (*cognitio speculativa*), there is another which is "an affective or experiential knowledge (*cognitio affectiva seu experimentalis*), whereby a person experiences (*experitur*) in oneself the taste (*gustum*) of divine sweetness and the delight (*complacentiam*) in divine will."[5] However, while using the patristic and medieval vocabulary of the "spiritual senses," Thomas stresses their analogical character by adding – often but not always – qualifying clauses, as in the phrases *quasi experimentalis* ("as it were experiential") and *quodammodo experimentalis* ("in a certain way experiential").[6]

Subsequently, in the sixteenth century, namely in the Renaissance, which was an epoch of humanism, the significance of human individuality emerged decisively. For instance, despite his disapproval of several philosophical opinions held by the great humanist Erasmus, Martin Luther relied on his own, rather idiosyncratic, experience of grace. That very experience caused a total reversal in his religious attitude and ushered in a vibrant act of faith and trust in Jesus.

This legitimatization of a person's lively and spirited faith recurs among the German Pietists of the seventeenth century and among the Methodists and the Shakers of the eighteenth century. At about the same time, among spiritual writers of the *Grand Siècle*, the French noun *la mystique* is coined to designate the private sphere of mysticism, which is often exalted to a degree that suggests a divorce from the rest of church life.[7] Moreover, notwithstanding the fact that most Catholic bishops at that time frown on the appeal to private experience, the word *experience* continues to be used, for instance by the late-eighteenth-century Jesuit Jean Grou, who wrote, "the great master of the interior life is experience" ("le grand maître de la vie intérieure, c'est l'expérience").[8]

It is in the nineteenth century that the concept of religious experience becomes central *in theology*, namely with Friedrich Schleiermacher, who has exercised an enormous influence upon what has been called liberal Protestantism. His longest work, *Der christliche Glaube* ("The Christian Faith") is written from the epistemological perspective of an experiential component, namely the "inward experience" (*innere Erfahrung*).[9] In this magnum opus, religion is divided between an outward and an inward side. He writes: "the organization of the communicative expressions of piety in a community is usually called *Outward Religion*, while the total content of the religious emotions, as they actually occur in individuals, is called *Inward Religion*."[10]

An all-important difference between Schleiermacher and Lonergan is the fact that the former extols religious experience at the expense of dogma. Religion (*Religion* in German) or piety (*Frömmigkeit*) equates to the consciousness (*Bewußtsein*) that is shared in the Church; belief (*Glaube*), far from possessing a permanent value, simply conveys this consciousness in a particular epoch. More will be said on Schleiermacher in Study 5. These preliminary observations are meant to help us realize how dissimilar Lonergan's interpretation of religious experience is from the father of liberal Protestantism – despite the highly significant points they have in common – namely first the difference between inward consciousness and its outward objectification, and second the very important role of religious consciousness for the understanding of Church doctrines.

In the wake of Schleiermacher, a subjectivistic construal of religious experience came to predominate in the writings of prominent Catholic authors such as the modernists in France and in England, and in the writings of Protestant authors such as William James in the United States as well as Ernst Troeltsch and Rudolf Otto in Germany. Interestingly, both Karl Rahner and Lonergan have been reproached for a subjectivistic stance (presumably akin to Schleiermacher's). Unfortunately Rahner is not faultless in this respect, as I shall try to show in Study 8. On the other hand, I think that this criticism is undeserved in Lonergan's case; we shall see why in the course of this essay.[11]

THE FUNCTIONING OF THE HUMAN MIND

Lonergan offers a conception of the human mind, which he calls "intentionality." This is key – without a clear grasp of the basic structure of human agency, it is virtually impossible to understand his concept of religious experience.

The word *Intentionalität*, which came from the Austrian philosopher Franz Brentano and was adopted by the German philosopher Edmund Husserl, refers to a "tension towards" reality – a tension that constitutes the life of the person. Drawing upon Thomas Aquinas's epistemology, Lonergan lays out how intentionality, as a dynamism, unfolds on four levels. A principal activity characterizes each level: experience, understanding, judgment, and decision. Each of these levels requires many other operations, which will be detailed in our next Study.

In the years following the publication of *Method in Theology*, Lonergan identified two movements in intentionality: from below upwards and from above downwards.[12] In the first case, from lower to higher, one starts by taking in data from the senses (sight, hearing, etc.), which in today's world may often be mediated electronically. While we share this first level with animals, the other levels are specifically human since they are rooted in acts of questioning. One is able to move from one level to the next by means of questions. Thus, one moves from level one (experience) to level two (understanding) by asking questions related to the data, such as: "What is that? What does that mean? How does that work? Why does that happen this way?" The answers to these questions are insights, which are acts of understanding, and are expressed in interrelated concepts that form hypotheses.

In turn, the hypotheses of this second level spontaneously lead us to ask questions of another kind, which allow a critical detachment with respect to our hypotheses. One thus progresses to the third level (judgment) when one asks: "Is that really the case? Is that true? Which hypothesis best reflects reality?" The answers given are for the most part only probable: they are judgments about reality, which is known in a manner that is probably correct yet imperfect and open to revision, as the history of science amply illustrates.

Finally, questions of yet another kind again lead us to progress to the fourth level (decision): "What needs to be done in a particular situation? Is there a good that emerges as a thing to be accomplished? Which action is worthy of being undertaken?" And, once a relevant value has been identified, "Must I be consistent and commit myself to it as well as to the people for whom this value makes a difference?"

The movement between levels that I have just described is from lower to higher. Yet human intentionality also operates from higher to lower. Lonergan adumbrates the actuality of that movement: "So it is that besides development from below upwards there also is development, if not from above downwards, at least from within an encompassing, enveloping worldview or horizon or blik."[13]

This second movement starts at the fourth level, the level of values, of love, of commitment to others. Here one lives within a horizon, that is, a set of interests, a particular sensitivity to aspects of one's life. This horizon enables us to more easily accept, at the third level, truths that agree with what we value, at the fourth level. Next, as we progressively accept these truths, we gain a deeper understanding of their significance, at the second level. Our horizon also influences the first level, making us more attentive to some data and experiences and less attentive to others. Moreover, still at the first level, we express that which we hold dear (fourth level), consider true (third level), and find meaningful (second level). We become both creators and communicators of data, which we hope are intelligible, true, and value-laden, through the use of the many forms of language at our disposal: scientific, technical, artistic, everyday language, etc.

REALMS OF MEANING

Since Lonergan considers religious experience as a realm of meaning, let us now lay out his unique position on realms of meaning, which was adumbrated in Study 2 and must be more fully described now. He differentiates several realms of meaning, which are basic kinds of human activity: common sense, theory, interiority, and transcendence, also called religion (see *Method,* 81–5 and 271–6). In each of those realms, human beings handle meaning in a specific manner. Later in the book, he adds two other domains of meaning: scholarship and art.[14] And he explains: "Any realm becomes differentiated from the others when it develops its own language, its own distinct mode of apprehension, and its own cultural, social, or professional group speaking in that fashion and apprehending in that manner" (272). Let us characterize each of the four basic types.

Fundamentally practical, common sense deals with things as concrete and in relation to us – that is, from the point of view of agents interested in achieving particular goals. In contradistinction to common sense, theory observes and inspects things in order to find their general characteristics and to devise abstract definitions; it aims at comprehending features of reality in the interrelations they have among themselves, in their connections, independently of the distinctive perspective of this or that observer. Interiority concerns the whole of the human subject, as practical, theoretical, religious, scholarly, or artistic, that is, as it consciously experiences its psychical, cognitive, and affective intentionality. Finally, as we saw in the preceding Study, in addition to this first kind of interiority, Lonergan identifies a second kind of interiority: transcendence, which is also called "religion" and which underlies the first kind. I shall have much to say about this presently.

Forms of common sense are innumerable, because every community – village, city, region, country – possesses a particular brand of common sense. Beyond common sense, people may become adept at theory. Theory began in the West with Socrates, who asked for definitions – neither too narrow nor too broad – of virtue, for instance. Socrates' demanding, intellectual requests baffled his fellow Athenians because their horizon was bounded by common sense. Plato and Aristotle considerably developed the field of theory, which at that time comprised both philosophy and science. It is only with Descartes that philosophy and science were distinguished.

Moreover, because physics was systematically figuring out its method in the seventeenth century, it became desirable to differentiate the worlds of meaning, especially science from common sense, as well as science from religion. Lack of differentiation accounted for the crisis that ended up with the condemnation of Galileo. From the standpoint of things related to common-sense observers, and for religious authorities who invoked the Bible, the sun moved around the earth, whereas the distinguished Italian scientist argued the opposite, basing himself not on common sense or on Scripture but on the standpoint of things interrelated among themselves, involving empirical measurements and theoretical reasons, which were appropriate in the sphere of physics.

Given the heritage of Plato in patristic times, Justin Martyr, followed by Clement of Alexandria and most other church fathers, soon realized that their teaching could no longer utilize exclusively scriptural categories, most of which belong in the realm of common sense; they would also require the assistance of philosophical categories. Had they been unwilling to discuss doctrinal matters theoretically, they would have been unable to meet the challenge of Greek and Roman non-Christian thinking; they would have been reputed intellectually inferior, incapable of using reason as competently as their adversaries or competitors – principally the Platonists, the Stoics, and the Gnostics.

Lonergan perceived a similar contest for the Church after the Second Vatican Council. That council had distanced itself from the traditional scholastic categories derived from the world of theory and it had preferred to talk with biblical words, which belong in the world of common sense. Although he greatly admired the intellectual feat of Thomas Aquinas and incorporated several Thomist elements into his own theology, he did not think one should cling to scholasticism. Likewise, he did not agree with those who remained content with a biblical approach that reflects representations going back as far as two thousand years. However central and fecund the word of God proves to be, it must be inculturated, that is, rephrased in terms of present-day numerous brands of common sense (see the chapter "Communications" in Lonergan's *Method in Theology*).

Instead, he argued that Christian theologians should accept the modern turn to the subject – anticipated by St Paul, St Augustine, and others – try to fathom its potential and adapt it to the design and purposes of theology. Solely the appropriation of a transcendental – that is, of a universal – understanding of the human person could allow theologians to transpose the common-sense idioms of the Bible into today's myriad sorts of common sense. Only a theology that is subject-centred but still respectful of the revelatory character of Christianity could mediate between ancient and contemporary forms of common sense, in which the divine message has been, is, and will be couched. Consequently, it is incumbent on theologians to become skilful at transiting from any realm of meaning to another. This requires being at home in all of the four basic realms, thanks to the acquaintance with one's operations and states in each of those spheres.

If we follow Lonergan's lead, religious phenomena will no longer be interpreted in a commonsensical or theoretical mode, namely from the standpoint of the first or of the second realm of meaning, but interiorly, from the standpoint of the third realm of meaning. Theological practice done from this standpoint will be more and more helpful in a worldwide mentality that is being vastly influenced by twentieth-century psychology. Still, the third realm of meaning, which employs psychological tools, must accord itself to the contents of the fourth realm, namely transcendence. Hence the significance of religious experience.

THE ASCENDING MOVEMENT TOWARDS RELIGIOUS EXPERIENCE

In *Method in Theology* as well as in Lonergan's subsequent writings, the concept of religious experience plays a key role. This section will lay out the several elements contained in this concept.

As explained in my section on the human mind, the subject moves through intentionality's four levels in two directions: in an upward movement and in a downward movement. The former starts with the first level, which is the sensitivity that we share with animals. Animals however are confined to a habitat, whereas we humans move beyond our immediate surroundings and have access to a world mediated by meaning. It is our capacity to question that enables us to go beyond the animal's (and the infant's) world of immediacy and, indeed, to go beyond ourselves towards what is not ourselves, as we progressively encounter meaning, truth, and value. Lonergan observes that, on the fourth level, the intentionality that transcends itself can be fulfilled when one lives in a state of love, either with one's husband or wife, with parents or children, with fellow citizens, or with God.

It is on the fourth level that Lonergan positions religious experience. Here, not only is one attracted to limited values but, more significantly, one apprehends ultimate value. This experience amounts to the religious aspect of the fourth level, namely the aspect concerned not with finite values but with infinite value. A unique affective state establishes itself: being in love in an unrestricted fashion. Lonergan avers that this affective state consists not in knowledge but in consciousness. "To say that this dynamic state is conscious is not to say that it is known. For consciousness is just experience, but knowledge is a compound of experience, understanding, and judging. Because the dynamic state is conscious without being known, it is an experience of mystery" (*Method*, 106). The consciousness he is talking about is experience not on the first but on the fourth level of intentionality: "It is this consciousness as brought to a fulfilment, as having undergone a conversion, as possessing a basis that may be broadened and deepened and heightened and enriched but not superseded ... So the gift of God's love occupies the ground and root of the fourth and highest level, of man's intentional consciousness. It takes over the peak of the soul, the apex animae" (*Method*, 107). However, when one becomes aware of this consciousness, there begins the knowledge of it, which Lonergan calls "faith." Faith is "the eye of religious love, an eye that can discern God's self-disclosures" (119).

THE DESCENDING MOVEMENT IN RELIGIOUS EXPERIENCE

So far I have described the movement from below upwards, which ascends towards the experience of being in love unconditionally. The complementary movement, from above downwards, is launched at the fourth level, more precisely in the religious aspect of that level, and it triggers various kinds of responses at the lower levels. It descends from hearing, so to speak, an inner word of transcendent love, to its outer forms of expression, until it reaches the stage in which new data are created. Chapter 4 of *Method in Theology* enumerates those religious discoveries. Unfortunately the succession of those discoveries remains partly implicit in Lonergan's account. Perhaps the sequence could be clarified as follows: a basic state of being in love unrestrictedly (prior word, also called inner word) → faith (the knowledge born of religious love) → the word as expressed (outer word) → belief (judgments of fact and of value to which one adheres) → action in the world (thanks to a self-transcendence that undoes decline and promotes progress in society).

In this sequence it is easy to observe a succession of mutual influences between the cognitive and the affective in the human person. In fact, at every level of intentionality, a combination of the cognitive and the affective is present. It is mostly at the lower three levels that cognitive operations predominate, and mostly at the fourth level that affective states predominate.

Incidentally, the primacy of love permits us to place Lonergan's view of religious experience within one of the medieval spiritual traditions, which culminates in the wonderful classic entitled *The Cloud of Unknowing*. He brings up the theme of the cloud a few times in *Method in Theology*. He refers twice to a fellow Jesuit's study on that little jewel, about which he avows: "I have found extremely helpful William Johnston's *The Mysticism of the Cloud of Unknowing* ... Readers wishing to fill out my remarks will find in his book a position very largely coherent with my own" (*Method*, 342, note

7; see 29, note 1, 266, and 278, note 4). Lonergan's description of religious experience equates it with mysticism; it has the advantage of situating mysticism with respect to the whole of human experience, that is, with respect to the overall intentionality.[15]

AN INTEGRATION OF FAITH AND REASON

Having spelled out the elements that Lonergan discerns within religious experience, let us pay some attention to another of his accomplishments, which consists in clarifying how faith and reason work hand in hand – something he does from the vantage point of the human subject.

After Luther, numerous theologians, spiritual writers, and catechists downplayed human reason and extolled personal experience. They reacted against the extreme emphasis on logic of the late Medieval Ages that is noticeable in Henry of Ghent, Scotus, Ockham, and the nominalists, as well as against the modern rationalism that is evident in Descartes. Those theologians, spiritual writers, and catechists turned their back on the intellect. They took away from the intellect a good portion of what belongs to it and they transferred that portion to the heart. Other theologians adopted – probably unwittingly – the conceptualism that Henry of Ghent had initiated, and this kind of thinking resulted in the narrow, static, and dogmatic neo-Scholasticism that dominated the Catholic agenda until the Second Vatican Council.[16]

By contrast, we find in *Method in Theology* a remarkable integration of faith and reason. Let us examine how Lonergan has achieved a synthesis that brings together intellectuality and affectivity. There are four points to be considered.

For one thing, religious experience is situated within the overall dynamism of human intentionality. It is definitely not isolated from the rest of human life. Lonergan locates it in the domain of transcendence. This domain is reached on the top floor of intentionality, namely on the fourth level, which for him is the level of affectivity par excellence, even though feelings are present at all levels. We can easily observe that, in his view, religious affectivity is not divorced from religious intellectuality. In fact, the vector that is "questioning" and the state of being in love are parallel: "Just as unrestricted questioning is our capacity for self-transcendence, so being in love in an unrestricted fashion is the proper fulfilment of that capacity" (106).

The second noteworthy thing is that, in chapter 11, entitled "Foundations," the author places religious experience at the very centre of theology, which is, after all, an intellectual enterprise. And yet this enterprise requires that the person of the theologian be transformed according to three conversions. Such a construal of theology applies not only to Christianity but to any religion that carries with it a belief in God (for instance, Judaism, Islam, Hinduism) and even to a non-theistic religion (such as Buddhism). Lonergan's ecumenism is broader than the dialogue between the Christian churches. It extends to all world religions, even though he himself did not engage in specific analyses of non-Christian religions. His contribution is methodological, elaborating the principles of a cross-cultural theology.[17]

At any rate, by paying attention to chapter 5, entitled "Functional Specialties," we find that Lonergan does not make of religious experience the sole basis of the theological enterprise. As explained in my previous Study, there are eight functional specialties, grouped into two phases. The first phase consists of research (assembling the relevant documents), interpretation (expounding the meaning of the texts), history (discerning the evolution of authors or of periods), and dialectic (lining up the oppositions between theological propositions and positions). The second phase consists of foundations (explicating the three conversions), doctrines (establishing what dogmas are to be accepted), systematics (arriving at a modest understanding of the contents of the dogmas), and communications (transmitting the religious message in a way that is at once respectful and critical of the common sense of the people addressed).

Furthermore, a third, all-important tenet of Lonergan's, which helps us to interpret religious experience correctly, is the thesis that "objectivity is simply the consequence of authentic subjectivity, of genuine attention, genuine intelligence, genuine reasonableness, genuine responsibility" (*Method*, 265; see 292). This position entails no objectivity on the first and on the second level of intentionality; only on the third level, the level of truth, is there cognitional objectivity, which must be completed by the full, existential objectivity of the fourth level. On the first two levels, we find merely inchoative objectivity. One becomes objective by obeying, not two, but four transcendental precepts: be attentive, be intelligent, be reasonable, be responsible (20).

Later in the same book, the author adds a fifth precept: be in love (268). As a result, alluding to the experience of otherworldly love, he makes bold to write: "religious conversion is the event that gives the name, God, its primary and fundamental meaning" (350). Nevertheless, we would err if we were to single out religious experience – here called "religious conversion" – as the exclusive and sufficient source of religious objectivity. The age-old temptation of illuminism, that is, of relying only on one's own inner light, precisely consists in segregating one's personal experience from the other levels of intentionality and setting it aside so as to consider its felt immediacy as an incontrovertible proof of its veracity.

CONCLUSION

We have noted the centrality of religious experience in Lonergan's theology. Although the biblical, patristic, and medieval writers fathomed religious experience in marvellous ways, they did not rely on it as much as the moderns do. It is obvious, then, that Lonergan is a modern thinker by virtue of having accepted the turn to the human subject, which we can observe in Luther, Descartes, and countless others in their wake.

Nonetheless, he knew that adopting this stance had its risks. Since the nineteenth century, the Catholic Church's authorities have been wary of theologies based on religious experience.[18] Given that the brilliant Schleiermacher, whose theology stems from religious experience, did not manage to avoid relativism and that most systems of thought whose foundation is religious experience have been incapable of providing for the possibility of reaching truth, we can say that, by comparison, Lonergan's contribution is remarkably sound both philosophically and theologically. Philosophically, it is grounded in a detailed epistemology, articulated in *Insight*, and summed up in the first chapter of *Method in Theology*; theologically, it is grounded in the gifts of love and light granted by the Holy Spirit.

Like Schleiermacher and so many other Christian thinkers, Lonergan situates religious experience at the core of theology.[19] However, unlike Schleiermacher, he thinks that a Christian community is not limited to the viewpoint of an epoch. For him, far from being subjectivistic, authentic subjectivity reaches objectivity. Given divine grace, the human person is capable of self-transcendence, and this attitude implies that one is open to what is said by other people and, indeed, by the Other. Consequently Lonergan sees the authentic subject not only as endowed with a receptivity to the wisdom of a religious tradition – a receptivity qualified by what the individual or the group happens to understand – but as willing to embrace the doctrinal corpus of a religious tradition. This doctrinal corpus, which is the natural development of the outer word, confirms and helps us deepen the inner word that has been experienced. In this way, objectivity, both theological and philosophical, is emphasized more by Lonergan than by most modern authors.

Moreover, by synthesizing the several components of human intentionality and by differentiating the realms of meaning, he manages to provide an account of the subjective side of Christianity that is admirably balanced and fair. He also elucidates the interrelations between affectivity and intellectuality. Man's loving impulse and questioning thrust are two dynamisms that work in tandem. Both are connected with the dogmatic side of Christianity, which is presented as an answer to the affective yearning and to the intellectual quest of humanity. For him, insofar as the reception of doctrines is accompanied by a lively search for understanding, the doctrines enable us to safeguard both love and truth.

Thus reason and faith are united in a way that differs from premodern accounts, even from the one we find in Thomas Aquinas, although it is obvious that Lonergan has been greatly inspired by his medieval mentor.[20] In fact, his vision is a transposition of Aquinas's thought into a conceptuality that is governed, not by theory (as in Aquinas), but by an intentionality analysis that has objectified the interiority. In this, Lonergan is confirmed as a modern thinker who refuses to jettison tradition – his objectification of interiority owes much to St Augustine and to John Henry Newman.[21]

NOTES

1 Thomas Merton, *The Wisdom of the Desert: Sayings from the Desert Fathers of the Fourth Century* (New York: New Directions Books, 1970), 11.

2 Gregory of Nyssa, *Ad Thalassium*, Prologue, §9, translated from the bilingual edition of *Questions à Thalassios* (Paris: Cerf, 2010), Series "Sources Chrétiennes," no. 529.

3 Pierre Miquel, *Le vocabulaire latin de l'expérience spirituelle dans la tradition monastique et canoniale de 1050 à 1250* (Paris: Beauchesne,

1989), and *Le vocabulaire de l'expérience spirituelle dans la tradition patristique grecque du IVe au XVIe siècle* (Paris: Beauchesne, 1989).

4 See Dionysius, *The Divine Names*, 2.9, 648B, and 3.2-3, 681A-684D; Thomas Aquinas, *Summa Theologiae*, I, q. 1, a. 6, ad 3; II-II, q. 45, a. 1, ad 2, and a. 2. With respect to Aquinas's *Summa Theologiae*, I refer to one of its parts: I, I-II, II-II, or III, followed by the question's number and by the article's number, whenever applicable. The "ad" designates a reply to an objection. I-II means the first half of the second part; II-II means the second half of the second part. Translations are mine, after having consulted two versions, namely the one by Fathers of the English Dominican Province and the one called Blackfriars.

5 Aquinas, *Summa Theologiae*, II-II, q. 97, a. 2, ad 2.

6 See A. Patfoort, "Cognitio ista est quasi experimentalis (*I Sent*, d. 14, q. 2, a. 2, ad 3m)," *Angelicum* 63 (1986): 3–13, and "Missions divines et expérience des Personnes divines selon S. Thomas," ibid., 545–59.

7 See Michel de Certeau, "Mystique," in *Encyclopedia Universalis* (Paris, 1971), vol. 11, 521–6.

8 Jean Nicolas Grou, *Spiritual Maxims*, trans. a monk of Parkminster (Delia, KS: Saint Pius X Press, 2014), "Author's Preface," 9. French title: *Maximes spirituelles, avec des explications* (1789), Avant-propos.

9 Friedrich Schleiermacher, *The Christian Faith*, trans. H.R. Mackintosh and J.S. Stewart (Edinburgh: T & T Clark, 1986), §14.1.

10 Schleiermacher, *The Christian Faith*, §6, Postscript.

11 On Rahner's and Lonergan's approaches to religious experience, see Louis Roy, *Transcendent Experiences: Phenomenology and Critique* (Toronto: University of Toronto Press, 2001), 128–41 and 177–8.

12 Lonergan, "Healing and Creating in History," in *A Third Collection*, ed. Frederick E. Crowe (New York: Paulist Press, 1985), 100–9, at 106.

13 Lonergan, "Religious Experience," in *A Third Collection*, 126.

14 I shall return to scholarship in the third section of this chapter. Insofar as art is concerned, Lonergan considers it as an irreplaceable mode of approaching and expressing reality, including religious reality; see *Method*, 61–4 as well as 72–3, 112, and 273. Moreover, from what he says about symbolic apprehension and expression, we may note that symbolism has much to do with art; see *Method*, 64–9 as well as 305–7.

15 In a book on Christian mysticism, I present the medieval debate about the priority of knowing or loving in mystical consciousness. See Louis Roy, *Christian Mysticism in a New Key: A Systematic Theology Approach* (New York: Crossroad, 2016), chapters 9 and 10.

16 I mentioned this problem of conceptualism in Study 1 and I will return to it later, especially in Study 8.

17 See his remarks on Wilfred Cantwell Smith and on Raimon Pannikar in *A Third Collection, passim*. See also the Index of Names.

18 On the Protestant side, Karl Barth and other Neo-orthodox theologians have vehemently opposed Schleiermacher and his liberal epigones. Like the Catholic authorities, they have been concerned about the subjectivism of the proponents of religious experience. However, in contradistinction to Catholics, who have defended the normativity of a Tradition safeguarded by the Holy Spirit, these Protestants have defended the paramount significance of a Revelation imparted by the Word of God.

19 See Louis Roy, *Le sentiment de transcendance, expérience de Dieu?* (Paris: Cerf, 2000), where Lonergan's concept of religious experience is differentiated into four main types and an effort is made to show the pastoral implications of a theology that takes seriously the transcendent experiences.

20 To assess the influence of Aquinas on Lonergan, see Lonergan's *Verbum: Word and Idea in Aquinas*, ed. Frederick E. Crowe and Robert M. Doran, volume 2 in *Collected Works of Bernard Lonergan* (Toronto: University of Toronto Press, 1997).

21 On Augustine's influence in matters of self-knowledge see Lonergan's Introduction to *Verbum*; on Newman's influence see Lonergan's *A Second Collection: Papers by Bernard J.F. Lonergan, S.J.*, ed. William F.J. Ryan and Bernard J. Tyrrell (Toronto: University of Toronto Press, 1996), 38, 273, 276, and *Caring about Meaning: Patterns in the Life of Bernard Lonergan*, ed. Pierrot Lambert, Charlotte Tansey, Cathleen Going (Montreal: Thomas More Institute, 1982), 13–14, 20, 46, 257.

Study 4

The Religious Quest and Faith

In his teaching, Lonergan repeatedly highlights the basic operations of the human mind, which occur in four hierarchical levels. As stated in our preceding Study, each of these four levels is characterized by a principal operation: (1) experience, (2) understanding, (3) judgment, and (4) decision. Lonergan enumerates several acts. (In the following quotation, I distinguish the four levels in square brackets.) "Operations in the pattern are [first level] seeing, hearing, touching, smelling, tasting, [second level] inquiring, imagining, understanding, conceiving, formulating, [third level] reflecting, marshalling and weighing the evidence, judging, [fourth level] deliberating, evaluating, deciding, speaking, writing" (*Method*, 6).

I would like to argue that by systematically elucidating those four levels of what he calls "conscious intentionality," and by relating them to religious experience, Lonergan makes an interesting contribution to the understanding of faith. This Study will also recall a few aspects of traditional theology that his thought helps us appreciate better. Moreover, it will show the complementarity between the path of creativity and the path of healing, along both of which human intentionality can tread. Lastly, I will develop the theme, present in Lonergan's works, of relatedness between persons, human and divine, and vis-à-vis the whole of reality.

LEVELS OF HUMAN INTENTIONALITY

Human intentionality is our built-in tendency to intend reality. Truth is manifold, for an aspect of it can be found on each of the four levels of intentionality as well as in religion. At each level, different criteria are spontaneously operative, which help us discern whether we are moving in the direction of truth: the first is taking account of the evidence; the second, asking questions and understanding; third, verifying and judging; and the fourth, pursuing what is worthwhile. Thanks to religious experience, these levels also apply to our openness to the infinite.

Let us revisit the levels of intentionality. On the first level, we want evidence. Anything that comes from our senses, imagination, and memory may be useful. What we hear people say, what we read, what we ourselves experience or experiment on, all this constitutes the level of data or evidence.

On the second level, we pursue understanding. We often receive data without actually grasping their meaning. We may, for example, do mathematics without really figuring out what the operations mean. We may think of ourselves as Christians, although with a very limited understanding of Christian life. But whenever we ask a question, we can feel in our mind a desire to know. Wonder has just been awakened; we seek to understand. What a difference between the expressionless attitude of a person who very rarely asks any question, the puzzled and eager face of a person who is raising a relevant question, and the flash in the eyes of a person who suddenly gets an insight!

The third level is the level of verification. We want to determine the validity of what we think we have understood. Does our idea or hypothesis correspond to the data? If it does, with what degree of probability? We have to qualify our affirmations and tell the difference between what is probable and what is certain. Wisdom entails accepting the merely probable in most cases and finding certitude in rare cases. It also entails believing other people, whether in science, in the field of common sense, or in religion. It is reasonable to believe when we have neither the time nor the capacity to verify for ourselves.

The fourth level is the level of decision and action. Prompted by our feelings, we value material things, living beings, and persons. We are attracted to them because of the utility, the pleasure, or the interest that we find in them, or because of their intrinsic beauty and lovableness. What Lonergan is pointing out is that the same eros of knowing that drives our desire to perceive, understand, and verify propels us further to decision and action.

Our lived experience clamours to insist that deciding and acting are not a simple affair. We know and yet often forget that self-interest rarely bequeaths the common good. Since history is a mixture of good and bad, of meaning and absurdity, a critique of society's ways is needed. Values often conflict with one another, either because some are actually disvalues or because a choice must be made between two or more values. We can follow the inspiration of our conscience, provided we weigh situations, notice other people's needs, and take into consideration our own talents and goals. So deliberation is sometimes difficult and sometimes easy. And according to Aristotle, virtue or excellence, which is acquired by practice, makes decisions and actions easier.

RELIGIOUS EXPERIENCE AND THE FOUR LEVELS

What Lonergan calls religion pervades the four levels of intentionality while culminating at the fourth. In this section, first I will highlight, perhaps more clearly than he does, the two sides – intellectual and affective – of religious experience; and second, I will relate religion to the four levels.

On the one hand, the basic question that humans ask concerning the mysterious ground of meaning, truth, and value, namely "the question of God" (*Method*, 101–3), shows that they are open to more than what they can grasp intellectually. It is impossible to answer this fundamental question by considering only our finite world. But this question is intelligent. Therefore those who want to respect all the requirements of human intelligence discover that they are related to an infinite Mystery. The function of the religions is to offer them an answer, either in symbolic or in conceptual language.

On the other hand, there are such phenomena as experiences of transcendence, in which people *feel* their openness to the infinite.[1] These experiences are more common than is acknowledged in our society. They are precious because it is in them that people's hearts are attracted to God. In such experiences, something other than the everyday is at work; for a Christian believer, it is the Holy Spirit.

Let us now inquire into how the process of coming to believe unfolds at each of the four levels of intentionality. Using Lonergan's categories, we can say that words, symbols, narratives, events, and people are religious data on the first level of intentionality. On the second level, such data give rise to apprehensions of meaning. Through education and acculturation, through conversation, through reading books and learning from the mass media, one gains insights into Christianity. Many aspects of it are seen to make sense insofar as they provide answers to one's aspirations and questions. One may have come into contact with the Church and have found light in the Bible, in liturgy, in catechesis. One may also have been struck by the quality of Christian witnesses, who are helpful, dedicated, and inspiring guides.

On the third level, since human reason and heart are fallible, intellectually perspicacious people realize that they cannot completely rely on their own judgments regarding religion and ethics. Hence the central role of a religious tradition. It is interesting to notice that in the last fifty years several Protestant exegetes have highlighted the formative function of various oral traditions prior to the writing of the New Testament texts.[2] Further, religious seekers can examine the credentials of Christianity (the beauty and profundity of its literature, the rich meaning it affords, the fruits it has brought about in the lives of the saints, etc.) and come to the conclusion that God has spoken through Jesus Christ and that such a revelation is worthy of our belief.

Anyone who knows the Catholic Church is confronted with her claim that thanks to the assistance of the Holy Spirit she is indefectible and infallible in matters of religious truth. (I will qualify this affirmation presently.) What is noteworthy, however, is that she views her testimony as inseparable from God's testimony. The risen Christ has granted his Holy Spirit to the Church: "The Advocate, the Holy Spirit, whom the Father will send in my name, will teach you everything and remind you of all I have said to you" (Jn 14:25).

While the foregoing is a simple claim regarding true judgment, it may be far from simple as a lived experience for the believer. There is and has always been theological discussion and disagreement in the Church. Nevertheless one can find a basic unity regarding the essentials of faith. A Catholic believer is someone who accepts the fundamental judgments of fact (on the third level) handed down by the Catholic tradition as lying beyond one's capacity to fully understand and verify them, but who is open to formulating and assessing different ways of expressing them in dialogue with other Christians and with all people of good will.

On the fourth level, the orientations of the Bible, of Jesus Christ, and of his disciples (what they called "the Way," Acts 9:2) are perceived as worthwhile, as desirable for one's own life. "Peter said to them, 'Repent, and be baptized every one of you in the name of Jesus Christ for the forgiveness of your sins; and you shall receive the gift of the Holy Spirit'" (Acts 2:38). This decision to greet God's love manifested in Jesus Christ and communicated by the Holy Spirit is on the fourth level because it entails choosing the means by which one is going to love Jesus and his Father, to be open to the guidance of the Holy Spirit, and to love one's fellow human beings in the light of the gospel.

Still, this decision is impossible without religious experience, which, as previously stated, is twofold. First, a person asks basic questions regarding the grounds of meaning, truth, and value. By doing so, one discovers that one is open to infinite meaning, truth, and value (God). And secondly, one affectively experiences the love of Jesus Christ and the Father's forgiveness and salvation. After hearing Peter talk about the death and the resurrection of Jesus, his listeners "were cut to the heart" (notice the feeling) and said to him and to the rest of the apostles, "Brethren, what shall we do?" (Acts 2:37). Paul also reacted with profound emotion to the transcendent value of Jesus' friendship and compassion. He refers to him as "the Son of God, who loved me and gave himself for me" (Gal 2:20). Such love grounds trust and makes people realize that the Holy Spirit has been acting in their heart.

CONTINUITY WITH PAST MASTERS

Lonergan's account of human intentionality has the advantage of continuity with great thinkers of the past. While materialists restrict their attention to experience, Plato concentrates on understanding, Aristotle explores judgment, and Augustine adds decision. Like the bishop of Hippo, Thomas Aquinas has these four operations. At various points in his writings we find connections between the senses (both external and internal) and understanding; between simple apprehension and judgment (respectively Aquinas's first and second operation of the intellect); and between the intellect (capable of understanding and judging) and the will (capable of deciding). Still, he does not combine the four basic activities in a single schema, as Lonergan does.

By employing the enlightening metaphor of levels, Lonergan gives us the full picture in a compendious manner and he helps us to reread very fruitfully ancient authors such as Plato, Aristotle, Augustine, and Aquinas, as well as modern ones like Newman. Indeed the New Testament includes elements that belong to each of the four levels. On the first level, the parables of Jesus are addressed to our imagination (Mt 13). Each of the successive levels is also illustrated by a different question. What gives rise to the second set of human acts is the question for intelligence, such as "How can this be?" (Lk 1:34). What gives rise to the third set is the question for truth, such as "Are you he who is to come?" (Mt 11:3). What gives rise to the fourth set is the question for deliberation, such as "What should we do?" (Lk 3:10, 12, and 14).

Plato shows us the enormous difference between perceiving and understanding. Heeding this difference, like most patristic and medieval writers, Aquinas distinguishes what is said of God metaphorically (*metaphorice dictum*) and what is said properly or literally (*proprie dictum*); the first kind of language is based on sense experience, while the second kind is based on the understanding of perfections. Scripture speaks metaphorically when it declares that Jesus is both "the Lion of the tribe of Judah" and "a Lamb" (Rev 5:5–6). It speaks literally when it refers to "the Father" and "the Son" (Jn 3:16) or when Jesus asserts that "there is only one who is good" (Mt 19:17).

This distinction is most helpful in the current debate prompted by the feminist critique of religious language. The validity of the metaphorical (issuing from perception, at the first level) is guaranteed by the literal (at the level of understanding). The importance of the literal can only be appreciated if we have realized that understanding adds much to mere perceiving. Literal names offered by divine revelation can safeguard the deposit of faith and guide current language usage. Only literal names can regulate inventiveness regarding new images. Otherwise, mere pragmatic decisions are made concerning words to be changed in liturgy, as will be demonstrated in Study 10. The new criterion risks being, "Let us adopt those new images of God, since they derive from our own human experience."[3]

The famous dictum by St Augustine, "Believe in order to understand," presupposes a fundamental distinction between the second and third level of human intentionality. On the second level, we ask questions such as "What is it?" On the third, we ask questions such as "Is it so?" Even children notice the difference between what is imaginable, meaningful and yet not necessarily actual (for instance, Santa Claus), and what is real (for example, their parents' rules). As Augustine and Newman insist, in the order of faith, assent constitutes the central act. People believe Christ, not because we find *everything* in his message equally meaningful, but in order to understand more and more of it.

Furthermore, Lonergan explains that it would be pointless to believe, were we not in love with the One we trust. Hence the significance of the fourth level of intentionality, as the precept "be in love" is one of the forms of the fourth-level precept "be responsible." Here he closely follows Augustine, who is at once the doctor of love and the doctor of grace. Both of them are fond of quoting Romans 5:5, "Hope does not disappoint us, because God's love has been poured into our hearts through the Holy Spirit who has been given to us."[4]

The strong emphasis laid on belief by the Catholic Church is balanced by her symbolic tradition. On the third level, belief is not blind, since it takes place in a context of prayer and *lectio divina*. By speaking of "real apprehension" ("real" in contrast to "notional"), Newman beautifully illustrates how the first and second levels do enrich the third, which he calls "assent."[5] On the first level, the imagination vividly represents the concrete scenes of the life of Jesus. Through the particular images and feelings, insights occur on the second level. Insights into Jesus, the Father, the Holy Spirit, and the lives of the saints are real apprehensions. Building on Coleridge and Newman, John Coulson emphasizes the paramount role of the literary imagination in opening up fresh perspectives on our world and on the meaning of existence.[6]

THE HEALING OF HUMAN INTENTIONALITY

Human intentionality was created pure and whole by God. Unfortunately it has been marred by original sin. Lonergan recognizes that human acts are distorted by several forms of bias: dramatic bias, which is psychic; individual bias, which fosters selfishness; group bias, which protects class interest; and general bias, the result of a pragmatism that prefers short-term gain to long-range solution (see *Insight*, 214–27 and 244–69). As a consequence, human intentionality stands in need of conversion. Conversion is brought about by divine grace, which operates first and foremost on the fourth level. It consists of the gift of a new heart. In its turn, this loving heart attunes a person to religious and worldly values, according to the right scale in which they must be situated.[7] About our wounded humanity and the divine solution, more will be said in Study 14, in the context of human rights.

When the heart is given a benevolent inclination towards God and the human race, and when each of the human values finds its own place in the order of love, healing takes place on the fourth level of intentionality. This level influences the third, in that one becomes willing to believe, to accept the truths revealed by the God with whom one is in love. Such truths are the judgments of fact that make up the Creed. For Lonergan, faith – "the eye of love" (*Method*, 117) – issues in judgments of value, and belief issues in judgments of fact. Based on those judgments, faith regulated by belief and seeking understanding engenders a great many insights on the second level of intentionality. At the same time, those insights are embodied in images, feelings, symbols, words, and artefacts on the first level of intentionality.

INTERIORITY AND RELATEDNESS

Inspired by Lonergan, this last section will expound two factors operative in human intentionality: interiority and relatedness. Not only is this pair relevant for our time, it can also play a normative function because it encompasses the two sides of a universally effective human intentionality, which is the nucleus of intelligent, reasonable, and responsible life. As relatedness, intentionality consciously heads towards what is other than itself; concomitantly, as interiority, intentionality is aware of itself intending otherness. Moreover, every time relationship and consciousness are equally valued, a mutual enhancement ensues.[8] When they are allowed to develop all the way without inhibition, it becomes clear that interpersonal love and contemplation – the most perfect cases of relatedness and interiority – go hand in hand and stimulate each other.

This account of interiority and relatedness as paired factors within intentionality has the merit of illustrating the complementarity of relatedness and interiority and, more specifically, the necessity of self-knowledge in order to spell out the range of relatedness. Furthermore, this adequate view regarding the epistemological and ethical potential of interiority enables us to unite what is so often kept apart or opposed, namely the natural and supernatural aspects of human experience. Far from being self-enclosed, human cognition and affectivity *naturally* seek to encounter the real. And far from being condemned to be restricted to itself, human intentionality is open to a *supernatural* elevation that does not abolish its intrinsic properties.

The dynamism of intentionality is oriented towards both the personal and the impersonal world. A sound differentiation of the sciences shows that the world is not the purely material bulk imagined by a reductionistic cosmology. An elucidation of the echelons of conceptuality found in physics, chemistry, biology, psychology, the various social sciences, and philosophy displays an increasing complexity (see *Insight*, 280–3). Chemistry, for instance, while not ignoring the laws of physics, nonetheless has recourse to a more embracing set of interlinked concepts. The same must be said of biology in regard to chemistry, of psychology in regard to biology, and so forth. At the heart of human studies one finds issues that cannot be unravelled without philosophical self-knowledge. Finally, because it is incomplete, distorted, and susceptible to a higher integration, the life of the spirit cannot be fully understood without acknowledging a higher, supernatural, level.

This hierarchical and dynamic vision of an evolutionary universe has affinities with the specific way in which humans undergo change (see *Insight*, 470–504 and *passim*). At every stage of development or transformation, the subject as integrator reaches a provisional form of coherence in its acquisitions. As operator, the subject moves from one stage to the next. For example, when questions for intelligence are asked, the subject proceeds from the perceptual to the intellectual level. When questions for reflection are asked, it shifts to the rational level. When questions for deliberation are asked, it raises itself to the existential level. When ultimate questions are asked, it enters into the religious dimension. Every time such a passage is made, that which precedes is not left behind, but is respected, taken along, and sublated as it is associated with a higher mode of human existence.

A strong and resourceful affective pull accompanies the intentional dynamism I have just sketched. The human person is not a "useless passion" (*passion inutile*, as Jean-Paul Sartre put it), but a meaningful passion, whose roots are neural, psychic, spiritual, and mystical. Halfway between the neural and the psychic, a censor preconsciously selects the affects and images that should eventually give rise to insights. Thus the neural contributes to the psychic life (see *Insight*, 214–23). As a principle of limitation – an aspect of finitude – the psychic collaborates with the intentional, which is a principle of self-transcendence. Mediating between the body and the spirit, the psyche provides a spatial-temporal springboard for human activities. Many negotiated interactions between the body and the spirit are needed so that a series of satisfying integrations are achieved. But besides integrations, new operations take place. These operations are the result of both the cognitive operators and the affective pull. In particular, the momentum of our operations comes in large measure from symbols, those combinations of images and feelings that propel us as we develop and as we emerge into superior ways of relating and being. At the fourth level, self-love based on self-esteem gives a person the inner security that is required for good judgments of value and courageous decisions.

CONCLUSION

As explained in Study 3 and elaborated in this Study, the path of creativity implies a movement upwards, which proceeds from the first level to the second and so forth. This movement is complemented by the path of healing, a movement downwards which descends from the fourth level until it reaches the first. However, these two movements can be differentiated into numerous sequences. Under the influence of the Holy Spirit, the human mind becomes very flexible, so that many interactions take place among the several levels it spans. The key to genuine faith is the emergence of self-transcendence, of real interest in others and in the Other, of sincere concern for people's progress in virtue and sanctity, of mutual solidarity and assistance during the lifelong process of personal development.

The task of pastors and educators consists in accompanying believers on the road towards Christian perfection. Lonergan's oeuvre can help them to know more fully the complexities of the embodied soul and to be competent guides in a world where many of our contemporaries are seeking self-knowledge and spirituality.

NOTES

1 See Louis Roy, *Le sentiment de transcendance, expérience de Dieu?* (Paris: Cerf, 2000) and *Transcendent Experiences: Phenomenology and Critique* (Toronto: University of Toronto Press, 2001).

2 See, for instance, James D.G. Dunn, *The Oral Gospel Tradition* (Grand Rapids, MI: Eerdmans, 2013), and his anterior books.

3 See Louis Roy, "Inclusive Language Regarding God," *Worship* 65 (1991): 207–15. I have returned to this issue in a book I am currently writing on God.

4 See, for instance, St Augustine, *The Trinity*, trans. Edmund Hill (Brooklyn, NY: New City Press, 1991), bk.VII, chap. 2, §5; bk.VIII, chap. 5, §10; bk. XIII, chap. 4, §14; bk. XV, chap. 5, §31; Lonergan's *Method*, 105, 241, 278, 282–3, 327, 340.

5 John Henry Newman, *An Essay in Aid of a Grammar of Assent*, ed. I.T. Ker (Oxford: Clarendon Press, 1985).

6 John Coulson, *Religion and Imagination "in aid of a grammar of assent"* (Oxford: Clarendon Press, 1981); he employs the word "imagination" in a broad sense, which includes apprehensions.

7 See *Method*, 117–18 and "Healing and Creating in History," in *A Third Collection: Papers by Bernard J.F. Lonergan, S.J.*, ed. Frederick E. Crowe (New York: Paulist Press, 1985), 100–9.

8 See Lonergan, "The Mediation of Christ in Prayer," in *Philosophical and Theological Papers 1958–1964*, ed. Robert C. Croken, Frederick E. Crowe, and Robert M. Doran, volume 6 of *Collected Works of Bernard Lonergan* (Toronto: University of Toronto Press, 1996).

Study 5

Faith and Belief

In *Method in Theology*, chapter 4, sections 7 and 8, Bernard Lonergan puts forward an all-important distinction between faith and belief. Does this distinction imply that he sides with liberal theologians who have extolled faith and relativized belief? If so, Lonergan would disagree with Thomas Aquinas, who insisted on never separating faith and the articles of belief. In this Study, first I will briefly delineate Aquinas's stance on this issue and mention its merits; second, I will characterize the views of two liberal theologians, Friedrich Schleiermacher (1768–1834) and Wilfred Cantwell Smith (1916–2000), and indicate their drawbacks; and third, I will ask whether Lonergan's position corresponds to that of Aquinas or to that of the liberal theologians, or whether it constitutes a third, distinctive position.

THOMAS AQUINAS'S POSITION

In his *Summa Theologiae*,[1] Thomas Aquinas introduces what he thinks are, following Augustine, the three elements of the faith-experience: *credere Deum*, to believe that God is such and such (= the material object); *credere Deo*, to believe God (= the formal aspect); and *credere in Deum*, to believe in God (= the affective side). In his commentary on Romans, he claims that the *credere Deo* is more properly the act of faith, showing its specificity.[2] In his commentary on John, he explains: "It is one thing to say: 'I believe that God [is such and such]' (credere Deum), for this indicates the object. It is another thing to say: 'I believe God' (credere Deo), for this indicates the one who testifies. And it is still another thing to say: 'I believe in

God' (credere in Deum), for this indicates the end. Thus God can be regarded as the object of faith, as the one who testifies, and as the end, but in different ways."[3]

The *credere in Deum* is ascribed to the will, whereas the first two phrases are facets of knowledge. *Credere Deum* is a matter of receiving the revealed propositions both in their symbolic and in their conceptual garb. *Credere Deo* refers to the ground of such an acceptance, to wit, the First Truth (*veritas prima*). Jesus Christ is the First Truth, the Word embodied in a human nature and thus made visible. To quote Aquinas again, Christ "was also full of truth, because the human nature in Christ attained to the divine truth itself, that is, that this man should be the divine Truth itself ... Thus it is said: 'In whom all the treasures of wisdom are hidden'" (Col 2:3).[4]

In *Summa Theologiae*,[5] Aquinas considers the intimate relation between the *credere Deo* (God as revealing) and the *credere Deum* (God as revealed). He writes that faith is grounded in the First Truth. Its formal object is compared to the middle term of a syllogism. The middle term appears both in the major and in the minor premises but not in the conclusion. It is the pivot that enables reasoning to tie up subject and predicate in the conclusion. Thus faith assents to propositions (God as expressed, which is the material object) because they are revealed by God (God as expressing, which is the formal object).

This link between the First Truth and the articles of faith has two advantages. First, the emphasis is laid on what might be considered an intellectual mysticism, namely the experience of the light thanks to which believers realize that they can totally trust God as truthful without any qualification.[6] "The light of faith makes one see (*videre*) the things that are believed"[7] or, more precisely, as the rest of reply 3 suggests, the light of faith makes one see *which things* must be believed. "For he [the believer] would not believe if he did not see that they were to be believed, either because of the evidence of signs or because of something else of this kind."[8]

The second advantage is that Christian beliefs are not devalued since they convey true judgments made in the light of the First Truth.[9] Aquinas claims that "the interior act of faith requires a firmness without any doubting, for such firmness proceeds from the infallibility of divine truth, on which faith finds support." He adds, "Faith must be simple, that is, without any mixture of error."[10] People cannot at the same time acknowledge the First Truth and entertain reservations about the beliefs that spell it out.

Still, as First Truth, the person of Jesus Christ is more important than the articles of faith: "Since whoever believes assents to someone's words, the person to whose words there is assent seems to hold the principal place (*principale*) and to be the end, as it were, in any form of belief. Those things are as if secondary (*secundaria*) that someone holds in willing to assent to that person. So he rightly has Christian faith who by his will assents to Christ in the things that truly belong to his teaching.[11]"

SCHLEIERMACHER'S POSITION

This section will not evaluate Schleiermacher's overall theology; instead, I shall concentrate on his views about faith and belief. Readers could find a very favourable treatment of his innovative thoughts on consciousness, feeling, and absolute dependence in two of my books, which highlight the implications of his original ventures for a philosophy of transcendent experiences and for a theology of mysticism.[12] As a matter of fact, since the beginning of my career I have been fascinated by this Protestant thinker's admirable contribution to modern theology.

If we compare him with Aquinas, we find that in the threefold constitution of the act of believing – *credere Deo, credere in Deum, credere Deum* – Schleiermacher lacks the first aspect: to believe God. For him, the most important aspect is the second one: to believe in God. As he announces in *The Christian Faith*, it is the experiential component, the "inward experience" (*innere Erfahrung*).[13]

However, in contrast to Aquinas, Schleiermacher infrequently alludes to the element of love which is the decisive factor in the *credere in Deum*. One of those very rare occurrences is "the love which wills to perceive" (§13, Postscript). This fact is surprising, since he speaks eloquently of "The Divine Love" in §166–7. For him, religious experience is self-consciousness, God-consciousness, the feeling of absolute dependence. Its kernel is not love, but the "facility of religious emotions" which, thanks to the redemptive influence of Christ, "becomes a permanent state" (§5.4). The believer thus passes from a state of "being bound" (*Gebundensein*) to "release" (*Erlösung*, §11.2, usually translated as "redemption." See the English translator's helpful remark). A permanent state of harmony seems to be preferred to love invested in mystical attentiveness throughout consolation *and desolation*, as Ignatius of Loyola would insist.

Schleiermacher locates faith-certainty, not in the *credere Deo*, but in an experience that has something in common with Aquinas's *credere in Deum*. Commenting on the "state of absolute facility" and on the "certainty (*Gewißheit*) that the influence of Christ puts an end to the state of being in need of redemption, and produces that other state [of absolute facility]," he declares: "this certainty is just faith (*Glaube*) in Christ," namely "the certainty which accompanies a state of the higher self-consciousness" (§14.1) – a certainty that is both inward (as simply conscious) and objective (as expressed). In the next paragraph, he writes: "faith is nothing other than the incipient experience of the satisfaction of that spiritual need [of redemption] by Christ" (§14.2). Faith is that "immediate (*unmittelbare*) certainty" (§33.3).

In Schleiermacher's theology, not only is the *credere Deo* absent but the *credere Deum* is considerably weakened. Belief (*credere Deum*) does not stem from the testimony of the First Truth (that is, from the *credere Deo*). Given its dependence upon an experiential and personal certainty, belief is greatly relativized.

In English we have two words for the Latin *fides*, namely *faith* (the experience) and *belief* (the proposition). Like Latin, the German tongue is in the semantic position of not having two distinct terms. Consequently, the German renders *fides* as *Glaube*. Like *fides*, *Glaube* includes an inner and an outer aspect. This is illustrated by the title of Schleiermacher's masterpiece, *Der christliche Glaube*. The English translation bears the title *The Christian Faith*. In this magnum opus, religion is divided up into an outward and an inward side: "the organization of the communicative expressions of piety in a community is usually called *Outward Religion*, while the total content of the religious emotions, as they actually occur in individuals, is called *Inward Religion*" (§6, Postscript).

As in his earlier addresses *On Religion: Speeches to its Cultured Despisers*, Schleiermacher bases his approach in *The Christian Faith* on "religion" (*Religion*). Yet, in the latter, mature work he emphasizes doctrine (*Glaubenslehre*) more than in his youthful *Speeches*. Here *Religion* or *Frömmigkeit* (piety) amounts to the *Bewußtsein* (consciousness) that is shared in the Church; *Glaube* (belief) conveys this consciousness at a particular epoch. The full title of Schleiermacher's later treatise denotes this contextualism: *Der christliche Glaube nach den Grundsätzen der evangelischen Kirche im Zusammenhange dargestellt*. Unfortunately the English edition leaves out most of it.

The full title can be translated as: *The Christian Faith systematically presented according to the principles of the Evangelical Church.*

In his *Brief Outline on the Study of Theology,*[14] Schleiermacher divides theology into three domains: philosophical, historical, and practical. Historical theology is subdivided into three parts: exegetical theology, Church history, and dogmatic theology (also called dogmatics or systematic theology).

Historical theology includes, first, "the knowledge of primitive Christianity" and "the knowledge of the total career of Christianity" (§85), and second, dogmatic theology, which I shall describe presently. Such historical knowledge must be taken into consideration. Some writings "are held capable of contributing to the original, and therefore for all times normative, representation of Christianity" (§103). "The collection of those writings which contain the normative representation of Christianity forms the New Testament canon of the Christian Church" (§104). Nevertheless, he does not understand this normativity in a definitive way: "the concept of normative value is also one which cannot be reduced to fixed, immutable formulas" (§108). He ascribes little significance to canonical writings[15] seemingly because in them we merely find the data out of which historical theologians can construct "the essence of Christianity," which is "attached to a certain history" (§21). Likewise, he sees orthodoxy as having little weight, with the true challenge for theologians consisting in combining an "orthodox" and a "heterodox" element since they must care for "true unity" and "free mobility" in the interpretation of doctrine (§203–4).

Dogmatic theology is the culmination of the whole enterprise. Schleiermacher holds the view that dogmatic theology merely represents "the historical knowledge of the present condition of Christianity," that is, "the knowledge of doctrine now current in the evangelical church" (§195; see §97). This means that "the knowledge of doctrine" of the German Evangelical Church of his time is to be preferred to the knowledge that the German Protestants had in previous centuries or to the knowledge that other churches currently profess.

Like Kant, Schleiermacher attempts to discover the universal in the subjective. According to *The Christian Faith*, "piety," or the "feeling of absolute dependence," is "a universal element of life" (§33). For all his efforts to balance the subjective with the objective – or "piety" with "belief" – he clearly leans on the side of a subjective faith and he does not consider church belief as permanently valid.[16]

He himself tells his readers that he selects the doctrines constitutive of his theology according to the following criterion: as "accounts of the Christian pious states of mind (*frommen Gemütszustände*)" (§15; I have modified the translation), they must play a role in sustaining the harmonious feeling of dependency.[17] Accordingly, he disregards the idea of creation and insists only on preservation. Logically, far from being supernatural, the action of God's grace in the believer is reduced to the level of a sustaining presence. Furthermore, the fact that his Jesus Christ is not divine implies that he rejects the councils of Nicea and Chalcedon. For Schleiermacher, the fall, the redemption, the resurrection, and the ascension do not count for much and even the Trinity is relegated to an appendix at the very end of his book (§170–2).[18]

WILFRED CANTWELL SMITH'S POSITION

For his part, Smith tirelessly denounces the modern understanding of an individual religion as a body of doctrines.[19] He extols living faith, which he calls religion (in the singular) as contradistinguished from religions (in the plural), that is, institutional religions. He condemns the fact that "the religious orientation has been reduced (and I stress that word) from an active faith to a passive belief, from the *form* of consciousness to an *object* of consciousness."[20] He vigorously combats the opinion that faith is reducible to an acceptance of beliefs. He equates faith with trust, commitment, response, and loyalty. He finds his clue in the etymology of the English verb "'to believe": "Literally, and originally, 'to believe' means 'to hold dear': virtually, to love … This is what its German equivalent *belieben* still means today."[21] Undoubtedly he has a point here – and a beautiful one indeed.

Moreover, he regards faith as generic, that is, as common to all, including philosophers and scientists, who look up to truth as worthy of being unconditionally pursued.[22] By contrast, beliefs are specific and so they diversify. In his use of the word "beliefs," however, one notices an ambiguity. Sometimes it means opinions; sometimes it means dogmatic propositions. Like Aquinas, Smith states that having faith is very different from having opinions. But Aquinas would disagree with Smith's relativization of dogmatic propositions.

Smith has no room for beliefs that would correctly transmit a divine revelation. Instead, he praises the creative power of human faith. He asserts: "It is faith that generates the tradition in the first place" and "it is the faith of Muslims that has made the Qur'an the Word of God."[23] Hence the perspicuously anthropocentric nature of theology: "This is *fides quaerens intellectum*, faith in pursuit of self-understanding, in the new and rich and enriching sense of *fides humana*, the faith, the involvement, the final truth of humankind."[24] In *Faith and Belief* Smith has a section on Thomas Aquinas. As Frederick Crosson perceptively notes, Smith misconstrues Aquinas's distinction between the formal and the material objects of faith. "Smith takes the distinction of formal and material objects of faith to be a distinction of immediately and mediately simple. The formal object of faith, he seems to think, is the prima veritas, God himself, purely simple, while the material object of faith consists of those things assented to which orient us to God: 'ritual and ceremony, the sacraments, scripture ... propositions, belief and other intellectual constructs.'"[25]

Crosson goes on to explain: "The distinction of material and formal objects of faith is not properly the distinction of mediately and immediately simple — though that distinction is coextensive with it – but rather the distinction between what is believed and the reason for believing it. And that reason is, simply, that it is spoken by God. So the difference can be expressed as that between what is believed and who is believed."[26]

Smith realizes that, within a confessional context, beliefs matter very much for religious people because they are profoundly bound up with faith. Yet, as a historian, he seems to accept a relativist account of belief. In order to show great respect for diversity (a laudable concern), he pays tribute to a common faith construed as a human attitude, an existential stance, accompanied with anti-intellectual connotations (that is, depreciation of beliefs understood as propositions). Faith appears to be untranslatable into statements that would have objective and universal validity. Hence James McClendon's and James Smith's correct observation: "there remains a difference, which [Wilfred Cantwell] Smith's account cannot make clear, between sincere attachment to a false belief and hypocritical profession of a true belief."[27]

Furthermore, beliefs have no set content, hence no normative value, since any particular belief takes on a different meaning in each believer's mind. Of course, Smith is right when he insists on variations of meaning, given that beliefs are appropriated by different persons. Nonetheless, the disquieting implication here is that the faithful can never express with precision the exact commonality in the meanings they are supposed to share.[28]

He ends up with a disjunction faith/belief, rather than a Thomist assumption of beliefs by faith thanks to a supernatural light shed on all aspects of reality. Given that he excessively relativizes judgments, his position – wittingly or not – does not depart from the one propounded by classical liberal theology since the time of Schleiermacher.

Interestingly, Lonergan reports that he heard Smith declare that "good rationalism is the basis of a world theology." Then, having acknowledged that Smith himself (presumably as a man of faith) is not a rationalist, since faith for him means feeling, Lonergan comments: "He thinks that rationalism is a good solid basis for world unity and, of course, very scientific. Scientists thought so too until they hit Quantum Mechanics."[29] Yet, apart from this criticism of Smith, Lonergan approved of Smith's thesis that "to live religiously ... may demand the totality of a person's response."[30] And on one occasion, after having heard Smith's response to one of his papers, entitled "Faith and Beliefs," Lonergan replied in a very irenic fashion, extemporaneously mentioning their "quite different interpretations of faith," owing to their dissimilar backgrounds (Reformed and Catholic). He explained that Smith equated faith with "involvement" (in the sense of personal commitment) whereas he himself was "interested in some sort of an intellectualist notion of faith."[31]

Still, several features of Smith's standpoint resembles Lonergan's, which seems also to smack of rationalism in its apparent devaluation of the authoritative character of belief. Hence the necessity of clarifying the latter's position.

LONERGAN'S POSITION

Chapter 4 of *Method in Theology*, entitled "Religion," introduces a distinction between the inner and the outer word (112–19 and 123). Of the latter, he writes, "By the word is meant any expression of religious meaning or of religious value" (112). Of the former, he writes: "Before it enters the world mediated by meaning, religion is the prior word God speaks to us by flooding our hearts with his love. That prior word pertains, not to the world mediated by meaning, but to the world of immediacy, to the unmediated experience of the mystery of love and awe" (112).

What is this prior, inner word? In Study 3, I situated it in a sequence of spiritual discoveries. I would now venture to say that it covers a twofold experience. First, an affective state that transcends our ordinary states: "being in love in an unrestricted fashion" (105), that is, "being in love without limits or qualifications or conditions or reservations" (106). Second, within this affective state, a distinctive quality of consciousness, as indicated by the phrase "a conscious dynamic state of love, joy, peace" (106). This particular quality consists in a fulfillment: "Being in love with God is the basic fulfilment of our conscious intentionality" (105). Lonergan situates such consciousness "on the fourth level of intentional consciousness" (106): "it is this consciousness [on the fourth level] as brought to a fulfilment" (107). Earlier, he speaks of a "basic fulfilment" (84). John Dadosky rightly emphasizes the adjective *basic*: "It is the *basic* fulfillment, but I presume Lonergan chose his words carefully, so we can say that it is not the *complete* fulfillment. Such fulfillment would pertain to the finality of human longing for the beatific vision."[32]

The two sides of religious experience – love and the felt consciousness that permeates it, which is felt – are concomitant. Nevertheless, such consciousness differs from knowledge: "the dynamic state is conscious without being known" (106). Accordingly, Lonergan defines faith as follows: "Faith is the knowledge born of religious love" (115). He distinguishes between two kinds of knowledge: "besides the factual knowledge reached by experiencing, understanding, and verifying, there is another kind of knowledge reached through the discernment of value and the judgments of value of a person in love" (115).

The latter kind of knowledge – knowledge derived from religious experience – consists of several components, which Lonergan does not differentiate. Still, based on his analysis of ordinary consciousness, we can differentiate religious consciousness in the same manner, that is, from below upwards and according to the four levels of intentionality. First, as soon as a person pays attention to one's conscious state, it becomes *awareness*.[33] Second, whenever it is named, such awareness acquires a meaning. Third, if it is pronounced to exist, it constitutes a judgment of fact. Fourth, if it is considered to be good, it makes up the content of a judgment of value.

Commenting on Pascal's famed phrase, "the heart has reasons which reason does not know,"[34] Lonergan construes "the heart's reasons" as "feelings that are intentional responses to values," in this case "an apprehension of transcendent value" (115; see 30–1 for the notion of intentional response). Unfortunately Lonergan does not clearly distinguish, in the response to transcendent value, between the feelings (the affective quality of consciousness) and the apprehension that we may have of them. Moreover, he does not spell out the components of that apprehension: affective awareness, meaning, and the two kinds of judgment (judgment of fact and judgment of value). His treatment of the intentional response is too compact.[35]

Lonergan seems to situate faith half-way between the inner and the outer word. Faith is more explicit than the inner word and less explicit than the outer word. Still, I would submit that the original being-in-love is not yet a "word." It is apprehended as a word from God only when we become aware of it. As I pointed out (a couple of paragraphs before this one), such awareness must be equated with the beginning of a knowledge. In the being-in-love, God tells us something. When our consciousness turns into an awareness, this lovingness becomes a word. Therefore, to designate the original, not yet known, being-in-love, I prefer the phrase "inner grace," which Lonergan uses later in the book (298).

Does the fact that faith is first and foremost an affective knowledge demote the outer word to a secondary place? Not for Lonergan, who declares: "One must not conclude that the outward word is something incidental. For it has a constitutive role" (112; on constitutive meaning, see 78). Elsewhere he makes it clear that "the constitutive role of meaning" is far from being secondary: "acts of meaning inform human living."[36] Talking about two persons in love, he explains: "It is the love that each freely and fully reveals to the other that brings about the radically new situation of being in love and that begins the unfolding of its life-long implications" (113). And on applying this interpersonal situation to love between God and us, he states: "One needs the word – the word of tradition that has accumulated religious wisdom, the word of fellowship that unites those that share the gift of God's love, the word of the gospel that announces that God has loved us first and, in the fulness of time, has revealed that love in Christ crucified, dead, and risen" (113). Lonergan insists on not separating the inner and the outer word: "God's gift of his love has its proper counterpart in the revelation events in which God discloses to a particular people or to all mankind the completeness of his love for them" (283). In any religious tradition, revelation is accounted for by the combination of two structures.

Speaking of "Christian religious experience," Lonergan distinguishes its two fundamental components as follows:

> As infrastructure it is the dynamic state of being in love in an unrestricted fashion, a conscious content without an apprehended object. Its suprastructure, however, is already extant in the account of Christian origins: God sending his only Son for our salvation through death and resurrection and the sending of the Spirit. The distinctiveness of Christianity lies in this suprastructure. To it the adherents of non-Christian religions may wish to ascribe the characterization of religious experience as being in love.[37]

The outer word brings about a focusing: "In the paschal mystery the love that is given inwardly is focused and inflamed, and that focusing unites Christians not only with Christ but also with one another."[38] How do people come to agree to religious beliefs? Lonergan answers: "Among the values that faith discerns is the value of believing the word of religion, of accepting the judgments of fact and the judgments of value that the religion proposes" (118). The importance of belief derives from the fact that, far from being solitary, religious experience is shared and that "community invites expression" (118). Moreover, countless believers acknowledge that "not only the inner word that is God's gift of his love but also the outer word of the religious tradition comes from God" (119). In a previous section on belief in general, Lonergan highlights the indispensable role of belief in daily life and observes that even scientists "do not suffer from a pointless mania to attain immanently generated knowledge of their fields" (43; see 41–7). "Immanently generated knowledge" refers to what individuals can verify for themselves – a very limited portion of science indeed.

Still, Lonergan maintains a primacy of faith over belief: "Beliefs do differ, but behind this difference there is a deeper unity. For beliefs result from judgments of value, and the judgments of value relevant for religious belief come from faith, the eye of religious love, an eye that can discern God's self-disclosures" (119).

What is absent here is the language of obligation, which we find in Aquinas (and in Newman for that matter). In Aquinas's view, believers see that some things are to be believed. This "seeing" depends on the insight that Jesus Christ, the First Truth, must be believed. This is the formal aspect of faith. In a religious quest, at some point an individual comes to the conclusion that believing has now become a matter of obligation for her or for him. Newman thus wrote to Mrs William Froude: "Faith then is not a conclusion from premises, but the result of an act of the *will*, following upon a *conviction* that to believe is a *duty*."[39]

Does Lonergan disagree with his mentors Aquinas and Newman in this respect? Admittedly, his language is less compelling than theirs. Nonetheless, if the eye of faith "can discern God's self-disclosures" (119; see the fuller quotation I gave, two paragraphs above), then the person makes judgments of fact and of value about them and must normally feel obliged to assent. A few lines which precede on the same page are clear about a divine revelation: "There is a personal entrance of God himself into history, a communication of God to his people, the advent of God's word into the world of religious expression. Such was the religion of Israel. Such has been Christianity. Then not only the inner word that is God's gift of his love but also the outer word of the religious tradition comes from God" (119). And he adds: "Finally, the word of religious expression is not just the objectification of the gift of God's love; in a privileged area it also is specific meaning, the word of God himself" (119).

In fact, in chapter 2 of *Method in Theology*, in a section on beliefs, Lonergan uses the vocabulary of obligation. After the step in which a person judges that someone else's statement deserves to be believed, there comes the step in which the person reaches "the conclusion that the statement ought to be believed." The reason is that "if believing is a good thing, then what can be believed should be believed" (46). Remarkably, the whole analysis of belief here is non-confessional; it is applicable to any religious situation or to any purely moral situation.

If, in *Method in Theology*, Lonergan refrains from proposing the traditional Roman Catholic view of faith as fashioned by Aquinas, it is because his goal is not to expound a theology according to any specific tradition.[40] He himself points out: "I am writing not theology but method in theology. I am concerned not with the objects that theologians expound but with the operations that theologians perform" (xii). His project is ecumenical, in the broadest sense, which includes even non-Christian theologies. "By distinguishing faith and belief we have secured a basis both for ecumenical encounter and for an encounter between all religions with a basis in religious experience" (119; see 332–3).

Towards the end of his chapter on religion, he writes: "in acknowledging a faith that grounds belief we are acknowledging what would have been termed the *lumen gratiae* or *lumen fidei* or infused wisdom" (123). He is right that such light of grace, light of faith, or infused wisdom, amounts, not to the outer word, but to the inner word, namely to the subjective experience. The role of the objective tradition is to explicate that religious experience and to situate it in a context of meaning and value.

By stressing the inner word, then, does Lonergan condone the anthropocentrism of Schleiermacher, of Smith, of liberal Protestantism, and of Catholic modernism?[41] In 1969 he noted the difference between those currents and "most of the traditional forms of Christianity":

> My account of religious beliefs does not imply that they are more than objectifications of religious experience. It is a view quite acceptable to the nineteenth-century liberal Protestant or to the twentieth-century Catholic modernist. But it is unacceptable to most of the traditional forms of Christianity, in which religious beliefs are believed to have their origin in charism, prophecy, inspiration, revelation, the word of God, the life, death, and resurrection of Christ.[42]

However, Lonergan seems to come dangerously close to liberalism and modernism when he approves of Karl Rahner for having stated that "in theology theocentrism and anthropocentrism coincide. On this basis, he [Rahner] desires all theological statements to be matched by statements of their meaning in human terms." Nonetheless, Lonergan warns us about a false interpretation, which Rahner also rejects: "Explicitly Father Rahner excludes a modernist interpretation of his view, namely, that theological doctrines are to be taken as statements about merely human reality."[43] Thanks to his critical realism, Lonergan's method decisively undercuts any immanentism or subjectivism.[44] Still, given the justified criticisms levelled against the anthropocentrism characteristic of liberal Protestantism and of Catholic modernism, I would suggest we refrain from speaking of

Lonergan's method as an "anthropocentrism," and we rather call it "an anthropological method" (in the transcendental sense that he adopts, which is not an idealism, but a critical realism).

CONCLUSION

On the one hand, Lonergan never belittles the validity of religious beliefs in the way Schleiermacher and Smith do.[45] Of course, it is not that, for them, beliefs are always unimportant; some are pronounced helpful. Still, they are not normative in the sense that they would possess a permanent validity. On the other hand, in *Method in Theology* he does not argue for specific beliefs. This decision of his follows from his theological methodology.

In chapter 12 of *Method*, he presents and endorses the First Vatican Council's position on the permanence of dogmas. He concludes: "It presupposes (1) that there exist mysteries hidden in God that man could not know unless they were revealed, (2) that they have been revealed, and (3) that the church has infallibly declared the meaning of what has been revealed. These presuppositions also are church doctrines. Their exposition and defence are tasks, not of a methodologist, but of a theologian (323–4). Why then does he introduce such theological "presuppositions" (as he calls them) in his methodological book? In order to make an epistemological point, which is a part of his method; the permanence of dogmas is not incompatible with their historicity (see 325). Let us note that this epistemological principle may very well apply to other religious traditions such as Hinduism, Buddhism, or Islam.[46]

We have no indications that later in his life Lonergan abandoned his robust dogmatic stance in Catholic theology itself.[47] Having situated it in the dynamic context of the multiple developments of doctrines (see 326), he had no need to forego his dogmatic stance.

NOTES

1 Thomas Aquinas, *Summa Theologiae*, II-II, q. 2, a. 2.

2 Aquinas, *Super Epistolam ad Romanos Lectura*, Caput 4, Lectio 1, no. 327, in *Super Epistolas S. Pauli Lectura*, ed. Raphael Cai (Turin: Marietti, 1953), vol. 1:58.

3 Aquinas, *Commentary on the Gospel of St. John*, trans. James A. Weisheipl and Fabian R. Larcher (Albany, NY: Magi Books, 1980; distributed by St. Bede's Publications, Petersham, MA), chap. 6, lecture 3, no. 901; translation slightly emended.

4 Aquinas, *Commentary on the Gospel of St. John*, chap. 1, lecture 8, no. 188.

5 Aquinas, *Summa Theologiae*, II-II, q.1, a.1

6 I am not saying that Aquinas's mysticism is intellectualistic. It also has a pronounced affective side, as in this sentence: "To know Christ's love is to know all the mysteries of Christ's Incarnation and our Redemption. These have poured out from the immense charity of God; a charity exceeding every created intelligence." Aquinas, *Commentary on Saint Paul's Epistle to the Ephesians*, trans. Matthew L. Lamb (Albany, NY: Magi Books, 1966), chap. 3, lecture 5, 144.

7 Aquinas, *Summa Theologiae*, II-II, q. 1, a. 4, ad 3.

8 Ibid., ad 2.

9 Romanus Cessario rightly insists on the inseparability of the First Truth and the articles of faith, in *Christian Faith and the Theological Life* (Washington, DC: The Catholic University of America Press, 1996), 57 and 62–3.

10 Aquinas, *Expositio Primae Decretalis*, no. 1142, in *Opuscula Theologica*, ed. Raymundo A. Verardo (Turin: Marietti, 1954), vol. 1:419. We find the same argument in his commentary on the *De Trinitate* of Boethius, q. 3, a. 1, ad 4, that is, in *Faith, Reason and Theology*, trans. Armand Maurer (Toronto: Pontifical Institute of Mediaeval Studies, 1987), 69.

11 Aquinas, *Summa Theologiae*, II-II, q. 11, a.1.

12 See Louis Roy, *Transcendent Experiences: Phenomenology and Critique* (Toronto: University of Toronto Press, 2001), chap. 4 and passim, and Mystical Consciousness: Western Perspectives and Dialogue with Japanese Thinkers (Albany, NY: SUNY Press, 2003), chap. 6.

13 Friedrich Schleiermacher, *The Christian Faith*, trans. H.R. Mackintosh and J.S. Stewart (Edinburgh: T & T Clark, 1986), §14.1; the other references will be given in my text.

14 Schleiermacher, *Brief Outline on the Study of Theology*, trans. Terrence N. Tice (Atlanta: John Knox Press, 1977).

15 Hence the criticisms addressed to Schleiermacher from an orthodox Lutheran standpoint, for example by Werner Schultz, *Schleiermacher und der Protestantismus* (Hamburg: Herbert Reich, 1957).

16 For an analysis of the rather shaky intellectual underpinnings of Schleiermacher's position, see Louis Roy, "Schleiermacher's Epistemology," *Method: Journal of Lonergan Studies* 16 (1998): 25–46.

17 In the *Brief Outline*, "the cultivation of doctrine" amounts to "the process by which the religious self-consciousness gains clarity" (§166).

18 See Charles C. Hefling, Jr, "The Meaning of God Incarnate according to Friedrich Schleiermacher; or, Whether Lonergan is Appropriately Regarded as 'A Schleiermacher for Our Time,' and Why Not," in *Lonergan Workshop*, vol. 7, ed. Fred Lawrence (Atlanta: Scholars, 1988), 105–77, at 126–52.

19 See William Cantwell Smith's several books, notably *The Meaning and End of Religion: A New Approach to the Religious Traditions of Mankind* (New York: Macmillan, 1963) and *Belief and History* (Charlottesville: University Press of Virginia, 1977).

20 William Cantwell Smith, *Towards a World Theology: Faith and the Comparative History of Religion*, (Maryknoll, NY: Orbis Books, 1989), 93.

21 William Cantwell Smith, *Faith and Belief* (Princeton, NJ: Princeton University Press, 1979), 105. In contemporary German, however, *belieben* means "to wish."

22 Cantwell Smith, *Faith and Belief*, 11, 16, and 129–42. On the other hand, he does not mean that "faith is everywhere the same"; there are "several types of faith" (11).

23 Ibid., 5 and 4.

24 Ibid., 6.

25 Frederick J. Crosson, "*Fides* and *Credere*: W.C. Smith on Aquinas," *The Journal of Religion* 65 (1985): 399–412, at 404, quoting Smith, *Faith and Belief*, 91.

26 Crosson, "*Fides* and *Credere*," 405.

27 James Wm. McClendon, Jr and James M. Smith, *Convictions: Defusing Religious Relativism*, rev. ed., 1994 (reprint, Eugene, OR: Wipf and Stock, 2002), 156.

28 See the very helpful piece by Dennis M. Doyle, "Objectivity and Religious Truth: A Comparison of Wilfred Cantwell Smith and Bernard Lonergan," *The Thomist* 53 (1989): 461–80.

29 *Caring about Meaning: Patterns in the Life of Bernard Lonergan*, ed. Pierrot Lambert, Charlotte Tansey, and Cathleen Going (Montreal: Thomas More Institute, 1982), 30 and 175–6.

30 Lonergan, "Religious Experience," in *A Third Collection: Papers by Bernard J.F. Lonergan S.J.*, ed. Frederick E. Crowe (New York: Paulist Press, 1985), 115–28, at 122.

31 Lonergan, "Faith and Beliefs," in *Philosophical and Theological Papers 1965–1980*, ed. Robert C. Croken and Robert M. Doran, volume 17 of *Collected Works of Bernard Lonergan* (Toronto: University of Toronto Press, 2004), 30–48, at 48.

32 John D. Dadosky, "Is There a Fourth Stage of Meaning?" *The Heythrop Journal* 51 (2010): 768–80, at 771.

33 Search for "awareness" in the Glossary and Index of Louis Roy's *Mystical Consciousness*.

34 Blaise Pascal, pensée 423 (see pensée 424) in *Pensées*, trans. A.J. Krailsheimer, rev. ed. (New York: Penguin Books, 1995). This numbering is based on Pascal's first copy, the order of which is followed by Louis Lafuma's edition: Pascal, *Oeuvres complètes* (Paris: Seuil, 1963).

35 For a critique of Lonergan's position on feeling and knowledge, see Louis Roy, *Transcendent Experiences*, 135–7 and 162–4.

36 Lonergan, "Theology in its New Context," in *A Second Collection: Papers by Bernard J.F. Lonergan, S.J.*, ed. William F.J. Ryan and Bernard Tyrrell (Toronto: University of Toronto Press, 1996), 55–67, at 61.

37 Lonergan, "Prolegomena to the Study of the Emerging Religious Consciousness of Our Time," in *A Third Collection*, 55–73, at 71. Underlying Schleimacher's excessive relativization of dogma, we find his inadequate epistemology. See Louis Roy, "Schleiermacher's Epistemology," *Method: Journal of Lonergan Studies* 16 (1998): 25–46.

38 "Philosophy of God, and Theology: The relationship between Philosophy of God and the Functional Specialty, Systematics," in *Philosophical and Theological Papers 1965–1980*, 162–218, at 170.

39 *The Letters and Diaries of John Henry Newman*, ed. Charles Stephen Dessain with others (Oxford: Clarendon Press, 1961–1984), vol. 12:228.

40 Except for a few very short passages in *Method in Theology*, quoted by Charles Hefling, "Revelation and/as Insight," in *The Importance of Insight: Essays in Honour of Michael Vertin*, ed. John J. Liptay Jr and David S. Liptay (Toronto: University of Toronto Press, 2007), 97–115, at 101.

41 On the difference between Lonergan and Schleiermacher in this respect, see David F. Ford, "*Method in Theology* in the Lonergan Corpus" in *Looking at Lonergan's Method*, ed. Patrick Corcoran (Dublin: The Talbot Press, 1975), 11–26, especially 14–17.

42 Lonergan, "Faith and Beliefs," in *Philosophical and Theological Papers 1965–1980*, 30–48, at 46–7.

43 Lonergan, "Theology and Man's Future," in *A Second Collection*, 135–48, at 148.

44 Much more successfully than Rahner; see Study 9 in this book.

45 Avery Dulles wrongly associates Lonergan's understanding of the relation of faith/belief with Wilfred Cantwell Smith's; see *The Assurance of Things Hoped for: A Theology of Christian Faith* (New York: Oxford University

Press, 1994), 194. Dulles contradicts himself when he states, on the one hand, that Lonergan "affirms a close connection between faith and beliefs" (154) and, on the other hand, that Lonergan "makes a sharp distinction between faith ... and beliefs" (173). The "close connection" is mentioned only once, whereas the "sharp distinction" recurs as a refrain in his comments on Lonergan.

46 See, for instance, John J. Makransky, "Historical Consciousness as an Offering to the Trans-Historical Buddha," in *Buddhist Theology: Critical Reflections by Contemporary Buddhist Scholars*, ed. Roger R. Jackson and John J. Makransky (Richmond, Surrey: Curzon Press, 2000), 111–35.

47 An instance of that dogmatic stance is Lonergan's treatment of the Council of Chalcedon in a lecture he gave in 1975 entitled "Christology Today: Methodological Reflections," in *A Third Collection*, 74–99.

Study 6
Meaning and Truth

In this Study I would like to apply Lonergan's distinction between meaning and truth, that is, between the second and the third level of intentionality, to the tension that exists between these two factors in contemporary Christian experience. Among many Westerners at the moment, interest in spirituality is based not on truth coming from outside but on personally discovered meaning. At the same time, Church authorities present their message as being the truth, namely as the revelation given by God. However, we shall soon see that personal meaning and revealed truth are far from being contradictories.

In a piece entitled "On Reincarnation," I used the distinction between understanding and judging, introduced by Aristotle and followed by Aquinas and Lonergan, to address the question whether belief in reincarnation is compatible with Christian faith. I then argued that even though reincarnation is *meaningful*, it is nevertheless not *true* because it is fundamentally opposed to the resurrection, a doctrine revealed by the Holy Spirit in the Bible.[1]

I am aware that my position on truth appears dogmatic. In current parlance, the adjective "dogmatic" is pejorative: it implies a doctrinal rigidity. This acceptation indicates something about Western culture, for which any claim to *religious* truth is insufferable, whereas similar claims to truth are acceptable in the natural sciences, in political practices (for instance, Western democracy as the best system everywhere), or in the sphere of human rights (as we shall see in Study 14). It is not too difficult to detect here a huge contradiction between our bias against truth-statements in religious matters and our easy acceptance of truth in other areas.[2]

It is normal for cultivated Christians to feel a tension between meaning and truth, given the state of our current thinking – moulded as it is by the eighteenth-century Enlightenment with its rejection of any specific revelation, supposedly because such revelation would be demeaning for human autonomy and perhaps linked to intolerance and violence.[3] In this context, I will now delineate three positions concerning the relationships between meaning and truth. The first stresses meaning at the expense of truth; the second stresses truth at the expense of meaning; and the third seeks a complementarity between meaning and truth. Thereafter, I will have recourse to Lonergan's inner word/outer word pair, so as to elaborate the relation between interior inspiration and exterior revelation. Finally, I will highlight the role of affectivity in the passage from meaning to truth.[4]

TWO INCOMPLETE POSITIONS

For the advocates of the first position, religion (which most of them nowadays prefer to call "spirituality") is a matter of meaning. One is interested in religious experiences, questions, ideas, and practices insofar as they give significance to one's life. In a manner that is rather individualistic, one selects, among all that is offered by various religious agencies or churches, only that which assists and enhances one's personal quality of life. The criterion of such choices is the very meaning that the individual's intelligence can understand and that his or her heart can be satisfied with. What the human mind retains as meaningful becomes *truth for them*, whether they manage to convince themselves of that truth, or they remain in doubt about it, or they hold it simply as some practical inspiration.

The drawback of this position is relativism. In this frame of mind, people take ideas to be true *relative to* the individuals who accept them. No one is ever sure that the beliefs of any group are better than the beliefs of another group. Consequently the individual takes a practical decision and declares, "I consider this particular belief to be true because it has meaning for me." Adolphe Gesché, who strongly emphasized the importance of meaning in faith and theology, nonetheless cautioned: "The promotion of meaning must always be controlled by truth's signature. Being meaningful does not suffice for making something true. If it did, this principle would amount to falling into a new positivist snare, namely a hermeneutical positivism."[5]

Likewise, Pope John Paul II, after evoking the questions that human beings raise about meaning, stated: "No one can avoid this questioning, neither the philosopher nor the ordinary person. The answer we give will determine whether or not we think it possible to attain universal and absolute truth, and this is a decisive moment of the search. Every truth – if it really is truth – presents itself as universal, even if it is not the whole truth. If something is true, then it must be true for all people and at all times."[6]

To give an instance in which a concrete truth was understood by a few dissidents as "universal and absolute," I will cite the profound personal transformation of Bartolomé de Las Casas. He abandoned his privileged status of *encomendero*, that is, owner of Indian labourers (practically speaking, slaves), in sixteenth-century Hispaniola (now the Dominican Republic) and later, as a Friar Preacher and a bishop, he dedicated fifty years to an uphill battle against the oppression of the natives by the Spaniards. It was not primarily because his conversion gave him *meaning* (although of course it did), but because the friars in Hispaniola had denounced the treatment of Indians as totally contrary to the *truth* of divine law, laid down in the Bible and exemplified in Jesus.[7]

Let us now consider those who adopt the second position. To them, religion is a matter of truth. They are mindful that the biblical prophets and writers insisted on the fact that they were not speaking in their own name but in the name of the Lord. In the wake of the authors of the New Testament, Christian believers know that Jesus Christ is not merely a man but also the Son of God, the one who manifests who the Father is and leads human beings to salvation. Those believers are convinced that, insofar as the interpretation of the Bible is concerned, the Church's councils uttered truths valid for all times because each of those councils concluded a long period of serious thinking and discussion sustained by the Holy Spirit.

The drawback of this position is dogmatism. This happens when such people take either Scripture or Church declarations literally. They are likely to fall into a fundamentalism of the Bible or of the Magisterium.[8] All doctrines are put on the same plane. It becomes impossible to distance oneself from minor doctrines, for instance from the rigid way moral principles are not infrequently applied.[9] In addition to being overly dogmatic, most of the time the position that I am describing is classicist.

Lonergan has much to say about classicism. While recognizing its remarkable achievements, he nevertheless criticizes classicism for seeing itself as *the* culture, superior to other interpretations of human life, none of which can count as culture. In fact, classicist culture, which was generally accepted in the West during the eighteenth and nineteenth centuries, is one particular culture. Hence Lonergan's attempt to interpret the notion of culture not in a normative but in an empirical fashion, taking account of the wealth of data about the cultures of humankind – data coming from history, social anthropology, and sociology. Given the importance of this issue, I will return to it in the next Study.

Let us conclude this section by briefly portraying the confrontation between the relativists and the classicists once more. The first position states: "This is true because it is meaningful." And since meaning varies according to individuals, groups, cultures, and epochs, it follows that truth also changes. The second position avers: "This is meaningful because it is true." And since truth must always be the same, one deduces that meaning cannot change. The first position is subjectivistic and relativistic; the second position is dogmatic and classicist.

MEANING AND TRUTH INTERTWINED

A third position, which synthesizes what is valuable in these opposites, is trying, these years, to find and express its identity. It could be characterized as an orthodoxy that recognizes cultural variations compatible with the Gospel. In the eyes of this supple orthodoxy, truth is immutable, while meaning fluctuates to a certain degree, that is, inasmuch as truth is grasped and articulated differently, although not contradictorily, throughout the ages.

It is important to notice the following healthy phenomenon: an ardent, well-oriented quest for meaning manifests itself as inclusive of a quest for truth. Hence, Henri Bouillard rightly deplores what he calls "the separation between fact and meaning" – a separation typical of a certain scholasticism, with its one-sided emphasis on fact, for both Catholics and Protestants since the seventeenth century. He proposes to replace this inadequate problematic with a new approach, which he dubs "discerning meaning in the fact."[10] In the context of this Study, the key to his approach is the interpenetration of meaning and truth. This interpenetration is founded both on the transcendental functioning of the human mind and on Christian revelation.

By paying attention to what Lonergan writes about the levels of human intentionality, we can learn much from him about the transcendental functioning of the human mind. Intentionality searches for meaning. It needs to understand what it experiences in everyday life as well as what is proposed by its cultural and religious heritage. In the face of events, of what it feels and conjectures, and of what it receives from the mass media, the human mind spontaneously asks: What is it? What does it mean? In all domains of human activity, including religion, meaning is the principal concern.[11] Believing is impossible without a minimum of understanding of that to which one adheres; and it is impossible to remain a believer without developing this kind of understanding.

Still, it is the selfsame human mind that entertains interrogations not only at the level of meaning, but equally at the level of truth, when it asks: Is what I have so far assumed really true? Perhaps I ought to think twice about it? What then emerges is no longer merely the desire to understand, but also the desire to verify.

Furthermore, any intelligent person becomes aware of the problem of error. Knowing a little about the history of ideas may help in this respect. It is not necessary to have studied all the great thinkers to note that they differ among themselves regarding virtually all the significant aspects of reality and of human life. If Plato, Aristotle, Plotinus, Spinoza, Kant, Hegel, and others did not succeed in verifying the whole corpus of their tenets, who can pretend to be capable of answering the essential philosophic questions in a manner that is satisfactory and true?

In light of this difficulty concerning truth, Lonergan twice made a case for the indispensability of belief, first in *Insight* (chapter 20, section entitled "The Notion of Belief") and second in *Method in Theology* (chapter 2, section entitled "Beliefs"). He stresses the very little percentage of "immanently generated knowledge," that is to say, of the knowledge personally acquired and verified in daily life, in scientific learning, and in religious education. He also stresses the high percentage of belief among people of common sense, among scientists, and among adepts of any religion of any spiritual movement. In *Insight* he raises the following question: "A fundamental methodological issue is whether each man should confine his assents to what he knows in virtue of his personal experience, his personal insights, and his personal grasp of the virtually unconditioned or, on the other hand, there can and should be a collaboration in the advancement and dissemination of knowledge" (726). And of course he acknowledges the necessity of collaboration: "If there is such a collaboration, then men not only contribute to a common fund of knowledge but also receive from it. But while they contribute in virtue of their own experience, understanding, and judgment, they receive not an immanently generated but a reliably communicated knowledge" (725). Whereas in *Insight* he treats the issue of belief in science and philosophy, in *Method in Theology* he broadens his scope so as to include the appropriation of "one's social, cultural, religious heritage," which "is largely a matter of belief" (41). In addition, he expounds five steps in the process of coming to believe (44–6).

INTERIOR INSPIRATION AND EXTERIOR REVELATION

The issue of meaning and truth remains insoluble until one acknowledges the priority of the experiential over the conceptual. It is often said that many people pay lip service to Christian revelation without putting it into practice; their conceptual discourse may be correct and yet their lived experience leaves much to be desired. Moreover, countless others, who deny any revelation, are nonetheless committed to justice; their lived experience is admirable and yet, from a Christian standpoint, their conceptual discourse is deemed inadequate, at least to a certain extent. In the realm of action, they behave, often unwittingly, in accordance with the ideals of Christian revelation while diverging from what they perceive as the content of that revelation. In both cases, we observe a discrepancy between orthodoxy and orthopraxis.

One can account theologically for the difference between these two groups by distinguishing, with Lonergan, between the inner and the outer word, whose complementarity I reported in Study 3. There is a definite complementarity between interior inspiration, which is the source of conviction and commitment, and exterior revelation, which is conveyed by the Judeo-Christian tradition. The former is the work of the Holy Spirit, who is active in hearts and intellects; the latter is the work of Jesus Christ, whose human nature actualizes God's project and makes it visible in our world. A good number of Christians, while distractedly hearing the message of Jesus, are deaf to the interior inspiration coming from the Holy Spirit. By contrast, a good number of justice-engaged atheists unknowingly follow that inspiration while rejecting aspects of the message of Jesus. Lastly, a good number of Christians accept both the interior inspiration and the exterior revelation.

John Henry Newman thus begins one of his Anglican sermons: "God the Son has graciously vouchsafed to reveal the Father to His creatures from without; God the Holy Ghost, by inward communication."[12] Personal inspiration and communal revelation can complete each other. On the one hand, one needs a minimum of inspiration if one is to become interested in revelation. On the other hand, external revelation confirms and supports the commitment of persons and groups interiorly touched by inspiration.

Notwithstanding this fruitful interaction, we should ask: Does the Christian message grant merely a pragmatic encouragement to the inspiration or is it a challenge issuing from the truth of God expressed in the Bible? This question takes us back to the fundamental objection: How can one reasonably think that God has revealed truth within a particular religious tradition and not in other traditions? In the wake of the Second Vatican Council, we can answer that Catholicism does not rule out the wisdom of other traditions, but offers criteria allowing believers to sort out elements of truth and elements of error in that wisdom.[13] This assurance does not imply the moral or spiritual superiority of Christians over non-Christians, but rather their acquiescence and deference to the word of God.

Of course it is this submission to the word of God that is disputed or rejected in numerous circles. In this regard, it is relevant to ask oneself whether the passage from meaning to truth, or from inspiration to revelation, may be basically ennobling. This passage not infrequently increases a more profound openness to reality. The word of God turns out to be cognitionally liberating: revelation makes it possible to discard the intellectual mistakes that handicap people's minds, and to envision dimensions of reality whose meaning has scarcely been adumbrated before, either because one has grasped only a part of it or because it transcends the range of the human mind.

AFFECTIVITY IN THE PASSAGE FROM MEANING TO TRUTH

The intellectual aspect of the passage from meaning to truth must ally itself with an affective experience. People can familiarize themselves with Christianity thanks to the mediation of witnesses whose speech and commitment possess meanings that draw non-Christians to them. In addition to this attraction, such witnesses refer others to Jesus. Indeed, it is only when one perceives the significance of Christ's person and message for one's life that one can envisage the possibility of accepting his teachings as true. Further, one must have been touched by his love, at once human and divine, so as to become capable of desiring to learn things from Christ that then begin to appear extremely important. It is a matter of friendship. Then a believer dares to affirm the Christian fact, namely the life, passion, and resurrection of Jesus, as presented by those who greet him as their friend and see themselves as friends in the Church. Such a faith affirmation is made possible out of love for Jesus, who himself lived this Christian fact and offers to all the ability to live it.

As Hans Urs von Balthasar insightfully put it, "the primal authority is the Son interpreting the Father through the Holy Spirit as divine love."[14] For those who recognize this authority of love, the words of Jesus open them up to other perspectives, and by means of those perspectives, open them up to the Other, who is the Lord.[15] God unveils himself in human history as different from what they used to imagine, for his otherness consists in an undreamed-of love.

If such an Otherness exists, then the meanings conveyed by the Christian tradition cannot be measured by human intelligence or enclosed in its natural horizon. Human reason ought never to claim the right to domesticate revelation. On the contrary, the reality proposed by revelation is defined by an Other who remains master of his word – this word being itself grounded in an unheard-of love. The divine possible is much more than the human possible. Hence, the quest for meaning faces the critical challenge of judging the real according to meta-scientific, meta-psychological, and even meta-philosophical criteria.

CONCLUSION

The itinerary succinctly described in these pages requires time. One should not succumb to the temptation of telescoping its stages. I have only intended, in this Study, to raise the issue of the relations between meaning and truth, to critique two options – which are unfortunately found widespread within present-day Churches – and to highlight an emerging alternative: a dynamic interaction between meaning and truth. This view, inspired by Lonergan, has the potential to be respectful both of the Christian uniqueness discovered in truth, and of the plurality of cultures exemplified in the variety of meanings.

NOTES

1 Louis Roy, *Coherent Christianity* (Ottawa: Novalis, 2005), 116–22; see also 42–3.

2 This epistemic attitude is perceptively pointed out by Lesslie Newbigin, *The Gospel in a Pluralist Society* (Grand Rapids, MI: Eerdmans, 1989), 15 and 23.

3 See Louis Roy, "Does Christian Faith Rule out Human Autonomy?" *The Heythrop Journal* 53 (2012): 606–23.

4 To keep as simple as possible this application of Lonergan's distinction between the second level of intentionality (here called "meaning") and the third level (here called "truth"), I will not take into account the intricacies of the highly differentiated analysis Lonergan offers in chapter 3 of *Method in Theology* or in "Is It Real?" *Philosophical and Theological Papers 1965–1980*, ed. Robert C. Croken and Robert M. Doran, volume 17 of *Collected Works of Bernard Lonergan* (Toronto: University of Toronto Press, 2004), 119–39.

5 Adolphe Gesché, "Théologie dogmatique," in *Initiation à la pratique de la théologie*, ed. Bernard Lauret and François Refoulé (Paris: Cerf, 1982), vol. 1, 271.

6 John Paul II, Encyclical Letter *Fides et Ratio: On the Relationship between Faith and Reason*, §27.

7 See Gustavo Gutiérrez, *Las Casas: In Search of the Poor of Jesus Christ*, trans. Robert R. Barr (Maryknoll, NY: Orbis Books, 1993). In Catholic Spain there was much discussion about the plight of the Indians, whereas in Protestant England there was no debate about the way the Indians were treated by the Americans of the colonies. In British political science, the *truth* that would have allowed people of good will to stand up against injustice towards the natives was simply missing or instead was replaced by *meaningful* maxims at the service of the powerful and the wealthy.

8 On fundamentalism, see Louis Roy, *La foi en dialogue* (Ottawa: Novalis, 2006), 127–9.

9 By contrast, for an example of flexibility in concrete ethics, see Thomas Aquinas, *Commentary on Aristotle's Nicomachean Ethics*, trans. C.I. Litzinger (Notre Dame, IN: Dumb Ox Books, 1993), Book Two, lecture 2, no. 259: "The teaching on matters of morals even in their general aspects is uncertain and variable. But still more uncertainty is found when we come down to the solution of particular cases."

10 Henri Bouillard, *Vérité du christianisme* (Paris: Desclée de Brouwer, 1989), 140–7.

11 See Lonergan's "Dimensions of Meaning," in *Collection*, ed. Frederick E. Crowe and Robert M. Doran, volume 4 of *Collected Works of Bernard Lonergan* (Toronto: University of Toronto Press, 1988), 232–45. See also Roy, *Coherent Christianity*, 135–7 and Study 1 in this book, section entitled "The Role of Meaning."

12 John Henry Newman, *Parochial and Plain Sermons* (London: Longmans, Green & Co., 1896), Vol. II, Sermon XIX, 217.

13 See Vatican II, the Declaration on the Relation of the Church to Non-Christian Religions (*Nostra Aetate*).

14 Hans Urs von Balthasar, *Love Alone*, trans. Alexander Dru (New York: Herder and Herder, 1969), 47.

15 See Louis Roy, *Self-Actualization and the Radical Gospel* (Collegeville, MN: The Liturgical Press, 2002), chapters 4–6.

Study 7

Neither Classicism nor Relativism

Throughout his oeuvre, Lonergan meets head-on an epistemological problem that can be solved by neither classicism nor relativism, namely the problem of objectivity in the social sciences, in philosophy, and in theology. His solution amounts to a rejection of both classicism and relativism in favour of an empirical notion of culture (*Method*, 302).

In his homily for the opening of the conclave of cardinals on 18 April 2005, right before being elected pope, Joseph Ratzinger warned against "the dictatorship of relativism" – a denunciation that was reissued by Pope Francis in his first address to the Diplomatic Corps on 22 March 2013 where he commented that "the tyranny of relativism ... makes everyone his own criterion and endangers the coexistence of peoples." In the eyes of most Christians, a philosophical standpoint that is relativist does not go along with the possibility that biblical revelation might be universally true. Still, responsible theologians cannot remain content with a mere dogmatic repudiation of relativism. Rather, the question to be raised concerns *the way* relativism can be overcome. Moreover, because it is too narrow, the classicism that has been prevalent for centuries in the Catholic Church cannot readily convey truths whose universality would be evident.

This Study deals with the issues at stake in the inadequacy of both classicism and relativism. The first section explains Lonergan's rejection of the classicist notion of culture and his understanding of the empirical notion of culture. Thereafter, it outlines some tenets that were paramount for him: method as supplanting theory; human intentionality as self-transcending; subjectivity in search of objectivity; the progression from a perspective towards a universal viewpoint; and the compatibility between historicity and permanence concerning religious truth. Each of these tenets plays a role in the overcoming of both classicism and relativism.

CLASSICISM ACCORDING TO LONERGAN

In the Introduction to *Method in Theology*, Lonergan wrote:

> The classicist notion of culture was normative: at least *de jure* there was but one culture that was both universal and permanent; to its norms and ideals might aspire the uncultured, whether they were the young or the people or the natives or the barbarians. Besides the classicist, there also is the empirical notion of culture. It is the set of meanings and values that informs a way of life. It may remain unchanged for ages. It may be in process of slow development or rapid dissolution. (xi)

He described the classicist notion of culture as follows:

> Classicist culture was stable. It took its stand on what ought to be, and what ought to be is not to be refuted by what is. It legislated with its eye on the substance of things, on the unchanging essence of human living and, while it never doubted either that circumstances alter cases or that circumstances change, still it also was quite sure that essences did not change, that change affected only the accidental details that were of no great account ... Classicist culture, by conceiving itself normatively and universally, also had to think of itself as the one and only culture for all time.[1]

Lonergan's stress on the limitations of classicism nevertheless did not prevent him from deeply appreciating humankind's great works, namely the classics. For him, the latter play the all-important role of fostering personal changes and of introducing an individual or group into a tradition of adequate interpretation (see *Method*, 161–2). So a non-classicist may very well be steeped in the classics.

In fact, classicist culture, which was generally accepted in the West during the eighteenth and nineteenth centuries, is one particular culture. Hence Lonergan's attempt to interpret the notion of culture not in a normative but in an empirical fashion, taking notice of the wealth of data about the cultures of humankind – data coming from history, social anthropology, and sociology. He portrayed the contemporary problem as follows: The contemporary notion of culture is empirical. A culture is a set of meanings and values informing a common way of life, and there are as many cultures as there are distinct sets of such meanings and values. However, this manner of conceiving culture is relatively recent. It is a product of empirical human studies. Within less than one hundred years it has replaced an older, classicist view that had flourished for over two millennia" (301). Later in the book, he remarked, "What ended classicist assumptions was critical history" (326). That is to say, the very practice of history and of other human studies placed centre-stage the fact that the meanings of life are ever in flux and past counting. For instance, literary criticism can easily demonstrate how two profoundly Christian tragedians such as Shakespeare and Racine nonetheless evidence worldviews that stand in contrast to each other. And even the New Testament authors convey meanings that are quite dissimilar in the way they point to equivalent truths.

Lonergan reproached classicism for seeing itself as *the* culture, in contrast to presumably inferior interpretations of human life, none of which, according to classicism, can count as culture. Moreover he listed the assumptions of modern scholastic theology, such as those of Melchior Cano, based on classicism: "Truth is eternal. Principles are immutable. Change is accidental ... It [Thomism] supposed the existence of a single perennial philosophy that might need to be adapted in this or that accidental detail but in substance remained the repository of human wisdom.[2]

Lonergan interpreted the post-Vatican II crisis as the difficulty of passing from a classicist conception to an empirical conception of culture. The former is the trademark of neo-scholasticism; the latter allows for a plurality of cultures and recognizes the legitimacy of Christianity being embodied in different contexts. In 1969, commenting on the classicists' resistance when it was suggested they ought to abandon their conception of culture, he remarked: "What is going forward in Catholic circles is a disengagement from the forms of classicist culture and a transposition into the forms of modern culture." And he humorously added: "This is a matter involved in considerable confusion. The confusion arises mainly because classicist culture made no provision for the possibility of its own demise."[3]

In fairness to Catholicism, however, we must acknowledge the predominance of the Enlightenment's secular classicism in the European elites' worldview from the eighteenth to the twentieth century. We can also mention the emergence, in our twenty-first century, of a new sort of classicism, taken for granted by billions around the globe, whose mentality looks the same cross-culturally after having been profoundly shaped by a uniform science, technology, the internet, and electronics.

Judging that "the classical mediation of meaning has broken down,"[4] on the one hand Lonergan did not accept the traditional, classicist, retrenchment that was less influential in the late 1960s and that has regained strength in the Catholic Church since that time. On the other hand he also did not agree with relativism in regard to Christian revelation, as he believed in the capacity that the human spirit has, when aided by the Holy Spirit, of discerning a kernel of truth inside the outer crust constituted by highly varied modes of expressing truth, while fully appreciating the meanings carried by those modes. Consequently, he did not underplay the challenge of discernment for serious theologians: "Our disengagement from classicism and our involvement in modernity must be open-eyed, critical, coherent, sure-footed. If we are not just to throw out what is good in classicism and replace it with contemporary trash, then we have to take the trouble, and it is enormous, to grasp the strength and the weakness, the power and the limitations, the good points and the shortcomings of both classicism and modernity."[5]

I will now outline some tenets that were paramount for Lonergan, which I mentioned in my introduction to this Study but will now repeat for the sake of clarity: method as supplanting theory; human intentionality as self-transcending; subjectivity in search of objectivity; the progression from a perspective towards a universal viewpoint; and the compatibility between historicity and permanence concerning religious truth. Each of these tenets plays a role in the overcoming of both classicism and relativism.

METHOD AS SUPPLANTING THEORY

This section builds upon what has been said about the realm of theory and the realm of interiority in the section entitled "Realms of meaning" in Study 3. A few years after the Second Vatican Council, Lonergan wrote: "Scholastic theology was a monumental achievement. Its influence in the Catholic church has been profound and enduring. Up to Vatican II, which preferred a more biblical turn of speech, it has provided much of the background of pontifical documents and conciliar decrees. Yet today by and large it is abandoned, partly because of the inadequacy of medieval aims, and partly because of the shortcomings of the Aristotelian corpus" (279; see also 327 and 329).

It is important to realize that what has to be "abandoned" is the confinement of theology to the realm of theory, with its Aristotelian logic. This requires moving from the theoretical mind to the methodical mind, in a manner that does not do away with the logical competencies of the medieval systematic mind, but rather sublates them by locating them within the larger context formed by what Lonergan called "the generalized empirical method." Thus he observed: "Among high cultures one may distinguish classical and modern by the general type of their controls: the classical thinks of the control as a universal fixed for all time; the modern thinks of the controls as themselves involved in an ongoing process" (29).

In effect, the methodical mind carries out a different control of meaning, exemplified by what one notices in the modern empirical sciences, where the procedures followed issue in results to the extent that original and pertinent questions have been asked – questions that allow data to be seen in a new way and that allow fresh hypotheses to arise. Unlike the theoretical mind, which tends to perfect and refine a static content, this new experimental mind accepts the imperfect, incomplete, and provisional character of knowledge. When this mind is applied to the history of religious ideas, it delves into the particular characteristics of texts, authors, and epochs. It is attentive as much to differences of contexts as to the unity of an evolving dogma.

Needless to say, theory goes hand in hand with classicism, whereas method goes hand in hand with the empirical approaches.

HUMAN INTENTIONALITY AS SELF-TRANSCENDING

The second paramount tenet that must be adverted to is the fact that, for Lonergan, self-transcendence is the goal of human intentionality (*Method*, 104–5). The latter is the urge, among human beings, to go beyond the strict limitations of their habitat and to learn how to live in a world mediated by meanings and values. People transcend themselves inasmuch as they ask questions for understanding, which make them discern intelligible patterns in the data perceptually collected; inasmuch as they ask questions for reflection, which make them determine the truth of their hypotheses; and inasmuch as they ask questions for deliberation, which make them assess values, courses of actions, and religious commitments.

As mentioned in an earlier Study, Lonergan calls this movement a "development from below upwards." One ascends, so to speak, a scale constituted by four levels: perception, understanding, reflection, and deliberation. Hence his four transcendental precepts: "Be attentive, Be intelligent, Be reasonable, Be responsible" (231).

He points out: "The transcendental notions, that is, our questions for intelligence, for reflection, and for deliberation, constitute our capacity for self-transcendence. That capacity becomes an actuality when one falls in love. Then one's being becomes being-in-love" (105). Among the various states of love – all situated on the fourth level of human intentionality – the love of God is supreme. Lonergan is fond of quoting Romans 5:5: "God's love flooding our hearts through the Holy Spirit given to us" (105).

From the religious component of the fourth level of intentionality is launched a "development from above downwards."[6] In this movement, thanks to the strength of the highest affective state, one accepts truths gained in education coming from family, companionship, school, media, or a religious tradition, then one manages to understand a good portion of what has been received, and finally one forges means of expressing all that has been acquired.

SEEKING OBJECTIVITY

Regrettably the human subject – perceiver, knower, doer, lover – is intellectually and affectively impaired. However, Lonergan's outlook on objectivity is grounded in the complementary fact that the inquiring human subject, spurred on, consciously or not, both by the Holy Spirit's inspiration and by the knowledge of a liberating divine revelation, spontaneously desires objectivity, as it naturally wants to respect and enhance reality. A sound exercise of subjectivity reaches out towards objectivity. A healthy subjectivity – or, more accurately, a healed subjectivity – heads towards objectivity. "Genuine objectivity is the fruit of authentic subjectivity. It is to be attained only by attaining authentic subjectivity" (*Method*, 292; see 265). The authentic subjectivity of people who transcend themselves is the sine qua non condition for coming out into objectivity.

The criteria of objectivity are "subjective" (35, 37, 39, 40), and this means they are neither subjectivistic nor objectivistic; human subjectivity need not be either subjectivistic or objectivistic. Unfortunately, subjectivism and objectivism both imagine the measurement of objectivity in a spatial way, after the model of perception.[7] Thereafter they part company: the former pronounces such (false) objectivity to be impossible, whereas the latter trusts common sense (despite its inadequacy in these matters) and declares such (false) objectivity to be possible. Hence Lonergan writes: "There is a subjectivity to be blamed because it fails to transcend itself, and there is a subjectivity to be praised because it does transcend itself. There is an objectivity to be repudiated because it is the objectivity of those that fail in self-transcendence, and there is an objectivity to be accepted and respected, and it is that achieved by the self-transcending subject."[8]

"Subjective," then, is not tantamount to "subjectivistic": subjectivism designates an individual subject's inability to transcend one's cognitive and affective anticipations, and her or his failure to grasp and express truth with an unbiased spirit. In contrast, authentic subjectivity enables genuine objectivity.

In *Insight* he underscores our capacity to affirm truth unconditionally and he observes that such unconditionality removes a judgment from the peculiar circumstances of its discovery and verification.

> Because the content of the judgment is an absolute, it is withdrawn from relativity to the subject that utters it, the place in which he utters it, the time at which he utters it. Caesar's crossing of the Rubicon was a contingent event occurring at a particular place and time. But a true affirmation of that event [is] an eternal, immutable, definitive validity. For if it is true that he did cross, then no one whatever at any place or time can truly deny that he did. Hence it is in virtue of absolute objectivity that our knowing acquires what has been named its publicity. For the same reason that the unconditioned is withdrawn from relativity to its source, it also is accessible not only to the knower that utters it but also to any other knower. (*Insight*, 402)

Later in the same work, Lonergan avers: "there is to any truth an essential detachability from the mind in which it happened to be generated, and an essential communicability" (*Insight*, 729). In *Method in Theology* he underlines the fact again: "what is true is of itself not private but public, not something to be confined to the mind that grasps it, but something independent of that mind and so in a sense detachable and communicable" (44–5).[9]

FROM PERSPECTIVES TOWARDS A UNIVERSAL VIEWPOINT

The fourth paramount tenet is Lonergan's reconciliation of perspectives with the movement towards a universal viewpoint in historiography.

Method in Theology dedicates two chapters to history, which have been prepared by the author's extensive reading of historians' reflections on historical knowledge. Under the heading of "Perspectivism" (214–20), he tells us that historians deal with the particular, whereas scientists (including those in the human sciences) deal with the universal. While maintaining his insistence on objectivity in the field of historiography, he acknowledges the fact that, unavoidably, historians work according to perspectives, namely specific viewpoints that determine the contexts in which they situate their topics.

On the one hand, perspectivism means that historians can never know everything about their subject matter because they must be selective regarding their materials. "Inevitably the historian selects what he thinks of moment and omits what he considers unimportant" (215). Consequently one can reach only "incomplete and approximate portrayals of an enormously complex reality" (219). Lonergan reminds us that "as in natural science, so too in critical history the positive content of judgment aspires to be no more than the best available opinion" (191), namely the probable. However, to avoid any collusion with relativism, "perspectivity" could be a better term than "perspectivism."

On the other hand, although historians begin within the bounds of definite perspectives, they are far from being definitively restricted by their angles of vision. Like all disciplines, the discipline of history is dynamic; it is practised by scholars whose viewpoint is moving and expanding. With training, well-guided research, and experience, they gradually enhance their ability to discover the past and to make it out in ways that are more and more adequate. Likewise, ethicists can discuss various principles and prioritize them according to what they deem most important for rightful action.[10]

Indeed, the capacity for progression and self-correction distinguishes perspectivism from relativism.

> Where relativism has lost hope about the attainment of truth, perspectivism stresses the complexity of what the historian is writing about and, as well, the specific difference of historical from mathematical, scientific, and philosophic knowledge. It does not lock historians up in their backgrounds, confine them to their biases, deny them access to development and openness. But it does point out that historians with different backgrounds will rid themselves of biases, undergo conversions, come to understand the quite different mentalities of other places and times, and even move towards understanding one another, each in his own distinctive fashion. (217)

This passage invites the following remark: Lonergan's recognition of the multiplicity of perspectives is filled with both modesty and hope. Let us notice, in the last quotation, his typical emphasis on the core importance of overcoming biases and going through conversions. This importance flows from his notion of horizon, which he introduces at the beginning of his chapter on dialectic:

> In its literal sense the word, horizon, denotes the bounding circle, the line at which earth and sky appear to meet. This line is the limit of one's field of vision. As one moves about, it recedes in front and closes in behind so that, for different standpoints, there are different horizons ... As our field of vision, so too the scope of our knowledge, and the range of our interests are bounded. As fields of vision vary with one's standpoint, so too the scope of one's knowledge and the range of one's interests vary with the period in which one lives, one's social background and milieu, one's education and personal development. So there has arisen a metaphorical or perhaps analogous meaning of the word, horizon. (235–6)

He rounds out his reflections on horizons with the following definition: "Horizons then are the sweep of our interests and of our knowledge" (237). Moreover, he states that differences in horizons may be complementary, genetic, or dialectical.

First, it frequently happens that the respective horizons of, say, a worker, a supervisor, a technician, an engineer, or a manager are complementary and in some measure include one another. Second, other horizons differ genetically: "They are related as successive stages in some process of development. Each later stage presupposes earlier stages, partly to include them, and partly to transform them" (236). Adept historians not only take into consideration complementary horizons, but above all consider as their main job to ascertain the connections between horizons that are genetically related. Thus Lonergan declares that the historian's task is "to grasp what was going forward in particular groups at particular places and times" (178). By "going forward" he means "process and development but, no less, decline and collapse" (178–9).

Third, dialectic has to do with another kind of difference in horizons, the analysis of which is a much more tricky business than the elucidation of a genesis. "There are fundamental conflicts stemming from an explicit or implicit cognitional theory, an ethical stance, a religious outlook. They profoundly modify one's mentality. They are to be overcome only through an intellectual, moral, religious conversion. The function of dialectic will be to bring such conflicts to light, and to provide a technique that objectifies subjective differences and promotes conversion" (235; see 128–30).

The horizons that are genetically related as well as the horizons that are dialectically conflicting exist not only among the people studied by historians but in scholars themselves. Hence the indispensability of personal development on the part of scholars. Lonergan's notion of a universal viewpoint sheds light on this progression. As made clear by the author of a remarkable book devoted to this topic, the universal viewpoint is "a heuristic structure," to wit, an orderly openness to reality. It characterizes a subjectivity in quest of objectivity. "Human knowledge is marked therefore by a double-pronged approach, a pincer movement, a scissors-action, with a lower blade arising from data and an upper blade descending from general anticipations."[11] The upper blade is not a static possession, but a distant goal. It consists in an asymptotic movement from a more or less limited standpoint towards universal science and universal history as the totality of the "to-be-known." Even if the universal viewpoint may be compared to a bird's-eye view, it definitely does not amount to a God's-eye view! We could rather place it halfway between sensory particularity and divine universality. Merely potentially universal at the beginning, only a portion of our knowledge becomes universal, step by step.

Although no interpretation can be context-independent, little by little scholars may try and enter into wider contexts. Provided we grasp the differences between various viewpoints, situating and marshalling the viewpoints broaden our own viewpoint and enhance our ability to diagnose with greater accuracy the fundamentally conflicting human condition. Making headway towards a universal viewpoint requires self-knowledge and knowledge of the other – two kinds of knowledge which increase as they interact. However, whereas *Insight* abundantly treats the "universal viewpoint,"[12] *Method in Theology* speaks only in one passage of "a comprehensive viewpoint," which has become the goal of the functional specialty called dialectic after having been enriched by integrating existential and religious components of human living.[13]

To sum up this section, we can say that if for Lonergan cognitional particularity and cognitional universality are compatible, it is because the richer the historians' erudition becomes, the more capable they become of understanding correctly other points of view and new sources of knowledge.

THE HISTORICITY AND THE PERMANENCE OF DOCTRINES

The fifth and last paramount tenet is Lonergan's acceptance of what he calls "pluralism." I interpret his version as being a *moderate* pluralism, in opposition to *radical* pluralism, which is the same as relativism. To understand his proposal for a moderate pluralism, we must pay attention to his treatment of the tension between the historicity and the permanence of doctrines (*Method*, 319–30).

This tension and its resolution is not solely a religious problem, but, in Lonergan's thought, a general epistemological fact. As was reported in Study 2, he states that human nature comprises two fundamental components: one a variable, historicity, which accounts for the multiplicity of cultures; the other a constant, natural right made up of the intentionality of the person. "A contemporary ontology would distinguish two components in concrete human reality: on the one hand, a constant, human nature; on the other hand, a variable, human historicity."[14] While human historicity causes change, the very capacity for changing resides in something abiding, or transcendental, namely human nature, comprised of the four levels of intentionality, which constitute our openness to the multifold reality of the world.

Lonergan accepts the historicity of dogmas in the theological field, which is but a particular case within the broader category of human historicity in general. The meanings that theologians come across were fashioned in particular but multiple contexts, and several of these contexts evolved in the course of discussions that took place prior or posterior to council pronouncements. Nevertheless, he holds that historians can identify, compare, relate, and contrast contexts. Sound hermeneutics and dialectic can make sense of their differences and oppositions. It is also possible to determine whether specific modifications have been cumulative or regressive.[15] In a lecture on pluralism, Lonergan stresses the validity of a statement in its original context despite its lack of complete meaningfulness in a new context: "It is true that contexts change, and it can happen that a statement that was true in its own context, ceases to be adequate in another context. It remains that it was true in its original context, that sound historical and exegetical procedures can reconstitute the original context with greater or less success and, in the same measure, arrive at an apprehension of the original truth."[16]

Given this process of ongoing reinterpretation, ought we to think that Christianity's self-understanding can fundamentally transform itself? To answer this question, Lonergan has recourse to a crucial distinction:

> There is a notable difference between the fuller understanding of data and the fuller understanding of a truth. When data are more fully understood, there result the emergence of a new theory and the rejection of previous theories. Such is the ongoing process in the empirical sciences. But when a truth is more fully understood, it is still the same truth that is being understood ... Now the dogmas are permanent in their meaning because they are not just data but expressions of truths and, indeed, of truths that, were they not revealed by God, could not be known by man. (325)[17]

Furthermore, Lonergan points out that the permanence of dogmas has often been wrongly construed, mostly in the Roman Catholic Church, within the limitations of the classicist frame of mind. "What is opposed to the historicity of the dogmas is, not their permanence, but classicist assumptions and achievements" (326). Consistent with such assumptions, there is just one culture, hence one way of articulating doctrines, and "the unity of faith is a matter of everyone subscribing to the correct formulae" (327). By contrast, he locates "the real root and ground of unity" in the inner word of God, the "being in love with God," as shaped by "the outward encounter with Christian witness," who testifies that "God has spoken through the prophets but in this latest age through his Son" (327, quoting Heb 1:1–2).

In his explication of "the real root and ground of unity," we find an echo of a medieval affirmation, that is, the one made by Aquinas, "The act of the believer does not reach its end in a statement, but in a reality ... Through them [the statements] we have knowledge of realities."[18] In Aquinas's view, endorsed by Lonergan, the statements point to the real character of revealed mysteries. In this vein, Lonergan writes: "the witness is to the mysteries revealed by God, and, for Catholics, infallibly declared by the church." And as he carefully balances permanence and historicity, he adds: "The meaning of such declarations lies beyond the vicissitudes of human historical process. But the contexts, within which such meaning is grasped, and so the manner in which such meaning is expressed, vary both with cultural differences and with the measure in which human consciousness is differentiated" (327).

What is required, then, is not pure repetition or sheer reassertion of dogmas, but "the transpositions that theological thought has to develop if religion is to retain its identity and yet at the same time find access into the minds and hearts of men of all cultures and classes" (132–3). The permanence of dogmas will be ensured by the conceptual transpositions which belong to the second phase of the theological method that Lonergan proposes. During this never-ending phase, implemented by four functional specialties called foundations, doctrines, systematics, and communications, "the theologian, enlightened by the past, confronts the problems of his own day" (133).

Inasmuch as problems have changed, we need new meanings, expressed in innovative formulations. So, harking back to the distinction between meaning and truth, explicated in our previous Study, we can say that while the truths remain the same, the meanings change to a certain extent. The meanings *do* change since the objects of belief are understood differently according to various milieus and according to various epochs. However, the meanings *do not* change insofar as conciliar texts propose definite, identifiable meanings in their respective historical context. One can sometimes go beyond the letter, but never against the intention that impelled the assertion of a dogma by the Church's solemn – also called extraordinary – magisterium. The intention is found in the living situation of a council, with its issues and concerns.

The First Vatican Council declared: "Let there be growth and abundant progress in understanding, knowledge and wisdom, in each and all, in individuals and in the whole Church, at all times and in the progress of ages, but only within the proper limits, i.e., within the same dogma, the same meaning, the same judgment."[19] Unfortunately the phrase from Vincent of Lérins, quoted by the council, "with the same dogma, the same meaning, the same judgment," has often been construed according to a classicist frame of mind.[20]

Actually, one cannot but detect a tension in the declaration: for one thing, "progress in understanding" is acknowledged; for another, the faithful are urged to cling to "the same meaning." It seems to me that the tension is resolved by saying that the meaning both changes and does not change. Consequently, while being faithful to anterior meanings defined as true, which do not change, what changes are the creative novelties (hence new meanings) regarding the expression of doctrines. "Historical consciousness" (154) – or "historical-mindedness"[21] – is the awareness that there has been and there still is cultural diversity throughout history. Hence the phenomenon of pluralism among cultures, philosophies, human studies, and theologies.

To further elucidate the nature of theological pluralism, he distinguishes three sources (326–30; see 271–81). First, we come across countless brands of common sense, that is, local mentalities. Second, aspects of human reality can be apprehended according to several modes called differentiations of consciousness: common sense, theory (also called science and system), interiority (which gives rise to method), transcendence (or religion), historical scholarship, and art. Third, we must take account of the degree to which people are converted.

The first two sources are positive, whereas the third is negative. "The real menace to unity of faith does not lie either in the many brands of common sense or the many differentiations of human consciousness. It lies in the absence of intellectual or moral or religious conversion" (330).

Lonergan's method provides some hermeneutical tenets by means of which he bequeathed us a way of overcoming relativism. His precious remarks deal with the intricate components of good or bad pluralism. Needless to say, acquiring and maintaining a differentiated mind and a converted spirit necessitates being actively involved in a never finished personal and communal enterprise.

CONCLUSION

Relativism has been a burning issue over the last few decades. Lonergan's thought provides intellectual tools that enable us to both understand the challenging difficulty of attaining the real and persist, patiently, with our quest for objectivity, not merely as an aspirational principle but as a concrete endeavour.[22] Facing this difficulty demands that we know the reasons why we must discard two antithetical extremes, namely classicism and relativism; it also entails that we put into practice the generalized empirical method, which was described in Study 1, thanks to which we can stretch out towards truth.

NOTES

1 Lonergan, "Belief: Today's Issue," in *A Second Collection*, ed. William F.J. Ryan and Bernard J. Tyrrell (Toronto: University of Toronto Press, 1996), 87–99, at 92 and 93.

2 Lonergan, "The Absence of God in Modern Culture," in *A Second Collection*, 101–16, at 109 and 110; see also 101 and 112–13.

3 Lonergan, "The Future of Christianity," in *A Second Collection*, 149–63, at 160.

4 Lonergan, "Dimensions of Meaning," in *Collection*, ed. Frederick E. Crowe and Robert M. Doran, volume 4 of *Collected Works of Bernard Lonergan* (Toronto: University of Toronto Press, 1988), 232–45, at 244.

5 Lonergan, "Belief: Today's Issue," in *A Second Collection*, 98–9.

6 Lonergan, "Healing and Creating in History," in *A Third Collection: Papers by Bernard J.F. Lonergan, S.J.*, ed. Frederick E. Crowe (New York: Paulist Press, 1985), 106.

7 On Étienne Gilson's "perceptionism" or "immediate realism" as not mediated by questioning, see Lonergan, "Metaphysics as Horizon," in *Collection*," §2, 192–203.

8 Lonergan, "Horizons," in *Philosophical and Theological Papers 1965–1980*, 10–29, at 13.

9 For a brief exposition of Lonergan's ideas about meaning and subjectivity, see Louis Roy, *Coherent Christianity* (Ottawa: Novalis, 2005), chap. 13.

10 See Todd A. Salzman and Michael G. Lawler, "Method and Catholic Theological Ethics in the Twenty-first Century," *Theological Studies* 74 (2013): 903–33, at 909–11 (on Lonergan's understanding of perspectivism).

11 Ivo Coelho, *Hermeneutics and Method: The 'Universal Viewpoint' in Bernard Lonergan* (Toronto, University of Toronto Press, 2001), 3; on the "scissors movement" see *Method*, 293.
12 See *Insight*, Index, "Viewpoint, universal."
13 See Coelho, 7 and 200; see also *Method*, 129, on "a comprehensive viewpoint," and 288, which mentions "a potential universal viewpoint."
14 Lonergan, "Natural Right and Historical Mindedness," in *A Third Collection: Papers by Bernard J.F. Lonergan, S.J*, ed. Frederick E. Crowe (New York: Paulist Press, 1985), 169–83, at 170.
15 As an illustration, see Lonergan, *The Triune God: Doctrines*, trans. from *De Deo Trino: Pars dogmatica* (1964) by Michael G. Shields, ed. Robert M. Doran and H. Daniel Monsour, volume 11 of *Collected Works of Bernard Lonergan*, (Toronto: University of Toronto Press, 2009). This big handbook was composed for his students in Rome in 1964; at that time, obviously he was not in a position to implement his (still only partially formulated) method; and yet that piece gives us a sense of how history and dialectic may contribute to theology.
16 Lonergan, "Doctrinal Pluralism," in *Philosophical and Theological Papers*, 70–104, at 76.
17 Still, the historical theologian begins with data (*Method*, 186–7 and 201–3); the point of the quoted text is that, for the systematic theologian, "dogmas ... are not just data" and should not be treated exactly in the way the empirical sciences base on data their merely probable conclusions ("a new theory").
18 Thomas Aquinas, *Summa Theologiae*, II-II, q. 1, a. 2, ad 2.
19 Dogmatic Constitution *Dei Filius*, DS 3020.
20 Vincent of Lérins, *Commonitorium primum*, in Corpus Christianorum: Series Latina, vol. 64, ed. Roland Demeulenaere (Turnhout: Brepols, 1985), 127–95; this author wrote this treatise around 434. See Thomas G. Guarino, *Vincent of Lérins and the Development of Doctrine* (Grand Rapids, MI: Baker Academic, 2013).
21 "The Transition from a Classicist World-View to Historical-Mindedness," in *A Second Collection*, 1–9. In "Natural Right and Historical Mindedness" on page 171, Lonergan tells us that the phrase "historical mindedness" comes from Alan Richardson.
22 Lack of space prevents me from demonstrating the convergence between Lonergan's plumbing of basic epistemological issues with the ground-breaking treatment offered by Karl Mannheim, *Ideology and Utopia: An Introduction to the Sociology of Knowledge*, trans. Louis Wirth and Edward Shils (San Diego, New York and London: Harcourt, 2nd ed., 1936).

Part Three

Application to Various Fields

Study 8

Some Implications for Theology

In Parts 1 and 2, I presented Lonergan's thought on method and on aspects of religion. Part 3 will be comprised of four studies which analyze implications of his method for theology, mysticism, liturgy, and education.

The Canadian Jesuit Bernard Lonergan and the German Jesuit Karl Rahner both lived from 1904 to 1984. Because of their intellectual acumen and their eagerness to face basic issues, their contribution to Catholic theology was considerable. Rahner, in particular, was actively involved in the writings of several documents of the Second Vatican Council and, by so doing, exercised a large influence on the Catholic Church's thinking. Moreover, his distinction between the transcendental and the categorial (often ambiguously rendered as "the categorical," thus suggesting a moral imperative), and his distinction between the unthematic and the thematic have been extremely helpful. In his many books, articles, and spiritual reflections, he shed light on virtually all aspects of Christian life. Like Lonergan, he is a giant of twentieth-century theology.

This Study discusses only two areas of Rahner's thought, namely his views on God and on theological pluralism, which evince his conceptualism. It employs Lonerganian tools to assess Rahner's approach to God. The first section introduces his epistemology, which misinterprets Thomas Aquinas's and does not agree with Lonergan's epistemology. The other sections link Rahner's epistemology to his views on the doctrine of God, the beatific vision, the Trinity, and theological pluralism.[1]

RAHNER'S AND AQUINAS'S DISCORDANT EPISTEMOLOGIES

Rahner's initial interests clearly resided in fundamental theology. His first two books are best interpreted in the wake of his fellow Jesuit, the Belgian Joseph Maréchal (1878–1944).[2] During the 1920s and 1930s, Maréchal carried out a systematic comparison of Thomas Aquinas and Immanuel Kant in the last three of his five "Cahiers" entitled *Le point de départ de la métaphysique*.[3] For him the human mind is essentially dynamic and its basic orientation manifests finality. In Cahier V, he stresses the fact that the human intellect spontaneously operates according to a purposeful ordering of its acts and its grasped objects towards truth. One can observe in its workings an undeniable orientation towards being in its complete intelligibility.[4] Because of the attention he pays to our acts, in particular to judging as discursive and not intuitive, Maréchal partly escapes the constriction of conceptualism. But, as Michael Vertin has demonstrated, his objectification of the consciousness that accompanies those acts is not so thorough as Lonergan's.[5]

Capitalizing on Maréchal's contribution, Rahner's first book, *Geist in Welt: Zur Metaphysik der endlichen Erkenntnis bei Thomas von Aquin*, published in 1939, is the result of his reading Thomas Aquinas with a sensitivity that is at the same time Kantian, Hegelian, and Heideggerian. From Kant, he borrows the sense of the a priori; from Hegel, the explication of the dynamic spirit; from Heidegger, being as a question.

As the title of the book, *Geist in Welt*, suggests, the human spirit belongs in the sensory world. It always operates in conjunction with the finite and it unfolds into the infinite. While being conditioned by a particular phantasm, the mind experiences an intellectual liberation by applying the general form to innumerable instances. A whole field of endless possibilities is thereby opened, the range of which is necessarily affirmed as unlimited, so that the mind finds itself oriented to the infinite in a "pre-apprehension" or "anticipatory grasp" (*Vorgriff*).[6]

Contrary to what several Thomists think, I have no difficulty with Rahner's thesis, based on Maréchal, that every judgment entails a *Vorgriff* of absolute being, even though he may too quickly identify being in general (Aquinas's *ens commune*) with infinite being (Aquinas's *esse tantum*), which Rahner also called absolute mystery.[7]

After all, did not Aquinas write, "All cognitive beings also know God implicitly in any object of knowledge?"[8] Nor do I hesitate to approve of Rahner's insistence on the *Beisichsein* (Being-Present-to-Self) as concomitant with the knowing process, pace Cornelius Ernst.[9] As is well known, self-awareness is a major theme in Lonergan also. Indeed I agree with many of the points made by *Spirit in the World*.

Lonergan defines cognitional theory as the answer to the question, "What am I doing when I am knowing?" For him, epistemology, which comes after the self-knowledge articulated as cognitional theory, is the answer to a subsequent question, "Why is doing that knowing?" Lastly, metaphysics is the answer to a third, basic question, "What do I know when I do it?" (*Method*, 25).

Rahner's epistemology, which correctly demonstrates the fact of the *Vorgriff*, that is, the openness of the human mind to being, unfortunately remains incomplete, because he moves too quickly into metaphysics without having the benefits of a thorough differentiation of human intentionality. His analysis of the functioning of the human mind fully recognizes the importance of questioning, and yet it overlooks insight and underrates judgment. Time after time in his works, he characterizes scientific knowledge as "conceptual." We shall see shortly that Rahner uses the adjective "conceptual" not as a simple shorthand for scientific knowledge but as a way to specify its nature.

The omission of what Aquinas calls *intelligere* is typical of modernity. In the sixteenth century, Cajetan had attempted a response to Scotus; the outcome had been an amalgam of Thomist and Scotist components of knowledge. Independently of Lonergan, the great historian Yves Congar found out that "Scotist vocabulary became the vocabulary of subsequent Scholasticism."[10] In the 1920s, because of the influence of Cajetan and of Suarez, virtually all the scholastic teachers were to a large extent Scotists insofar as epistemology was concerned. In an interview entitled "The Importance of Thomas Aquinas," Rahner mentions the influence of Suarez on the Jesuit School.[11] He does not discuss the epistemology of Scotus or of Suarez; nonetheless, these authors are important for him. For example, he adopts Scotus's position regarding the reason why the world was created and the necessity of the Incarnation even without original sin, and he disagrees with Suarez's interpretation of a text by Ignatius.[12] The young Rahner was deeply influenced by the conceptualism not only of the modern scholastics, but also of Kant and Hegel, who shared conceptualism's overlooking of insight.[13]

Whenever Rahner talks about knowledge in the scientific sense, he centres it around the concept, as Kant and Hegel did. In "Thomas Aquinas on Truth," a piece written in 1938 which sums up the results of *Spirit in the World*, he writes, "Thomas stands, rather, in the line of the tradition of Aristotle, Thomas, Kant, and Hegel in regarding this principle of truth as consisting in a formal *a priori* of the spontaneous intellect itself."[14] Throughout this article, several times he suggests that Aquinas, Kant, and Hegel's epistemologies are the same, while indicating but one area of discrepancy between Aquinas and Kant.

More specifically, he wrongly reports that Aquinas's *simplex apprehensio* is "the forming of a concept."[15] So far as I can observe, I don't find in Rahner's oeuvre any reference to the excitement and pleasure of having insights (the *apprehensio* or *intelligere* of Aquinas), an enjoyment that turns to joy in the case of interpersonal knowledge. Even in Rahner's late writings, the act of understanding is overlooked; the unthematic, transcendental self-presence and the conceptual, categorial objectification are juxtaposed, without any insight to account for the passage from the former to the latter.[16]

Even where we should expect to find the recognition that the act of understanding is much more than entertaining ideas (that is, in the section entitled "The Light of the Active Understanding," in the article entitled "Thomas Aquinas on Truth"), the insight is ignored and the concept remains central. There Rahner writes: "The intellect gives conceptual form to this material [sense impression], and so makes it that which is *intelligibile actu*, that which is known at the conceptual level and emerges as a synthesis of the sensory material and the *a priori* of the intellect.[17]

In the wake of Maréchal, Rahner rightly stresses the importance of judgment. Nonetheless, he exaggerates the capabilities of perception. He writes, "According to Thomas sensibility as such, to the extent that it apprehends the existing thing at all, apprehends it *as it truly is in itself*." There is "a finite act of perception that 'takes in' an individual object as such as it presents itself *in its own identity*."[18] "According to it [Aquinas's theory of cognition] sensibility is a finite experience in which a finite *being* reveals itself and is 'taken in', a kind of knowledge in which a sensible object is possessed in its manifestation of itself *as it is in itself*."[19]

If sensibility or perception already reaches reality, does judgment become redundant? In Rahner's opinion, no. The limitations of sensibility derive from the "obtuse particularity" of things, from "their lack of reference to anything beyond themselves." Sensibility cannot "stand back, so to say, from the impression it has received and from its object, and ... judge of it as it is in itself ... What sensibility experiences is always a genuine reality, yet it cannot express any judgement upon it, which means that strictly as such it never rises to a level at which it is capable of being true or false."[20] Therefore, judgment is needed so as to bring together perception and conception: "every one of our judgements and every one of our concepts contain two elements: a sensible element and an intellectual one (representation and conception)."[21] Notice the non-difference, in Rahner's sentence, between the judgment and the concept.

Although Rahner never discusses Scotus's epistemological texts, he adopts a position which resembles the one propounded by the "subtle doctor." The latter's account of knowledge can be fleshed out as follows. Out of the sensible species, the intelligible species emerges, thanks to an abstractive process. The universal concept – or essence – is the intentional content of the intelligible species. It is present in the intelligible species before the *intelligere* occurs, and it puts the knower in direct relation with the object. Objectivity, or truth, is obtained before the acts of understanding and judging; it is not constituted by these acts. In his eagerness to guarantee objectivity, Scotus places the decisive moment at the beginning of the process, when the extra-mental and yet universal object sets off the intelligible species that will soon impress the mind.[22] It is a matter of what Lonergan calls the "already out there now real." It is no wonder that Scotus diminishes the function of both understanding and judgment in the access to truth – the two are reduced to establishing the nexus between concepts that already exist, prior to being connected.[23] Of course, Scotus does not deny the presence of *quaestiones* and acts of *intelligere*; still, they do not play an important role in his epistemology.

For Scotus the concept comes *before* the act of understanding, whereas for Aquinas it makes its entry only *after* the act of understanding. As the result of an insight (*intelligere*), which takes place in the *receptive* intellect, followed by a "saying" (*dicere*), Aquinas's concept is a "word" (*verbum*) which turns out to be much richer than Scotus's concept. In line with the latter, Rahner locates truth at an early stage, that is, in the work of the *active* intellect. The "principle of truth" consists "in a light of the understanding itself which permeates and informs the material of the sense knowledge, and raises it in acts of judgement to the level of objective apprehension and conceptuality."[24] In this telescoped account, the "understanding" is left unexplained and the "saying" that gives its meaning to the "word" is absent.

In his long monograph entitled *Verbum*, Lonergan offers an exact reading of Thomas Aquinas's epistemological texts. The gist of Aquinas's position is as follows. There is already a certain generality (not yet a universality) achieved by the *cogitativa*, which unifies the particular data of the various senses. This half-sensitive and half-intellectual potency is also named the *ratio particularis* or the *intellectus passivus*. In connection with this generalized image or phantasm, the active intellect produces a form (*forma*) or likeness (*similitudo*) called *species intelligibilis* because it is susceptible of being understood. At this phase the species is about to shine in the phantasm. Insight (*intelligere*) occurs in the intellect as receptive (*intellectus possibilis*) when the intellect is actuated, in the very act of understanding, by the *species qua intelligitur*. Such understanding can be either a simple apprehension (*apprehensio*) expressed in a definition (*definitio, ratio, intentio*, which possesses a universality) or a reflective apprehension (*compositio* or *divisio*, which grasps the sufficient ground for affirming or negating a specific state of affairs) expressed in an intellectual commitment (*iudicium, enuntiatio, propositio affirmativa seu negativa*). At each of these two stages, the intellect says to itself what it has grasped in an inner word (*verbum interius*, also called *conceptio, conceptum, conceptus*). Like the preceding apprehension, the inner word is either simple (stating the meaning) or complex (positing the truth of a synthesis between subject and predicate).

Rahner's neglect of the twofold apprehension (simple and reflective) and of the corresponding twofold concept (definition and judgment) has deplorable philosophical and theological consequences. I will underline a few *theological* consequences in the rest of this Study. To finish the present section, however, let me call attention to an instance of *philosophical* consequence. Rahner declares: "Thomas's teaching is not completely consistent. If, for example, he had really taken seriously his own theory of the *anima forma corporis* (the soul as the form of the body), then he would not have been able to speak in general of an *anima separata* (a soul separated from the body)."[25] While Aquinas recognizes that prior to the resurrection of all, the state of *anima separata* is a very imperfect one, almost against nature, he nonetheless maintains it because his belief in the spiritual and subsistent character of the soul derives from his account of the acts of insight and judgment.[26]

THE DOCTRINE OF GOD

The shortcomings of Rahner's epistemology become evident when we examine his view of how human beings know/do not know God. Although he thinks that by and large he follows Aquinas's teaching on this topic, he departs considerably from the Angelic Doctor. As many commentators have observed, Aquinas walks a tightrope as he combines affirmations and negations regarding God. He maintains that our analogical knowledge of God is valid. For his part, Rahner downplays kataphatic (or affirmative) language and insists on apophatic silence. In his excessive emphasis on negations, he pushes centre-stage Aquinas's doctrine that we cannot comprehend God. By incomprehensibility, however, Rahner seems to mean unknowability. For Aquinas, the fact that God is incomprehensible entails that we shall never understand him perfectly, whereas for Rahner, it entails that the human intellect will never know God, who will always remain hidden. His strategy consists in overcoming human conceptual knowing by surrendering to absolute mystery. Consequently, he voices disagreement.

In "The Mystery of the Human Person," Rahner voices disagreement with Aquinas and exclaims: "How could Aquinas say that the essence of happiness consists in an act of the intellect, when he knew that God is incomprehensible; when he prayed: "I worship you, O hidden godhead," and knew that in the beatific vision God's incomprehensibility does not disappear?[27]

In Aquinas's theology, the incomprehensibility of God is beautifully balanced by his intelligibility. His God is both *incomprehensibilis* and *infinite cognoscibilis*, "infinitely knowable."[28] In Rahner's theology, this infinite knowability drops out of the picture and God undergoes, as it were, an everlasting eclipse. For him, the believers' experience of the mystery is more an experience of darkness than an experience of light. In the phrase "super-luminous darkness" which repeatedly recurs in his writings, "darkness" is the substantive whereas the luminousness is nothing but the accompanying adjective.[29]

Naturally Rahner understands Aquinas's doctrine of incomprehensibility to be primarily an anthropological statement. Yet he goes too far when he concedes, "Only in a highly derivative and tenuous sense should one regard divine incomprehensibility as an 'attribute' of God himself."[30] In another piece, he is more precise:

> We cannot however understand this incomprehensibility as a special characteristic of God, which he has *together with* the other attributes different from that, which then yield the fullness of meaning for which we yearn. These other attributes of God, which we declare to be the meaning of our existence, are themselves incomprehensible; this incomprehensibility is not one attribute of God alongside others, but the attribute of his attributes.[31]

Doesn't Rahner open the door to an ambiguity which many of his readers may fail to notice? Without saying so explicitly, he frequently crosses the line between an affirmation about our knowledge and an affirmation about God. For instance, he concludes an article quoted above with this extraordinary assertion, "the intellect only achieves its own fullness of being when in hope and love, in a freedom which properly belongs to it, it surrenders itself to incomprehensibility as its own beatitude."[32] "Incomprehensibility" has two undistinguished meanings here, both problematic. In the first sense, how could surrendering to *our* cognitional limits make us happy? Instead, it seems that Rahner has in mind our recognition that *God in Godself* is incomprehensible – the second sense of incomprehensibility. But again, how could this recognition make us happy? He writes, "man can reach final bliss only with a God who is incomprehensibly greater than himself and for that very reason the true blessedness of man."[33] I would agree partly with him if he is saying that to trust freely and fully, with hope and love, in God's incomprehensible *and therefore infinite goodness* is what makes us happy.

To contrast the two theologians, for Rahner, happiness consists in trustfully loving the God we do not understand; for Aquinas, happiness consists in gratefully loving the God whose goodness we understand more and more. Out of a deep sense of mystery, then, two incompatible conclusions may be derived. For Rahner, God and the world are so profoundly *unintelligible* that what we know and shall know amounts to a mere human construction which fails to actually characterize reality. For Aquinas, God and the world are so profoundly *intelligible* that what we shall know in heaven is infinitely vaster than the little we know on earth.[34]

On this issue, the Lutheran theologian Eberhard Jüngel voices a moderate, friendly criticism of Rahner's position. Having affirmed that God in himself is not darkness but rather light, Jüngel insists that our awareness of God's hiddenness is a consequence of revealed knowledge.

> And this is utterly different both from the non-knowledge of God and from the knowledge that presents itself on the basis of human self-knowledge, namely that God is unknowable. Under no circumstances does revelation allow *theological* insight into the hiddenness of God to be understood on the model of Immanuel Kant's famous statements concerning reason which has reached its own limits ... The hiddenness of God is something other than his incomprehensibility.[35]

In my opinion, Jüngel rightly disagrees with Rahner because he understands Rahner's "incomprehensibility" to mean unknowability, in the manner of Kant. Furthermore, Jüngel is ill at ease even with the concept of hiddenness and he prefers to make mystery the paramount concept.

> I disagree with Rahner's equation of mystery and hiddenness, which has its parallel in the equation of mystery and incomprehensibility. Though the mysteriousness of God certainly increases with knowledge of him, it is nevertheless not evident that mystery should mean hiddenness, indeed, that being *brought to light* should simply be 'an alternative formula' for *being taken back into the darkness of incomprehensibility*.[36]

So Jüngel retains Rahner's notion of mystery to indicate the limits of our knowledge of God and tones down hiddenness in order to preserve the fact of our knowing God through revelation: "One would be wise not to let the revelation of the hiddenness of God be the last word, but rather to introduce some differentiations within the concept of the *hiddenness* of God, to allow one to speak of overcoming the hiddenness of God in a way that does not in any way touch the mystery of God."[37]

Let us now observe how Rahner reads the declaration of the fourth Lateran Council (1215), which says: "We firmly believe and confess without reservation that there is only one true God, eternal, infinite (*immensus*) and unchangeable, incomprehensible (*incomprehensibilis*), almighty and ineffable, the Father, the Son and the Holy Spirit" (DS 800). That council also stated, "For between Creator and creature no similitude can be expressed without implying a greater dissimilitude" (DS 806).

In his piece, "The Hiddenness of God," the *incomprehensibilitas* underlined by that council and subsequently reiterated by Aquinas is rendered by *Unbegreiflichkeit*, a German word which is ambiguous.[38] On the one hand, it means incomprehensibility, that is, ruling out full grasping or encompassing;[39] on the other hand, given that *Begriff* is the concept, *Unbegreiflichkeit* also suggests unconceptualizability – a semantic shift from the daylight of Aquinas's intellectualism[40] to the night of conceptualism, in which the antithesis conceptualizable/unconceptualizable is taken for granted. Instead of Aquinas's view, Rahner seems to adopt here Kant's view that human knowledge (*Erkenntnis*) consists in the concept (*Begriff*) to which a sensible intuition (*Anschauung*) must correspond.[41] Accordingly, anything that lies beyond the conceptual – mostly God – is hidden in the sense of being unknowable.

THE BEATIFIC VISION

Throughout his essay, "The Hiddenness of God," Rahner contrasts the unthematic presence of divine truth with a conceptualistic view of knowledge. The inadequate account of knowledge that he rejects is "conceptual mastery" (229, 238, 240), "a model of knowledge in which an object is penetrated and mastered" (231), "theoretical understanding" (231, 239), "seeing through an object" (233). Rahner's problem stems from this caricature of rationality. The following text is typical. "Rationality *as such* is not directed in the first instance to the particular content of a proposition; rather it is ordered, in a constantly new way, to the methods and validity of the connection of propositions to one another. It is aimed, therefore, at least approximately and within distinct areas of human consciousness, at the building of systems."[42]

Given this distrust of rationality, wrongly equated with the conceptual and reduced to establishing connections between general propositions, Rahner is bound to proclaim that "the ending is the advent of God who is the enduring mystery and is accepted in love" (239). His dissatisfaction with conceptual knowledge leads him to assert the primacy of love not only on earth (as Aquinas does) but also in heaven.

Rahner's depreciation of insight and judgment depends on his own assumption, which we examined earlier, that knowledge is basically a matter of acquiring and linking concepts in a controlling manner. If knowing equates with this sort of conceptualization, which is taken to precede understanding, of course it has no place in the vision of God. Hence, Rahner mistakenly characterizes Aquinas's intention as follows: "to force man out of the brightness of the dimension which he can comprehend, and into the mystery of God where he no longer grasps but rather is grasped, where he no longer rationalizes but rather adores, where he no longer controls but rather is himself subject to a higher control."[43]

By contrast, for Aquinas the eternal happiness is the result of seeing (*videre*, analogically understood as understanding, *intelligere*) in interaction with *amare* (loving). In personalist terms, because we love God, we want to know him; constantly receiving insights (freely given by God) into the Trinitarian life, we appreciate and love the divine Persons ever more. As Walter Principe notes:

> For Aquinas, the integrity or full perfection of beatitude necessarily "requires" an accompanying overflow from vision of God into blissful delight, love, and joy such that nothing other than God's infinite goodness could ever attract the human heart (1–2.4.1, 5.4, 11.3). And if the essential act of beatitude is for him the intellectual vision of God, this act of vision itself is a great *good* that human persons seek and attain through love: then, on reaching this vision, the object of their affective longing and desire, they experience its perfect completion in affective bliss (1–2.3.4; 1.12.1).[44]

One should read the articles of the *Summa Theologiae* just referred to and compare Principe's understanding with Rahner's version: "Thomas sees the nature of the beatific vision as *consisting of intellectual knowledge alone*. In doing so, he denies nothing of the reality. But I think that, if Thomas had on this question made radical use of the interchangeability of being as true and being as good (*ens verum et ens bonum*), he might have formulated otherwise or possibly even seen more clearly the nature of the beatific vision."[45]

Incidentally, in his remarkable essay on the spiritual senses in the Middle Ages, Rahner wonderfully details Bonaventure's position regarding ecstasy. In this life, ecstasy, as the highest mystical state, is intrinsically affective. Rahner does not point out – and in that context does not have to point out – the fact that for this Franciscan doctor, the beatific vision consists of both intellectual beholding and loving.[46] However, not having taken note of this fact, he may have remained unaware that his own view of the beatific vision contradicts not only Aquinas's but also Bonaventure's. In fact Rahner's stance is indebted to Scotus, for whom beatitude formally consists in an act of the will.[47]

One additional point calls for comment. Two aspects of Rahner's representation of human knowledge must be criticized. First, it is conceptualistic and second, it is monolithic. Instead of opposing knowledge and a quasi-irrational experience of the mystery, he should have differentiated *several kinds of knowing*. Thinkers such as Thomas Aquinas, Polanyi, and Lonergan all distinguish between discursive and non-discursive knowing. However, in Rahner's oeuvre, I have found one felicitous exception: he correctly differentiates the Ignatian discernment of divine will from the "cognition of the rationally discursive and conceptually expressible kind."[48] Conceptualistic though the language remains, yet here he points in the right direction, that is, to a differentiation of knowing. Had he pursued this line, he might have avoided his antithesis between two caricatures, namely of scientific knowledge and of religious trust apparently dissociated from thinking.

THE TRINITY

In addition to the beatific vision, the treatise on the Trinity is a subject matter where Rahner betrays the fact that he does not share Aquinas's understanding of the Word.[49] About the Trinity he writes that "the supreme mystery is also the most obscure."[50] Construing Augustine's "speculative concepts" as "essential concepts," and lamenting that they are not "personal" concepts, he concludes that "they do not work."[51] Let the readers ponder this statement by Rahner: "Any attempt today to present the Christian doctrine of the Trinity must involve a "liberation" of the usual traditional propositions from their 'splendid isolation,' in which they have been encapsulated in scholastic theology."[52]

Elsewhere he indulges in disparaging and even caustic remarks on "the Augustinian-psychological speculations."[53] His skepticism is consistent with his disregard of the insight, which supplies the analogy for the generation of the Son. The Word is indeed the expression of an unrestricted act *of understanding* and, *pace* Rahner, not a matter of "conceptual objectivation" (again understood in the Scotist sense).[54]

THEOLOGICAL PLURALISM

Rahner's view of theology in the contemporary world can also be situated in the context of his epistemology. He asserts that "all the single insights of life (however modest, ambitious, loving, unsentimental, industrious, critical, 'positive,' intelligent, and so forth they may be) will never form a whole. We do not then imagine that there could be a well-tempered synthesis of all these disparate insights which could cater for them all."[55]

If he is thinking of an overall Hegelian synthesis, or of a positivistic erudition based on a huge amount of merely juxtaposed data, how can we not but agree? But how about the joy of acquiring, even here on earth thanks to a succession of related insights, a worldview which becomes more and more coherent? Let us think of Aquinas's *intelligere multa per unum*, interpreted by Lonergan as the "synthetic character of understanding."[56] I am afraid Rahner replaces such *fides quaerens intellectum* (faith seeking understanding) by an act of hope consisting in a transcendental decision in favour of God.[57] In fact, he is rather insistent:

> Yet, how simple Christianity is. It is the determination to surrender to God's incomprehensibility in love ... A Christian is a true and most radical skeptic. If he really believes in God's incomprehensibility, he is convinced that no individual truth is really true except in the process (which necessarily belongs to its real essence) in which it becomes that question which remains unanswered because it asks about God and his incomprehensibility. The Christian is also the individual who can cope with this otherwise maddening experience in which (to formulate it with poor logic but accurate description) one can accept no opinion as wholly true or wholly false.[58]

At the end of his career, Rahner adopts a somewhat relativistic stance regarding theology. He registers the coexistence, in the mind of many contemporary believers, of faith with "skeptical relativism." Bravely addressing the widespread epistemic situation of Catholics who dissent from several church doctrines, he does not see such denials as extreme cases, however many, for which remedies must be sought. In an essay where he discusses this issue, he extols the graced transcendental (namely the human openness to God, through which people subjectively receive revelation), without mentioning the importance of the categorial (namely the objective categories or words in which revelation is expressed).[59] Usually, he accords a secondary and yet real significance to the categorial. But not here. Once more, he departs from Aquinas, for whom first truth cannot be dissociated from the articles of belief.[60] For the Angelic Doctor, those articles are judgments, not concepts in the Scotist sense, as Rahner construes them.

Rahner accepts the fact of theological pluralism and intelligently strives to show that it precludes neither dialogue nor acceptance of church pronouncements.[61] Although his form of pluralism is not to be equated with relativism, it is more intractable than the form of pluralism that Lonergan acknowledges.[62] In a dialogue with William Dych, Lonergan respectfully begs to disagree with Rahner's construal of theological pluralism. It is in method that Lonergan finds the possibility of limiting theological pluralism. In a rebuttal of Rahner's very words,[63] Lonergan says: "I believe one will find ways to control the present uncontrollable pluralism of theologies, one will cease to work alien, alone, isolated, one will become aware of a common site with an edifice to be erected, not in accord with a static blueprint, but under the leadership of an emergent probability that yields results proportionate to human diligence and intelligence."[64]

CONCLUSION

Despite some overlapping, the discrepancy between Aquinas and Rahner as well as between Lonergan and Rahner is more significant than has been acknowledged in transcendentalist circles.[65] It has to do with the fact that Lonergan moved out of the conceptualism of his day and became a Thomist in epistemology, whereas Rahner unwittingly remained a Scotist in seeing conceptualization as the kernel of rationality. Perhaps this difference between the two thinkers can be explained by having recourse to the distinction between cognitional theory and epistemology, which I reported at the beginning of this Study. While the Lonergan of *Verbum* paid sustained attention to cognitional theory as the door to Aquinas's epistemology and metaphysics, the Rahner of *Geist in Welt* concentrated on epistemology and metaphysics, without dwelling long enough on cognitional theory.

Furthermore, in his disappointment with conceptualism as operative in scholastic theology, he overemphasized the attitude of trust in an irrationalist fashion. I cannot but speculate that the relativism of his latter years might be the consequence of his conceptualism because, in the conceptualists' accounts of human knowledge, concepts are not clearly connected to data by insights and judgments. In contrast to Rahner's view, reality for Lonergan is reached by perception, insights, and judgments according to relations between such acts – relations that he spells out in an elaborate fashion.

I readily recognize that Rahner made a significant contribution to the understanding of Catholic faith.[66] Unfortunately, since the last decades of the twentieth century, his moderate anti-intellectualism and anti-dogmatism have become, in the minds of the Rahnerians of the left, a green light for an unbridled creativity accompanied by an anti-dogmatism more pronounced than Rahner's. Against his best intentions, his lack of cognitional theory has fostered disrespect for Christian insights of the past and has legitimized the primacy of the imagination in its free choice of symbols.[67] His continual stress on the unknown Mystery and on human transcendentality has brought about a relativization of the ecumenical councils, of the doctors of the church, and of the magisterium. Evidently Rahner would disapprove of that trend among his disciples. Nevertheless the seeds of that deviation from sound doctrine are found in his deficient epistemology.

NOTES

1 See the lucid article by a competent philosopher, Andrew Beards, "Rahner's Philosophy: A Lonerganian Critique," *Gregorianum* 87 (2006): 262–83.

2 On Maréchal, Rahner, Lonergan, and others, see Otto Muck, *The Transcendental Method*, trans. William D. Seidensticker (New York: Herder and Herder, 1968). However, Lonergan distanced himself from Muck's "*generalized* notion of transcendental method by determining the common features in the work of those that employ the method. While I

have no objection to this procedure, I do not consider it very pertinent to an understanding of my own intentions. I conceive method *concretely*. I conceive it, not in terms of principles and rules, but as a normative pattern of *operations* with cumulative and progressive results" (*Method*, 13–14, note 4; italics are mine).

3 Joseph Maréchal, *Le point de départ de la métaphysique* (Paris: Desclée de Brouwer, and Bruxelles: L'édition universelle, 2nd ed., 1937). Excerpts translated into English are offered in *A Maréchal Reader*, trans. Joseph Donceel (New York: Herder, 1970).

4 See Gerald A. McCool, *The Neo-Thomists* (Milwaukee: Marquette University Press, 1994), chap. 6: "Joseph Maréchal," esp. 127–35.

5 Michael Vertin, "Maréchal, Lonergan, and the Phenomenology of Knowing," in *Creativity and Method: Essays in Honor of Bernard Lonergan, S.J.*, ed. Matthew L. Lamb (Milwaukee: Marquette University Press, 1981), 411–22.

6 Karl Rahner, *Spirit in the World*, trans. William Dych (New York: Continuum, 1994). On July 30, 2014, Harvey Egan wrote to me: "Bill Dych insisted that *Geist in Welt* be translated as spirit-in-world, NOT 'the' World. Rahner insisted that in some way the human person *is world*, not merely in the world. The editor's choice evokes a separation between spirit and world. I agree with Dych." See also Rahner's 1941 book, *Hearer of the Word: Laying the Foundation for a Philosophy of Religion*, trans. Joseph Donceel, ed. Andrew Tallon (New York: Continuum, 1994).

7 Rahner, *Spirit in the World*, part 2, chap. 3, §6; see J.A. DiNoia, "Karl Rahner," in *The Modern Theologians: An Introduction to Christian Theology in the Twentieth Century*, vol. 1, ed. David F. Ford (Oxford: Basil Blackwell, 1989), 183–204, at 191–2.

8 Thomas Aquinas, *De Veritate*, 22, 2, ad 1; quoted by Rahner in "Thomas Aquinas on Truth," in *Theological Investigations* (New York: Seabury Press, succeeded by Crossroad, 23 vols., 1961–1992, henceforth *TI*, followed by vol. and pages), 13:13–31, at 28. Aquinas explains, "Just as nothing has the note of appetibility except by a likeness to the first goodness, so nothing is knowable except by a likeness to the first truth."

9 Cornelius Ernst, "Translator's Introduction," in *TI* 1:v–xix, at xii, note 1, with a criticism of *Spirit in the World*, 69.

10 As pointed out by Lonergan in *Philosophy of God, and Theology*, "Lecture 2: The Functional specialty 'Systematics,'" in *Philosophical and Theological Papers 1965–1980*, ed. Robert C. Croken and Robert M. Doran, volume 17 of *Collected Works of Bernard Lonergan* (Toronto: University of Toronto Press, 2004), 188, note 28. Lonergan refers to Yves

M.-J. Congar, *A History of Theology*, trans. Hunter Guthrie (Garden City, NY: Doubleday, 1968), 130–1.

11 With few exceptions, for instance Pierre Rousselot, who broke away from conceptualism in *L'intellectualisme de saint Thomas* (Paris: Alcan, 1908), English translation: *Intelligence: Sense of Being, Faculty of God*, trans. Andrew Tallon (Milwaukee: Marquette University Press, 1999). See Paul Imhof and Hubert Biallowons, eds., *Faith in a Wintry Season: Conversations and Interviews with Karl Rahner in the Last Years of his Life*, trans. and ed. Harvey D. Egan (New York: Crossroad, 1986), 41–58, at 42 and 48.

12 See Rahner's "The Logic of concrete Individual Knowledge in Ignatius Loyola," in *The Dynamic Element in the Church* (New York: Herder, 1964), 84–170, at 137–41.

13 Helpful though some studies of Rahner's philosophy are, nevertheless they do not mention his conceptualism. For instance, Jack Arthur Bonsor, *Rahner, Heidegger, and Truth: Karl Rahner's Notion of Christian Truth, the Influence of Heidegger* (Lanham, MD: University Press of America, 1987); Robert Moloney, "Seeing and Knowing: Some Reflections on Karl Rahner's Theory of Knowledge," *The Heythrop Journal* 18 (1977): 399–419; and Thomas Sheehan, *Karl Rahner: The Philosophical Foundations* (Athens: Ohio University Press, 1987).

14 Rahner, "Thomas Aquinas on Truth," 20–1; it is Rahner who repeats Aquinas's name.

15 Ibid., 17. Those of my readers who are perhaps beginning to be put off by my criticisms of Rahner ought to consider that one of his fellow Jesuits, who commends Rahner's writings, nonetheless envisions the possibility that Rahner may have done violence (*Gewaltsamkeit*) to some of Aquinas's texts. See Johannes B. Lotz, "Zur Thomas-Rezeption in der Maréchal-Schule," *Theologie und Philosophie* 49 (1974): 375–94, at 389.

16 For example, Rahner's "On the Theology of the Ecumenical Discussion," *TI* 11:24–67, at 36–40; *Foundations of Christian Faith: An Introduction to the Idea of Christianity*, trans. William V. Dych (New York: Crossroad, 1984), 16–17.

17 Rahner, "Thomas Aquinas on Truth," 24.

18 Ibid.; italics are mine.

19 Ibid., 19; italics are mine.

20 Ibid., 20.

21 Ibid., 18.

22 See Giorgio Pini, "Scotus on Concepts," a lecture given at Boston College on April 20, 2001.

23 See *Verbum: Word and Idea in Aquinas*, ed. Frederick E. Crowe and Robert M. Doran, volume 2 of *Collected Works of Bernard Lonergan*, (Toronto: University of Toronto Press, 1997), 39, note 126; see "Scotus" in the Index of Concepts and Names,

24 Rahner, "Thomas Aquinas on Truth," 21. Rahner here speaks of "understanding," but not in Aquinas's sense of *intelligere*.

25 Imhof et al., *Faith in a Wintry Season*, 52.

26 On this topic, see L.-B. Geiger, "Saint Thomas d'Aquin et le composé humain," in *L'âme et le corps*, ed. Odette Laffoucrière (Paris: Fayard, 1961), 201–20. On the spirituality of the human central form, see Lonergan's *Insight*, 538–43 and "Spiritual" in the Index.

27 Rahner, *The Content of Faith* (New York: Crossroad, 1993), 80.

28 Aquinas, *Summa Theologiae*, I, q. 12, a. 7; see his *Commentary on the First Epistle to Timothy*, no. 269, in *Commentaries on St. Paul's Epistles to Timothy, Titus, and Philemon*, trans. Chrysostom Baer (South Bend, IN: St. Augustine's Press, 2007).

29 Rahner, "The Concept of Mystery in Catholic Theology," *TI* 4:36–73, at 42; "Poetry and the Christian," *TI* 4:357–67, at 358 and 359.

30 Rahner, "An Investigation of the Incomprehensibility of God in St Thomas Aquinas," *TI* 16:244–54, at 252.

31 Rahner, "The Human Question of Meaning in Face of the Absolute Mystery of God," *TI* 18:89–104, at 94. In this text and in other upcoming quotations, italics are the author's.

32 Rahner, "An Investigation," 254.

33 Rahner, "The Human Question," 103.

34 Rahner seems to have abandoned his early Thomistic position that "being is being-able-to-be-known (*Sein ist Erkanntseinkönnen*)" (Rahner, *Spirit in the World*, 67) or that "one cannot ask about being in its totality without affirming the fundamental knowability, in fact a certain *a priori* knowness of being as such" (68), that is, "a thoroughgoing determination of knowing by being" (liii).

35 Eberhard Jüngel, "The Revelation of the Hiddenness of God," *Theological Essays II*, trans. Arnold Neufeldt-Fast and J.B. Webster (Edinburgh: T&T Clark, 1995), 120–44, at 124–5.

36 Ibid., 125–6. The last words are a quotation from Rahner, "An Investigation," 250.

37 Ibid., 126.

38 Rahner, "The Hiddenness of God," *TI* 16:227–43, at 231.

39 I am indebted to Professor Hermann J. Pottmeyer for letting me know that the root metaphor of *begreifen* is the human hand seizing or capturing something.

40 May I call attention to Lonergan's praise of the *Summa*: "the intellectualism of St. Thomas ... shines as unmistakably as the sun on a noonday summer hills of Italy." See *Verbum*, chap. 5, Epilogue, 226.
41 Immanuel Kant, *Critique of Pure Reason*, trans. Norman Kemp Smith (New York: St Martin's Press, 1929), B146.
42 Rahner, "Faith, Rationality and Emotion," *TI* 16:60–78, at 61; Rahner's italics.
43 Rahner, "On Recognizing the Importance of Thomas Aquinas," *TI* 13:3–12, at 8.
44 Walter Principe, "Affectivity and the Heart in Thomas Aquinas' Spirituality," in *Spiritualities of the Heart: Approaches to Personal Wholeness in Christian Tradition*, ed. Annice Callahan (New York: Paulist Press, 1990), 45–63, at 52.
45 Imhof et al., *Faith in a Wintry Season*, 49.
46 Rahner, "The Doctrine of the 'Spiritual Senses' in the Middle Ages," *TI* 16:104–34, esp. 117–25; Bonaventure, *Breviloquium*, part 7, chap. 7.
47 Duns Scotus, *Opus Oxoniense*, IV, dist. 49, q. 3 and q. 4.
48 Rahner, "The Logic of Concrete Individual Knowledge in Ignatius Loyola," 94–5, including note 9.
49 My ex-colleague at Boston College, Matthew Lamb, reported to me that Rahner had confessed to him that he did not understand St Thomas's *emanatio intelligibilis*, namely the emergence of the *verbum*.
50 Rahner, "Remarks on the Dogmatic Treatise 'De Trinitate,'" *TI* 4:77–102, at 77. See Matthew Levering, "Wisdom and the Viability of Thomistic Trinitarian Theology," *The Thomist* 64 (2000): 593–618.
51 Rahner, "Remarks," 85–6.
52 Rahner, "The Mystery of the Trinity," *TI* 16:255–9, at 256.
53 Rahner, *The Trinity*, trans. Joseph Donceel (New York: Herder, 1970), 19, 47–8; see also 115–20 (with two footnotes on Lonergan's *De Deo Trino*), where he does not reject and yet severely restricts the fruitfulness of the psychological analogy.
54 Ibid., 48.
55 Rahner, The Content of Faith, 80.
56 Lonergan, *Verbum*, 65–6.
57 See, for instance, Rahner's "The Foundation of Belief today," and "Faith Between Rationality and Emotion," *TI* 16:3-23 and 60–78.
58 Rahner, The Content of Faith, 81.
59 Rahner, "On the Situation of Faith," *TI* 20:13–32, esp. 28–9.
60 Thomas Aquinas, *Summa Theologiae*, II-II, q. 1, a. 1–2; see Romanus Cessario, *Christian Faith and the Theological Life* (Washington, DC: The Catholic University of America Press, 1996), 53–7 and 62–6.

61 Rahner, "Pluralism in Theology and the Unity of the Creed in the Church," *TI* 11:3–23. One of the commentators who are most sympathetic to Rahner is nevertheless ill at ease with this aspect of Rahner's thinking; see Gerald A. McCool, "Person and Community in Karl Rahner," in *Person and Community: A Philosophical Exploration*, ed. Robert J. Roth (New York: Fordham University Press, 1975), 63–86, esp. 79–83.

62 For a contrast between Rahner and Lonergan on theological pluralism, see Guy Mansini, "Experiential Expressivism and Two Twentieth-Century Catholic Theologians," *Nova et Vetera*, English Edition, 8 (2010): 125–41.

63 Rahner, "Reflections on Methodology in Theology," *TI* 11:68–114, at 74.

64 Bernard J.F. Lonergan, "A Response to Fr. Dych," in *Theology and Discovery: Essays in Honor of Karl Rahner, S.J.*, ed. William J. Kelly (Milwaukee: Marquette University Press, 1980), 54–7, at 55. Unlike McCool and Lonergan, Mary E. Hines, Paul G. Crowley, and Richard Lennan do not see any problem with Rahner's construal of doctrinal pluralism; see the special issue on Rahner in *Philosophy and Theology* 12 (2000), no. 1.

65 Gerald McCool repeatedly fails to recognize that epistemological discrepancy. Regarding Aquinas and Rahner, see his piece, "Karl Rahner and the Christian Philosophy of St. Thomas Aquinas," in *Theology and Discovery*, 63–93; regarding Lonergan and Rahner, see McCool's "Twentieth-Century Scholasticism," in *Celebrating the Medieval Heritage: A Colloquy on the Thought of Aquinas and Bonaventure*, ed. David Tracy (The Journal of Religion, vol. 58, Supplement, 1978), S198–S221, at S218–S219. See also McCool's "The Philosophical Theology of Rahner and Lonergan," in *God Knowable and Unknowable*, ed. Robert J. Roth (New York: Fordham University Press, 1973), 123–57; on 126, McCool contrasts Rahner and Lonergan with the conceptualist Thomists, but on 132–3 and again on 143–4 his Rahner speaks the language of conceptualism; on 145 even his Lonergan has become a conceptualist!

66 See my positive appraisal of the transcendental openness to the infinite, in Louis Roy, *Transcendent Experiences: Phenomenology and Critique* (Toronto: University of Toronto Press, 2001), chap. 8, entitled "Maréchal, Rahner, and Lonergan"; see also my occasional use of Rahner's ideas in Study 10, on liturgy.

67 See Elizabeth A. Johnson, *She Who Is: The Mystery of God in Feminist Theological Discourse* (New York: Crossroad, 1994). Misled by Rahner, she incorrectly thinks that Aquinas's position on God amounts to "a theological agnosticism" (109), of which she approves. Having left out

Aquinas's key distinction between metaphorical and proper words, she puts forward only pragmatic criteria for discerning the respective validity of what she hails as "a revelry of symbols" (118). Notice the entire deregulation of images (117–20). On this issue, see also Louis Roy, "Inclusive Language Regarding God," *Worship* 65 (1991): 207–15.

Study 9

Some Implications for Mysticism

In recent years, there has been keen interest in the subject of mysticism as one aspect of the human experience. Neurologists, psychologists, sociologists, philosophers, and theologians have all made noteworthy contributions to the discussion. My aim in this Study is to show how Lonergan's theory of understanding and love makes possible a realistic, balanced, and open view of mystical consciousness, Christian or otherwise. I will set aside any discussion of the very worthwhile contributions from neurology, psychology, sociology, and theology. I will limit myself to the realm of the philosophy of religion, and more precisely, to the method that Lonergan called "intentional analysis."

I shall discuss the following topics: three kinds of consciousness, a common misunderstanding of mysticism, the connections between ordinary consciousness and mystical consciousness, and the intimate relationship between the cognitive and the affective in mysticism.

THREE KINDS OF CONSCIOUSNESS

Lonergan deals with consciousness in his masterpieces, *Insight* and *Method in Theology*, as well as in the fifth part of a treatise entitled *The Ontological and Psychological Constitution of Christ*.[1]

Let us name the three kinds of consciousness.[2] The first, which I will designate as *consciousness-of*, is the one we have *of* things and *of* people, at each of the four levels of intentionality. We can speak of it as one form of consciousness, even though normally Lonergan calls it "intentionality." Still, one instance of consciousness-of would be his usage of "consciousness" in the phrase "polymorphism of human consciousness" (see "Consciousness" in the Index of *Insight*). The second kind is *consciousness-in*, the one we experience *in* our daily activities, a self-presence that permeates all our acts and affective states since we consciously act and feel. And the third one is *mystical consciousness*, the one we reach when we attain a stage beyond our customary acts and states. In contrast to mystical consciousness, the first two kinds (consciousness-of and consciousness-in) pertain to *ordinary consciousness*. Mystical consciousness is vertical, while ordinary consciousness is horizontal.

However, these three kinds of consciousness are continuous, as they operate within the fabric of our lives, where they coexist prior to any reflective formulation. If we notice the presence of our consciousness-in or of our mystical consciousness, this consciousness automatically transforms itself into *awareness*, that is, an act of adverting to this consciousness, and as soon as we become interested in this awareness, we are launched into a reflection on consciousness. (The distinction between *consciousness* and *awareness* is not Lonergan's, but mine; however, I believe that it reflects his thought. What I refer to as *awareness* is simply the beginning of what he calls the "objectification" of consciousness.)

Consciousness-of becomes introverted when it reflects upon consciousness-in or upon mystical consciousness. To talk about consciousness presupposes an attention to consciousness. We are aware of consciousness-in or of mystical consciousness in this paying attention, where we find the data of consciousness. These are interior data, that is to say, they are our cognitive acts and our affective states as we experience them. These are not to be confused with the data of the senses, which come from the exterior. We will soon return to this point of confusion.

There is a normalcy associated with being continuously immersed in consciousness-of, since it is the one that our intentionality, oriented towards objects, exercises naturally. The fact remains that this dynamism is also a conscious intentionality. It has two sides: the intending of objects (consciousness-of) and the consciousness of being a human subject that is intending objects (consciousness-in). In addition to a *consciousness-of*, which is directed outward, each one of us is in touch with a *consciousness-in*, which is interior. Juxtaposed with a consciousness *of* objects is a consciousness *in* our own acts and our own states.[3] It falls to philosophy to explore this interior dimension, our conscious subjectivity. When the latter has been delved into and formulated, we obtain a knowledge of our interiority.

It is this consciousness-in that allows us to realize that we accomplish cognitive and affective acts, and to remember these acts, which are directed at particular objects (consciousness-of). If consciousness-in were not part of our experience, evidently we would never become aware of it. Lonergan refers to this non-reflective consciousness as the *conscientia-experientia*, consciousness-as-experience, to distinguish it from the initial intentional consciousness, namely the intending of objects, the *conscientia-perceptio*, consciousness-as-perception.[4] The latter is perceptual because it starts with perception, that is to say, through direct contact with data coming from outside, which are objectified as soon as we attempt to understand them. For Lonergan, the identification of *conscientia-experientia* with *conscientia-perceptio* amounts to a significant mix-up.

Consciousness has a wider scope than awareness. In this instance, awareness refers not to consciousness as still unattended-to, but to attended-to consciousness. The former constitutes consciousness that is said to be "non-positional," in Jean-Paul Sartre's sense; this belongs not to the area of consciousness-of, but rather to the area of conscious acts and states as yet unexpressed. Hence his idiosyncratic phrasing, *conscience (de) soi*, "consciousness (of) self."[5] These unexpressed acts or states are sensory perceptions, feelings, thoughts, and so on. The latter form of consciousness, said to be "positional," is the same consciousness, but at the moment when the subject pays attention to it for the first time.

Thus, there is a consciousness that exists prior to any awareness of it. This consciousness becomes awareness when a subject turns its attention to its bodily or mental states and acts (in which the subject is conscious). At this stage, consciousness-in begins to transmute itself into an embryonic form of consciousness-of. Awareness therefore constitutes the first step of consciousness-of, which lends itself to a further, more complete objectification during later steps. In other words, awareness is at the halfway point between pure consciousness and objectified consciousness.

In fact, we often experience moments of awareness. We can become aware of any of the acts or states that happen in our intentionality. It is in this way that we become aware of a pain, of a question, of an insight, of being drawn towards a value or a person, etc. Most of the time, we are happy to simply name that which drew our attention, without going beyond the meaning we inherited from others. Still, from time to time, our awareness pushes us to better understand what we are experiencing: we talk to a doctor about our pain, we discuss our question with a colleague, we let someone know about our insight, we confide in a friend that we are attracted to a value or a person, etc.

In relating this point to what was said earlier, we can say that the four levels of intentionality constitute consciousness-of. Within this dynamism that is intentionality, which aims at a consciousness-of, we find consciousness-in, because consciousness-of does not operate unconsciously. The knowing and feeling subject consciously wonders about and attains objects of interest, both cognitively and affectively. Beginning with consciousness-of, transcendental self-knowledge draws on consciousness-in and objectifies it.

In a study of Zen, a Western monk explains the difference between the *I*, the pre-known subject, and the *me*, the subject that we become aware of and that gradually becomes known:

> We can distinguish ourselves as the subject thinking and the object thought, or, more simply, as "I" and "me." Whenever we act or think, it is I who act or think; but whenever we think of ourselves acting or thinking, the subject of our thought is "me" – even though, be it noted, we may speak of ourselves and often (without sufficient analysis) think of ourselves as "I." The "I" and "me" are substantially identical, but cognitively, at the normal level of knowledge, they are distinct. This might be expressed by adopting a term from Buddhist psychology, the I and me exist in "nonduality." Put another way: whenever I think or act unself-consciously, it is *I*; whenever I think or act self-consciously, it is *me*.[6]

The *I* operates spontaneously in consciousness-of, which is intentional, because it intends objects to be known and appreciated. When one becomes aware of the way in which the *I* functions, the *I* begins to be objectified: it becomes a *me*. At this point, my endeavour can become a philosophical understanding of what I am as a subject. Since this philosophical understanding points to all intentional subjects in the way they function as subjects, it has universal implications; it transcends individual and cultural characteristics; it must therefore be considered *transcendental* knowledge, as in the thought of Kant, Husserl, and Lonergan.

A COMMON MISUNDERSTANDING OF MYSTICISM

The inordinate interest in paranormal phenomena, in the wake of William James's classic, *The Varieties of Religious Experience*, conceals the mistaken idea that there is some kind of access to a consciousness that, in a common sense understanding, would simply be "objectal," by which is meant that it is object-directed. Many authors, whose work involves an understanding of consciousness as a state imbued with content, consider the evolution of consciousness as the acquisition of a state of mind characterized by a greater openness to the bizarre, such as extrasensory perception. In my opinion, they err by confusing a higher consciousness with receiving particular *contents*, be they psychic, cosmic, or religious. They therefore disregard the subjective consciousness, which permeates the whole of the activity by which we access content. As a result, it is necessary to reject these misleading contributions put forth by researchers who are obsessed by their exploration of a consciousness that possesses objects, without being able to discern the transcendental aspect of human consciousness, from which human subjectivity originates.

Only the path of the person's self-knowledge as a knowing and acting subject allows us to properly understand mysticism from an intellectual perspective. Familiarity with our consciousness-in enables us to be open to mystical consciousness, which turns out to be precisely the source of our intentionality, that is, of consciousness-of. That is how Bernard McGinn, one of Lonergan's former students and the author of a series of books entitled *The Presence of God: A History of Western Christian Mysticism*, comes to define mysticism: "an immediate consciousness of the presence of God."[7] McGinn prefers not to use the word "experience," in order to avoid any suggestion that mystical life could be perceived as some kind of contact or encounter with the divine considered as object – as infinite, incomprehensible, and ineffable as that object may be.[8]

Unfortunately, Lonergan's employment of the word "experience" often leads to confusion for readers who may have overlooked the various meanings he attaches to this word. One must note how careful he is, never speaking of an "experience of God" but rather of a "religious experience" (*Method*, 105–7).[9] He does, however, use the term "object" but clearly specifies the way in which God can or cannot be said to be an "object" (*Method*, 341–3).[10]

We are inundated with essays that purport to examine mystical consciousness by presuming that consciousness always involves being conscious *of something*. Misled by this object-oriented model, which is current in the social sciences, many researchers in the area of religious experience take it for granted that mysticism equates with a special category of phenomena perceivable thanks to an expanded consciousness. It is alleged that in paranormal events, a more perceptive consciousness accesses new objects coming from outside, or receives particular revelations taking place inside. But a little familiarity with the great spiritual teachers should suffice to make us realize that although true mysticism may sometimes be associated with such phenomena, its essentials belong elsewhere.

In Hinduism, for example, paranormal and supranormal phenomena are regarded with circumspection: "Their religious significance is seen as ambiguous. According to the most authoritative masters, they are not intrinsic to mystical life and may even hinder it, especially if they are sought after for their own sake. Thus the Yoga Sutras approve of the practitioners' interest in them only temporarily, because such pursuit is an impediment to the full liberation of the mind."[11]

The same cautiousness is typical of many Christian writers. Notable in this regard is the fact that John of the Cross construes rapture (*arrobamiento*) or ecstasy (*éxtasis*) – they are the same for him – as resulting from the limited endurance of the human body. Far from simply delighting in rapture, the soul suffers so much that it hankers after a state in which it would be separated from the body. As he explains, the intake of the soul at its sensory level is so restricted that it is prevented from receiving an abundant spiritual communication. True, he does not disparage ecstasy, yet he puts no stock in it. He also remarks that such phenomena cease when the meditators have reached perfection.[12]

This position is echoed by William Johnston, who sums up the views of an authority on mysticism: "The French Jesuit, Joseph de Guibert (1877–1942), for example, maintained that ecstasy was by no means an integral part of the mystical ascent. It was, he claimed, simply a consequence arising from the weakness of the human organism unable to stand such a powerful inflow of spirit without losing the use of its physical and psychological faculties."[13]

And with respect to Zen, Johnston notes: "It is significant, too, that in Zen, even in the deepest spiritual experiences, physical ecstasy is virtually unknown. If anything like this does rear its head, it is promptly crushed. Indeed, the whole Zen training is calculated to counteract anything like ecstasy."

Johnston then proceeds to highlight a more profound sense of the word "ecstasy": "It is an experience that is undoubtedly present also in the deepest stages of Zen: an extraordinarily powerful uprising of spirit in the human mind and heart and the transition to a new level of consciousness. It is this that I call ecstasy … For the medieval mystics, ecstasy (the Greek *ekstasis* or *standing out*) was a going out from, or a relinquishing of, the self. This is the root meaning of the term."[14]

Accordingly, the term ecstasy means a "new level of consciousness." We find it not only in Zen but also in the works of Plotinus and Eckhart. It is equivalent to Lonergan's self-transcendence.

ORDINARY CONSCIOUSNESS AND MYSTICAL CONSCIOUSNESS

In this section I will develop Lonergan's thought in order to better understand the relationships between different kinds of consciousness. The consciousness that directs our daily life is directed outward and is pragmatic: it hears, observes, imagines, reacts to emotions, remembers, asks questions, analyzes, discusses, makes judgments, and makes decisions. This consciousness takes on a more disinterested stance when it becomes scientific or artistic. For example, the scientific mind distances itself from immediate needs and endeavours to know data independently from how they are used. Thanks to the artistic mind, the painter's eye and the musician's ear perceive fresh and unlimited possibilities through shapes and sounds.

Whether pragmatic, scientific, or artistic, ordinary human consciousness involves a double receptivity: from the world and from itself. These two aspects of receptivity are concurrent; an interest in reality is accompanied by an immediate presence to oneself as a receptive and proactive subject. Ordinary consciousness is therefore a double consciousness: a presence to others and a presence *in* oneself (which becomes a presence *to* oneself as soon as it is reflective). It is double in that our outward-directed consciousness (consciousness-of) is accompanied by an interior consciousness *in* our acts and feelings (consciousness-in). Participating in ordinary consciousness, this self-consciousness (consciousness-in) enables self-knowledge (awareness, reflective consciousness).

Ordinary consciousness, which functions in a *horizontal* plane, opens us up to another form of consciousness, this one *vertical*, underlying ordinary consciousness. This is religious consciousness, or more precisely, mystical consciousness. Consciousness-in mediates between consciousness-of and mystical consciousness. Whereas consciousness-of is entirely finite, consciousness-in is not; and whereas mystical consciousness is entirely infinite, consciousness-in is not. Accordingly, we can say that consciousness-in amounts to an *indefinite* dynamism.[15]

While it may be accompanied by extraordinary phenomena, this mystical consciousness turns out to be a fairly straightforward concept. Here are a few of its traits.

First, mystical consciousness is characterized by a centring. It is focused, unified, unfragmented. In prayer, it involves a dissatisfaction with thoughts and feelings. It turns out to be indifferent to the complexity of images, emotions, memories, logical connections. The belief that God lies beyond any exterior relationship leads to the subject's cognitive activity being reduced to a minimum; sometimes it disappears completely. The Spirit fills the person, enabling her or him to partake in the divine life. Because God inhabits the deepest centre of the human self, one is aware of a loving union, or even a shared identity with the Mystery, which is both immanent and transcendent.

Second, mystical consciousness implies a detachment from the *me*: the *I* remains, but forgets itself. "It is no longer I who live, but Christ who lives in me," writes Saint Paul (Gal 2:20) – a statement considered as indicative of mystical union by the great Zen philosopher Nishitani.[16] This detachment is not an absence of interests or preferences, but a putting into perspective of one's attachments as the result of the intensification of desire, a desire that enjoys a form of consciousness that is specifically religious, that is drawn to develop in a mystical manner. The centring on God leads to a de-centring with respect to the *me*, with respect to other people who would act as psychological crutches for us, with respect to any value that would correspond to an idol. Thus, what emerges as important is not the individual who seeks to build themselves up by their own means, but all of humanity called to penetrate the great Mystery.

Third, as already mentioned, ordinary consciousness is horizontal; it consists in a presence to the world and to the self. Mystical consciousness is vertical; it finds the Mystery in the depths of the self. Because one is horizontal and the other vertical, these two kinds of consciousness, far from being in competition, may coexist and even intermingle. Mystical consciousness enters ordinary consciousness, sometimes causing interference, but usually enriching it. Mystical consciousness gives ordinary consciousness a special quality: stillness, patience, a renewed ability to listen and to love the other, an enhanced dynamism for the pursuit of objectives that are in line with God's will.

Fourth, no longer satisfied with ordinary consciousness, human desire intensifies and is granted a consciousness that is specifically divine. Not without fear, desire readies itself for great renunciations that will allow this divine consciousness to grow within this desire. The Gospel – or any other authentic religious tradition – warns that its adepts must leave everything behind. On the other hand, when all things have been put into perspective, they will be returned a hundredfold, as promised by Jesus or other great spiritual masters, so that they may be enjoyed fully. When mystical consciousness permeates ordinary consciousness, the latter is imbued with undreamed-of flavours.

THE COGNITIVE AND THE AFFECTIVE IN MYSTICISM

At every level of intentionality, a combination of the cognitive and the affective is present. It is mostly at the first three levels that cognitive operations predominate, and mostly at the fourth level that affective states predominate. This fourth level holds within it both an interhuman dimension and a religious dimension. On the one hand, the height of the interhuman dimension is an affective state, a "being-in-love" between spouses, between parents and children, and even between citizens. On the other hand, the height of the religious dimension is found in a similar affective state, but in this case, the being-in-love is "without limit, without restriction, without condition, without reservation" (*Method*, 106). This loving state shatters our previous horizon and creates a new horizon within which our values and our beliefs are transformed. This state is said to be *dynamic* because it has an affective impact on our values and a cognitive impact on our beliefs (*Method*, 105).

In writing about these matters, Lonergan distinguishes between consciousness and knowledge: "To say that this dynamic state is conscious is not to say that it is known. For consciousness is just experience, but knowledge is a compound of experience, understanding, and judging" (*Method*, 106). He then describes how mystical consciousness affects knowledge:

> Faith is the knowledge born of religious love.
>
> First, then, there is a knowledge born of love. Of it Pascal spoke when he remarked that the heart has reasons which reason does not know. Here by reason I would understand the compound of the activities of the first three levels of cognitional activity, namely, of experiencing, of understanding, and of judging. By the heart's reasons I would understand feelings that are intentional responses to values … Finally, by the heart I understand the subject on the fourth, existential level of intentional consciousness and in the dynamic state of being in love. The meaning, then, of Pascal's remark would be that, besides the factual knowledge reached by experiencing, understanding, and verifying, there is another kind of knowledge reached through the discernment of value and the judgements of value of a person in love. (*Method*, 115)

These two fundamental tendencies – the affective and the cognitive – leave their mark not only upon our ordinary consciousness but also upon our mystical consciousness. We all have a tacit consciousness of our cognitive operations and our affective states; this consciousness becomes explicit with the awareness that emerges as we attend to this implicit consciousness. This awareness marks the beginning of what Lonergan calls "knowledge."

CONCLUSION

Lonergan's theory of knowledge and of love makes it possible to understand mystical consciousness, Christian or otherwise.[17] As we have seen, there is a clear distinction to be made between this mystical consciousness and both self-consciousness (consciousness-in) and the consciousness of exterior objects (consciousness-of). Far from being completely ineffable, mystical consciousness can be explored and known objectively, particularly in its connections with the consciousness that we have of ourselves. Furthermore, Lonergan's analysis of human intentionality accounts for both the cognitive side and the affective side of one's openness to Transcendence. It also allows for a deeper appreciation of the discoveries of thinkers such as Plotinus, Meister Eckhart, Schleiermacher, Sartre, or even Zen masters.[18]

NOTES

1 Lonergan, *The Ontological and Psychological Constitution of Christ*, trans. Michael G. Shields, volume 7 of *Collected Works of Bernard Lonergan* (Toronto: University of Toronto Press, 2001), 157–89. See also "Christ as Subject: A Reply," in *Collection*, ed. Frederick E. Crowe and Robert M. Doran, volume 4 of *Collected Works of Bernard Lonergan* (Toronto: University of Toronto Press, 1988), 153–84. See also Salvino Biolo, "A Lonerganian Approach to St. Augustine's Interpretation of Consciousness," *Science et Esprit* 31 (1979): 323–41.

2 See Louis Roy, *Mystical Consciousness: Western Perspectives and Dialogue with Japanese Thinkers* (Albany, NY: SUNY Press, 2003).

3 Basing himself on Alfred North Whitehead, John B. Bennett distinguishes between *awareness of* and *awareness with* in "A Suggestion on 'Consciousness' in Process and Reality," *Process Studies* 3 (1973): 41–2.

4 See Lonergan's *The Ontological and Psychological Constitution of Christ*, 172–3, and "Christ as Subject: A Reply," 163–6.

5 Jean-Paul Sartre, *Being and Nothingness: An Essay on Phenomenological Ontology*, trans. Hazel Estella Barnes (New York: Philosophical Library, 1956), lvi, see lii–lviii.

6 Dom Aelred Graham, *Zen Catholicism* (New York: Crossroad, 1994), 130.

7 Bernard McGinn, *The Foundations of Mysticism* (New York: Crossroad, 1991), xix; see his section "The Nature of Mysticism: A Heuristic Sketch," xiii–xx.

8 In *Mystical Theology: The Integrity of Spirituality and Theology* (Oxford and Malden, MA: Blackwell, 1998), Mark A. McIntosh rightly rejects "experientialism," which he understands as the endeavor to scrutinize one's own personal experience in prayer, which presumably evidences a self-centred disposition. Unfortunately his excessive reaction against the experiential owes much to Denys Turner, *The Darkness of God: Negativity*

in Christian Mysticism (Cambridge, UK: Cambridge University Press, 1995) and makes him misconstrue what great mystics such as Bernard of Clairvaux said about mysticism as experience. In so doing, he falls into the common misunderstanding of mysticism that I am criticizing in this section, namely a "consciousness-of" or an "experience-of" God.

9 Likewise, Thomas Aquinas speaks of *patiens divina* and not of *patiens Deum* (for example, in his *Summa Theologiae*, IIa IIae, q. 45, a. 2, where he quotes Dionysius's *pathōn ta theia* in Latin (*pati divina*) from *De Divinis Nominibus*, 2.9).

10 See also Lonergan, "Natural Knowledge of God" in *A Second Collection: Papers by Bernard J.F. Lonergan, S.J.*, ed. William F.J. Ryan and Bernard J. Tyrrell (Toronto: University of Toronto Press, 1996, reprint), 117–33, more particularly 121–4.

11 Joseph Maréchal, "Vraie et fausse mystique," *Nouvelle Revue théologique* 67 (1945): 275–95; the citation at page 287.

12 John of the Cross, "The Spiritual Canticle," in *The Collected Works of Saint John of the Cross*, trans. Kieran Kavanaugh and Otilio Rodriguez, rev. ed. (Washington, DC: ICS Publications, 1991), Stanza 13 §1–6, and Stanza 19 §1.

13 William Johnston, *Silent Music: The Science of Meditation* (New York: Harper & Row, 1974), 72, in reference to Joseph de Guibert, *The Theology of Spiritual Life*, trans. Paul Barrett (New York: Sheed and Ward, 1953), Part 7, chap. 4. Aquinas had already expressed this view in his *Summa Theologiae*, II-II, q. 175, a. 1.

14 Johnston, *Silent Music*, 73.

15 For a distinction between finite, indefinite, and infinite, see Louis Roy, *Transcendent Experiences: Phenomenology and Critique* (Toronto: University of Toronto Press, 2001), 156–60.

16 Keiji Nishitani, "Ontology and Utterance," *Philosophy East and West* 1 (1981): 29–43, at 35–43.

17 About Lonergan's personal experience, see Gordon Rixon, "Bernard Lonergan and Mysticism," *Theological Studies* 62 (2001): 479–97.

18 See Louis Roy, *Mystical Consciousness*.

Study 10
Some Implications for Liturgy

In liturgical celebrations, both Catholics and Protestants tend to be divided into conservatives or progressives. In Catholic liturgy, for instance, one of the problems is that many of the scholars and pastors who have been spiritually and theologically trained in a scholastic framework have reacted against it and adopted another outlook which strongly emphasizes the symbolic structure of religious experience. While this insistence is highly commendable in itself, it can unfortunately be interpreted in the manner typical of philosophical idealism.

A similar difficulty can be discerned among mainline Protestant churches, with which evangelical congregations beg to disagree. When this is the case, the implication is that for the liberals religion is first and foremost a matter of human interpretation, hope, and solidarity, whereas for the evangelicals religion has everything to do with coming to terms with the living God of the Bible. In liturgy as well as in other areas of church life, the stress on horizontal relationships, which has prevailed in the second half of the twentieth century, has been such as to jeopardize the vertical relationship to God.

Intellectually, what is at stake is an understanding of grace and mediation. In the history of Christian thought there have been at least four basic ways of apprehending the role of religious mediation: naïve realism, extrinsicism, immanentism, and critical realism.[1] My analysis of these four positions has been inspired by Lonergan's epistemology, complemented by that of other authors. What I shall be characterizing in this Study are general intellectual orientations as they are taken and acted upon by numerous believers. After examining the first three positions, I shall argue that only the fourth one can afford us a theological vision in which the horizontal and vertical relationships central to liturgy are appropriately related.

NAÏVE REALISM

According to this worldview, sense perception is the paradigm of human contact with reality. Any other access to the real is thought analogically as another kind of perception. Hence, anything that is encountered, known, and loved must be directly present, including "spiritual" or "supernatural" beings. One does not acknowledge the role of symbols created as intermediaries by the human soul to relate to the real in multifaceted ways. On the contrary, reality is pictured as directly available in signals or signs, which indicate the physical or spiritual presence of beings that are real because they move and influence people.[2] Thus God's or the saints' or the devil's action is felt as taking place right here in someone's experience prior to any question or reflection.

One can find in an American philosopher of religion a sophisticated discussion of mystical experiences based on such an unsophisticated position as naïve realism. For the author, experiences of God and sense experiences must be alike.[3] In the same vein, a French bestseller by André Frossard bears the title, *Dieu existe, je l'ai rencontré*, which can be translated: "God exists, for I have met him."[4] Marie-Dominique Chenu facetiously commented on this title by stating: "God exists, for I have *not* met him." I shall return to this little squabble at the end of my fourth section.

For naïve realism, there is no religious mediation: God's presence, albeit hidden to the senses, is immediate, directly perceived, and felt. As a matter of fact, religious experiences of naïve realists *are* based on intermediaries (hymns, exhortations, testimonies, rituals, etc.). The problem is that they are not understood to be mediations because no distinction is made between divine grace and man-made means of expression. This is what Tad Guzie calls "concretism": "In the concretist fallacy, there is no distinction between the events of the revealing experience and the symbols or doctrines which express that revelation. This fallacy is observed in the fundamentalists of every era, who identify the symbols of our own making with the reality of God. If you don't believe the way I do, you don't believe in the one true God.[5]" Needless to say, this orientation is so weak intellectually that present-day Catholic liturgists easily repudiate it. I shall therefore concentrate on the dialectic that is going on among the next three conceptions of grace.

EXTRINSICISM

The French philosopher Maurice Blondel seems to have been the first Christian thinker to have exposed aptly the defects of extrinsicism. In 1903, he wrote:

> Does the supernatural consist, as the extrinsicist thesis implies, in a notional relationship determined and imposed by God, there being no link between natural and supernatural but only an ideal juxtaposition of heterogeneous and even impenetrable elements which only the obedience of our minds can bring together? In that case the supernatural subsists only if it remain extrinsic to the natural, and if it is proposed to us from outside, its whole value residing in the fact that it is *above* nature.[6]

Extrinsicism is based on a medieval distinction between nature and grace which, in modern times, has hardened into a separation, "as two layers so carefully placed that they penetrate each other as little as possible."[7] They are pictured as two juxtaposed worlds, each with its commensurate end and kind of activities. For instance, Ripalda (1594–1648) reifies the supernatural dimension when he writes that it is a *substantia supernaturalis*, "a supernatural substance."[8] In popular piety, this substance has been looked upon as a spiritual treasure which can be quantitatively increased, thanks to one's merits, but remains foreign to the human mind's quest for meaning.

Karl Rahner characterizes this conception in the following manner. Although Catholics know, through the teaching of faith, that God grants them supernatural life, many of them assume that the intellectual and ethical acts which are naturally theirs are left totally untouched by grace. These acts "are referred to the supernatural only by their objects (by faith, by a pure intention etc.)."[9] Talking about the believer who has espoused this view of the relationship between the natural and the supernatural, Rahner adds: "But the space where he comes to himself, experiences himself and lives, is, as regards the data of consciousness, not filled by this grace. His experience of his spiritual and moral acts in their proper reality (in contrast to their proposed objects, which are distinct from the acts) remains exactly what it would and could be, if there were no such thing as a supernatural 'elevation' of these acts.[10]"

The distinction temporal/spiritual, which has been historically useful insofar as it guarantees the validity of laypeople's decisions over against excessive clerical jurisdiction, has unfortunately also involved a separation in modern Catholicism.[11] For one thing, religion has been reduced to the spiritual. Grace is sanctification taking place only in the soul. In the sacraments, God produces spiritual effects automatically (*ex opere operato*); he is imagined to be locally present and active in the things, words, and gestures that constitute the Christian rituals.[12] For another, human action has been looked upon in terms of religious duty, as a field in which Christian commandments should be applied. According to this view, in a first step, the sacraments mediate God's grace to the internal life of the soul; in a second step, meritorious obedience mediates God's will to the external field of human action. As a consequence, the sacramental experience is not intrinsically related to daily experience because the two are thought to be heterogeneous domains. The result is that the mediation between the Mystery and the human realm has become very tenuous.

Curiously enough, although this conception is based on the dichotomy natural/supernatural, the piety that goes along with it takes its revenge; in the lived experience of the Mass, in the benediction of the Blessed Sacrament, in the saying of the rosary, etc., there is a definite religious enjoyment, a taste for sacred music, silence, recollection. In principle, since extrinsicism maintains that there cannot be any experience of God prior to the resurrection, such religious feelings should be pronounced purely natural. In practice, however, the believers spontaneously regard them as part and parcel of the link they have with Christ. Thus, the contradiction between this theory and its practice calls into question the adequacy of the theory. Furthermore, the emotional rewards of this way of relating to God explain, at least in part, the vehement indignation of conservative Catholics whenever their piety is threatened by the position that has come to be characterized as immanentism.

IMMANENTISM

In his analysis of extrinsicism, Rahner suggests the hypothesis that "modern naturalism," or "modern lack of interest in the supernatural," may very well have emerged "on the basis of such a view of grace, which must be to some extent nominalist."[13] When late medieval nominalism, sixteenth-century Lutheranism, and seventeenth-century scholasticism had all agreed, for different reasons, on the opposition between nature and grace, it was logical for Spinoza, followed by the eighteenth-century Enlightenment, to extol the natural and reject a supernatural which seemed no longer needed for the happiness of humankind. Several subsequent Western thinkers have deemed not only the supernatural but also God to be incompatible with human freedom, construed as the rock of the natural.[14] In the nineteenth century, however, German idealism, coupled with romanticism, allowed many Christians to escape atheism in the wake of Schleiermacher and Hegel. The price to be paid, however was the abandonment of the supernatural and of the personal God of the Bible.[15] The God of idealism could not indeed threaten human autonomy. So Nietzsche pronounced him culturally dead.

For a long time, Catholicism by and large stayed immune to philosophical idealism.[16] From approximately 1870 until 1945 extrinsicism reigned in Catholic theology and piety. According to de Lubac, it was in the nineteenth century that scholastic theologians began to replace the adjective "supernatural" by the noun "supernature," "thus completing in their language a deviation of thought whose history was already long." In the first part of the twentieth century, the terminology nature/supernature became "more and more encroaching."[17] But after the Second World War, mostly thanks to de Lubac's book *Surnaturel*, the inadequacy of extrinsicism was increasingly exposed.[18] A profound need was felt to bring out the aspects of Christian life that extrinsicism had systematically neglected: the secular, the historical, the existential, the interpersonal, the bodily, the symbolic.

The rejection of the supernatural is explainable by the shortcomings of extrinsicism.[19] The vigorous reaction against the latter has thrust many theologians into the opposite extreme: immanentism, whose typical instances in the nineteenth century were the liberal Protestantism in the Lutheran Church and the Broad party in the Church of England. As is well-known, Newman combatted what he called "liberalism" as being the immanentism that resulted from exaltation of an autonomous human nature at the expense of the reality of God and of the supernatural.[20]

Of course, in Christian writings and liturgies tainted by immanentism, the vocabulary still includes biblical words such as God, grace, sin, salvation, etc. But having repudiated a naïvely realistic metaphysics and having come under the influence of philosophical idealism, one cannot intellectually account for the absolute transcendence of God and for the distinction natural/supernatural, which presupposes the absolute transcendence of God. The ontological uncertainties regarding God and his self-gift bring about a heavy stress on the indirect character of religion. Talking about "the music-lover listening to Bach or the Christian believer participating in a Eucharist," Charles Davis perspicaciously detected this issue by asking: "Are they responding to the concrete reality of the object presented, and thus entering into a direct, personal relationship with it? Or, are the mediating elements themselves the object of attention, so that the relationship with the mediated reality has become indirect?"[21]

According to the latter view, typical of religious idealism, mediations (people, events, words, gestures, music, works of art) occupy the whole field of religious consciousness, to the exclusion of the living God to whom they no longer effectively refer. Religion becomes a dimension of this earthly life, which in practice is considered to be more real than God. Therefore mediations are seen as intermediaries between the non-religious aspects and the religious dimension *of human life*, rather than between human life and God.

Guzie, for example, has little sympathy for those who raise the question whether Catholic worship has lost a sense of the sacred. He concedes that there is a loss of mystery whenever a celebration is "poor and unprepared." Nevertheless, he does not in the least deplore the jettisoning of "certain stimuli that used to make us attentive to the presence of God: sanctuary bells, organ music, certain kinds of chanting, certain regalia, even certain smells like the fragrance of incense." He degrades to the level of "stimuli" what any good scholar of religion would regard as symbolic mediations. And on what ground does he dismiss them? He declares: "The sacredness of a sacrament is not to be found in some kind of otherworldliness, or in stimuli that are only experienced in the church building. The real mystery is that we, though many, are one body in Christ in this everyday world."[22] Over against this "otherworldliness," he very much emphasizes the horizontality of religious mediations: "There is a place in any liturgy for moments which direct our attention 'upward.' But any liturgical celebration is in its total thrust 'horizontal.'"[23]

Guzie has very little room for verticality in liturgy. The reason why he repeatedly stresses horizontality seems to be that for him the sacraments are not individualistic but communal events. But if this sound liturgical principle leads him into downplaying the verticality, it is because he associates verticality with individualistic piety. One should ask, however, is there anything individualistic about the "stimuli" he has listed? Have they not for centuries been communally experienced? We should agree that, prior to the recent liturgical reform, there was a need for new symbols which would express the horizontal bonds among the participants united in Jesus Christ. Still, it is difficult to understand why this legitimate horizontality should relegate verticality to such a secondary place. There is no necessary link between verticality and individualism. As I shall argue in the next section, there can be a verticality that arises from a communally celebrated horizontality.[24]

Guzie repudiates "otherworldliness," not only because he associates it with individualistic piety, but also because he lacks the adequate epistemology and ontology that would enable him to make sense of what is otherworldly in Christianity. In a previous book, he points out that two basic questions present themselves. There is "the empirical question: What is that out there?" and there is "the human question: What is that for man?"[25] One can ask these two questions with respect either to the eucharistic bread and wine or to the eucharistic action.[26] If we focus on the bread and wine, as has been done since the early Middle Ages, we lose sight of the fact that the eucharist is an action done by the Christian assembly. If we raise the second question in the context of the eucharistic action, we ask about its meaning.

One should welcome this shift from the sacred things to the eucharistic action, which has become standard doctrine among liturgists and which is helpful for the understanding of the sacraments. Yet, this shift has often been accompanied by a mistaken sacramental belief and a misguided philosophical transition.

The mistaken *sacramental* belief is that a liturgical action ought to be expressed first and foremost in terms of horizontal communication. Along with Guzie, many other liturgists and pastors do not realize that vertical symbols, whose expressiveness is not directly interhuman, can be communally lived in a sacramental setting as the signs of the community's relationship to God. Their concept of liturgical action is not broad enough to include immanent acts of knowing and loving which do not always have to be translated into the kind of uttered words and bodily gestures typical of horizontal communication.

The misguided *philosophical* transition has been from extrinsicism to idealism. The contrast between "the empirical question," which refers us to what is "out there" (Guzie's very words), and "the human question," which refers us to the symbolic, is typical of the Kantian tradition.[27] It would be unfair to reproach Guzie for having tried and managed to shed some light upon liturgical issues by using this inadequate philosophical context. At least the Kantian two-levelled account of human knowing has enabled him to discard the one-levelled account offered by naïve realism.

Nonetheless, Kant's transcendental philosophy has its deficiency, which must be succinctly noted here. In contrasting the "empirical" and the "human" levels of knowing, Guzie fails to underscore the all-important act that Lonergan locates on the third level of intentionality, namely judgment. Unfortunately, in Kant's epistemology, judgment is merely a reduplication of the act of understanding.[28] In contrast to this position, for Lonergan, that which has been understood as meaningful still has to be verified and affirmed as true. Moreover, theologians who do not explore this third level fall short of establishing clearly that everything which is affirmed as true and real is contingent and limited, and that there must be a necessary and unlimited Being whose unknown essence is "to be." Therefore, far from being "otherworldly" in Guzie's pejorative sense, verticality is central in Christian worship, precisely because God is absolutely transcendent and uniquely real.

Guzie's position resembles that of Louis-Marie Chauvet, the leading sacramentologist in France since the 1980s.[29] On the one hand, Chauvet puts forward a trenchant refutation of the narrow, impersonal, instrumentalist construal of the sacraments as automatically producing their effects, which we find in modern Catholic theology before the Second Vatican Council, but which he wrongly attributes to Thomas Aquinas.[30] However, he indirectly – and rightly – criticizes several of the tenets that have just been described here as typical of naïve realism and extrinsicism. On the other hand, he proposes a very rich vision of the sacraments, situated within a symbolic order, and he highlights the central role of language as openness to reality. Thus several aspects of his sacramentology resemble Lonergan's account of symbolism and of mediation, as will be evident, I hope, in the rest of this Study.

While not being as liberal as Guzie, Chauvet has unfortunately espoused the philosophy of language of Martin Heidegger[31] who, as Oliva Blanchette has demonstrated, repudiated the conceptualism of

Scotus and Suarez in their treatment of being.[32] His repudiation of that erroneous approach to reality led Heidegger to replace it with a view of being as it is disclosed in language, especially in poetry. We find this view applied by Chauvet in his account of the sacramental experience. Liam Walsh sums it up as follows:

> For Chauvet the symbolical that is in sacraments belongs to the existential rather than the representational order; it is that which furnishes the typical and only authentic mode of human existence, the only access to the mystery of being. It occurs primarily in the field of language; it is bodiliness [*sic*] in action; it is the play of images and rites; it is history in the telling and in the making; it is the stuff of community relationships.[33]

The problem is that Heidegger's philosophy, adopted by Chauvet, does not provide us with criteria to sift the truths and falsities that may lie in the contents of literary works.[34] The same concern ought to apply to the issue of the validity of the individual or collective interpretations of those who participate in liturgies, including the presider's interpretations – a concern that Chauvet ignores. One can detect the influence of an epistemological idealism in his assertion that the human relation to the real is culturally constructed – a half-truth (see my Study 2, section "A Subjectivity in Search of Objectivity") – and in his assertion that a common code of values and norms is a matter of convention, which seems to be a consensual account of truth rather than a critical-realist account.[35]

I would like to round off this section by saying a word on two sacramental theologians who declared being indebted to Lonergan's thought, namely Bernard Cooke and Joseph Martos. Strangely enough, they do not seem to be aware of the issue of horizontality/verticality in liturgical practice. For instance, Cooke strongly insists that the sacraments are related to *human beings'* interpretations of their experiences, leaving aside the ways in which they are related to God.[36] And Martos concurs:

> For Cooke, the purpose of the sacraments is to transform the meaning of those fundamental human experiences … Jesus transformed the meaning of human existence and thereby transformed the very reality of that existence. And for those who knew him and believed in him, the experience of life changed so

> radically that their reality too was altered. They proclaimed him as their savior, the Christ. He was for them a sacrament.[37]

There is an ambiguity here as to whether such a transformation ought to be construed within the framework of idealism or of critical realism.

CRITICAL REALISM

Human intentionality is rooted in the immediacy of questioning and of our other spiritual acts, and unfolds thanks to the mediation of all the stages that constitute its journey. Whenever unhampered, it becomes realist in a critical manner. It differs from naïve realism in that it takes seriously the mediated character of knowledge. It differs from idealism in that it bases its openness to finite being as well as to God on a critical appropriation of the fact that people normally attempt to judge correctly both in matters of fact and in matters of value, and often succeed in doing so.

When it is put at the service of revelation, critical realism can ground the transcendent reality of God and ascribe a definite experiential and ontological status to grace. In this last section, I shall undertake to show the connections that exist between this theological pronouncement and the role of mediation in human life and in Christian liturgy.

Let us begin with its opposite, immediacy.[38] The most obvious case of immediacy is perception: "seeing is immediate to what is being seen, hearing to what is being heard, touch to what is being touched" (*Method*, 28). As infants, we all begin our life immersed in a narrow world of immediacy. But as soon as we use our imagination and our thinking power, we enter the larger world mediated by meaning. In this world, images, words, and symbols exercise their function of mediators: they mediate what they mean, and what they mean is something other than themselves. We must beware lest we envision this mediation in a spatial way: the mediated is not physically carried into our brains item by item, but it is highly and complexly organized so as to be understood as making sense and judged as being true. Both this creativity of the human mind, which the idealist philosophers have admirably highlighted, and the concern to attain what is real, to which they have paid less attention, lead us far beyond the world of perceptual immediacy.

This is not to say, however, that everything beyond perceptual immediacy is mediated. Our intellectual activity is spontaneously purposeful: it aims at understanding and at knowing correctly. It asks: What is this? Is this true? Is this worthwhile? Such questions lie at the root of the human spirit. They evidence a foundational desire or intention to find and respect being. Hence, the questioning that constitutes human intentionality and that directly tends towards being is immediately related to being, whereas the answers in which being is partially reached are mediated by our questions and our other intellectual operations.[39]

Therefore, besides the immediacy of perception and the mediatedness of full knowledge, there is the twofold immediacy of our intentionality. First, thanks to questioning, which evidences desire, intentionality directly aims at being. Second, intentionality is also in touch with itself because it is conscious of its operations. Such consciousness is immediate, but it becomes mediated when it is adverted to in its manifold aspects, understood in its inner connections, affirmed, and consented to. This point was elaborated in the preceding Study. In sum, human knowing is a compound of immediacy and mediatedness. In different ways, we are directly present to what is perceived, to our intention of being, and to our own conscious acts. Nevertheless, nothing becomes explicitly known unless it is mediated by our acts.

Mutatis mutandis, the same conjunction of immediacy and mediatedness is found in our relationship to God. Let us consider, in the first place, the human quest for God. In contrast to what Feuerbach, Marx, and Freud thought, the question of God is not derivative from other human needs. It stems from the unrestricted desire to know and to rejoice in everything that exists. Since this fundamental desire operates consciously, we are actually open to God as source of our light and love. And yet the appropriation of the way we raise and pursue the question of God is mediated by the long series of events which make our intellectual biography. The end of the section on immanentism above offers a rapid sketch of the basic steps that lead to the affirmation of the transcendent reality of God.

In the second place, the same procedure governs a sound theology of grace. On the one hand, the immediate experience of being in love in an unrestricted fashion is foundational, corresponding to a unique affective fulfilment (*Method*, 105–6). On the other hand, in order to be known and willed, this basic religious experience, which is the great gift of God, must be mediated by persons, events, words, symbols, etc. The central mediator is Jesus Christ who, in a special way, introduces the believers into a process of mutual self-mediation. Self-mediation is the fact that they transform themselves as they render themselves meaningful and good by way of their decisions, deeds, and sufferings. In addition to this personal engagement, this process is always reciprocal, since it cannot be done except in interaction with other people.

Thus, as Jesus progressively discovered and accepted his own mission, by humanly becoming a second Moses in his ministry and a suffering servant in his passion, he did it *for us* in order to show the only path through which human nature could be granted "the divinely originated solution to the problem of evil."[40] Because of what he became for our sake, in our turn we can become ourselves for his sake. Furthermore, such mutual self-mediation extends to all interpersonal relationships: whenever we act and suffer for the sake of the body of Christ, we allow our brothers and sisters to become fully themselves according to the purpose of the Father.[41]

As immediately present in us, grace, or the gift of God's love, is poured into our hearts by the Holy Spirit. As mediated through the process of mutual self-mediation, grace is freely cultivated by its recipients thanks to all the means that link them up with Jesus Christ. In the context of critical realism, these two sides of the same reality may be formulated as follows. First, what is unmediated – God's presence in the gift of his love – is most real, even though it in itself belongs, not to the world mediated by meaning, but to the realm of transcendence because it entails a participation in God's own life. Second, Jesus Christ, the central mediator, as well as the symbolic mediations that make him visible and reveal our meaningfulness and worth, relate us to God in a real, albeit not perceptual way, in complementarity with the inner gift of the Holy Spirit.

The conjunction between the mission of the Spirit and the mission of the Son brings together, both in ordinary living and in liturgy, the verticality and the horizontality of Christian symbolism, according to the embodied character of Redemption. Because of the Incarnation, there is no separation between the verticality and the horizontality. The vertical relationship between God and us is embodied in all the human operations and feelings by means of which we horizontally interact and constitute ourselves as humans. Horizontality is thus granted its inalienable importance by being celebrated as a gift of God. There is also no separation between the supernatural and the natural. Supernatural acts are nothing else than elevated *human* acts, be they vertical or horizontal. If there is indeed a distinction between these aspects of our experience, it is due to the fact that, logically and ontologically, the gift of God's own life, proclaimed in the New Testament, lies totally beyond the capacity of human nature.

It is such a view of graced intentionality that has enabled Joseph Flanagan to see, more deeply than Northrop Frye himself, the full significance of anagogic symbols.[42] Such symbols have an eschatological function. Their role in liturgy consists in suggesting, in a way that vividly speaks to the whole person, that human life on earth is not self-sufficient, that meaning and love are partial, unstable, and coupled with destructive tendencies, that desire and fear cannot be kept within the confines of this world, that nature may eventually be completely transformed and transcended, that the imaginative power of humankind looks towards Mystery and towards Redemption, that Christ stands in relationship to all parts of the universe and all stages of history according to a mode of presence that crosses the boundaries of space and time.

If we transpose what Frye writes about anagogic symbols into the key of critical realism,[43] we can make the following assertions. Far from throwing us back upon ourselves as creators of symbols who would merely express their own meanings in an idealist framework, mediations relate us to a real God whose Spirit touches us in the immediacy of desire and grace. They also relate us to a real God whose incarnate Word challenges us towards self-transcendence, conversion, and self-sacrificing love. Symbols do not contain their own meaning in an immanentist way; they expose us to the Mystery in a realist manner. They are not screens onto which purely human meaning would be projected; they are windows opening up to "the holy city, new Jerusalem, coming down out of heaven from God" (Rev 21:2).

In the light of what has been established in this section, let us revert to the disagreement between Chenu and Frossard. On the one hand, Chenu's position could be interpreted (wrongly) as suggesting an idealist stance, whereas Frossard's could be interpreted (equally wrongly) as an instance of naïve realism. On the other hand, one ought to decipher what each is rightly holding. Thus, with the former, who states: "God exists, for I have *not* met him," I would say that the uniqueness of God entails the fact that one cannot meet him in a perception-like experience. With the latter, who states: "God exists, for I have met him," I would say that, because of its dynamic and open structure and because of its being elevated by grace, human intentionality can meet God, for one can be conscious of being in love with God and of desiring to know him.

CONCLUSION

Let us now retrace our steps. Firstly, we saw at the outset that present-day Catholic sacramentologists are sophisticated enough not to account for the sacramental experience in terms of naïve realism. Secondly, following the rejection of modern scholasticism by most theologians, unfortunately most Christians cannot make sense of the distinction natural/supernatural, which extrinsicism had transformed into a separation. Thirdly, under the influence of philosophical idealism, many liturgists find it normal to underline horizontal relationships in such a way that the vertical relationship is hardly expressed any more. Religiously speaking, this orientation causes an impoverishment in the life of faith, which prayerfulness and spiritual counselling should partly remedy. Theologically speaking, this Study has tried to expose the immanentist rationale that underlies this orientation.

Lastly I have endeavoured to show that an awareness of the supernaturally elevated human intentionality, in its unmediated and mediating functions, can justify another liturgical orientation that emphasizes vertical symbolism. The use of critical realism should enable theologians and pastors to situate horizontal symbolism within its actual context, which is the verticality of the incarnate Mystery. "Very truly, I tell you, you will see heaven opened, and the angels of God ascending and descending upon the Son of man" (Jn 1:51; see Gen 28:12).

NOTES

1 See Lonergan, "Beyond Extrinsicism and Immanentism," in *Early Works on Theological Method 1*, ed. Robert M. Doran and Robert C. Croken, volume 22 of *Collected Works of Bernard Lonergan* (Toronto: University of Toronto Press, 2010), 103–27. In that context, Lonergan's characterization of "extrinsicism" referred to logic, whereas my definition

will come from the one Rahner coined in his discussions on grace. However, Lonergan's characterization of "immanentism" perfectly fits in with my understanding of that view.

2 See Susanne K. Langer, *Philosophy in a New Key* (Cambridge, MA: Harvard University Press, 1957), x and 57–9.

3 William J. Wainwright, *Mysticism: A Study of its Nature, Cognitive Value and Moral implications* (Madison: University of Wisconsin Press, 1981), xiii, xiv, 83, 84, 161, 184. See Louis Roy, "Wainwright, Maritain, and Aquinas on Transcendent Experiences," *The Thomist* 54 (1990): 655–72.

4 André Frossard, *Dieu existe, je l'ai rencontré* (Paris: Fayard, 1969).

5 Tad W. Guzie, *The Book of Sacramental Basics* (New York: Paulist Press, 1981), 124.

6 Maurice Blondel, "History and Dogma," in *The Letter on Apologetics and History and Dogma* (London: Harvill Press, 1964), 283; see Henri de Lubac, *A Brief Catechesis on Nature and Grace* (San Francisco: Ignatius Press, 1984), 37–8.

7 Karl Rahner, "Nature and Grace," in *Theological Investigations*, vol. 4 (New York: Crossroad, 1982), 165–88, at 167.

8 Quoted by J.P. Kenny, *The Supernatural* (Staten Island, NY: Alba House, 1972), 80.

9 Rahner, "Nature and Grace," 168.

10 Ibid., 166.

11 See Jacques Maritain, *Integral Humanism* (Notre Dame, IN: University of Notre Dame Press, 1973). See also Gustavo Gutierrez, *Theology of Liberation* (Maryknoll, NY: Orbis Books, 1973), 53–77 for a presentation of Maritain's understanding of the spiritual/temporal distinction, followed by a critique of its subsequent use in various church circles. It is not clear, however, whether Gutierrez himself rejects "a rigid distinction of planes" (58) or "the distinction of planes model" (64). His stress on "unity beyond all distinctions" (70; see 72) seems to recommend an abolition of the distinctions, which would place him among the immanentists whom I shall describe later in this Study. John F.X. Knasas, "The Liberationist Critique of Maritain's New Christendom," *The Thomist* 52 (1988): 247–67, sides with Maritain against Gutierrez. In contrast to Gutierrez and Segundo's interpretation of the Second Vatican Council as having moved away from these distinctions, see the more historically-minded account by de Lubac, *A Brief Catechesis*, 177–90. See also Juan Luis Segundo, *The Liberation of Theology* (New York: Orbis Books, 1976).

12 The principle of *ex opere operato* was originally intended to guarantee the validity of the sacraments despite the personal unworthiness of

priests. In practice, it has oftentimes sanctioned liturgies whose homilies are meaningless and whose gestures are devoid of symbolic value. On sacramental efficacy, see Piet Fransen, "How Can Non-Christians Find Salvation in their Own Religions?" in *Christian Revelation and World Religions*, ed. Joseph Neuner (London: Burns & Oates, 1967), 67–122, at 70–4.

13 Rahner, "Nature and Grace," 169.

14 See Louis Roy, "Does Christian Faith Rule out Human Autonomy?" *The Heythrop Journal* 53 (2012): 606–23.

15 See Karl Barth's critique of liberal Protestantism in *The Humanity of God* (Atlanta: John Knox Press, 1960), 11–33.

16 With the exception of the Catholic Tübingen School in its critical acceptance of Schleiermacher, during the second quarter of the nineteenth century.

17 De Lubac, *A Brief Catechesis*, 33–4.

18 See Henri de Lubac, *Surnaturel* (Paris: Aubier, 1946).

19 In addition to Gutierrez, we may mention Hans Küng, *Does God Exist?* (New York: Vintage Books, 1981), 518–22 and Eulalio R. Baltazar, *Teilhard and the Supernatural* (Baltimore: Helicon, 1966), 15–73. According to Baltazar, 26–7 and 30, but not for Henri de Lubac, *The Religion of Teilhard de Chardin* (New York: Desclee, 1967), 121–31, esp. 125, Teilhard de Chardin dispenses with the distinction natural/supernatural.

20 John Henry Newman, *Apologia Pro Vita Sua* (Oxford: Clarendon Press, 1967), 269–78. I would not disagree, however, with *everything* he included in the label "liberalism."

21 Charles Davis, *Body as Spirit* (New York: Seabury Press, 1976), 17.

22 Guzie, *The Book of Sacramental Basics*, 62.

23 Ibid., 61–2, 74–5, 79.

24 "Horizontality" and "verticality" are not theoretical distinctions for a systematic theology of grace, but are evocative of two basic kinds of relationship expressed in the liturgical setting. Vertical symbols may include more than old ones such as bowing, genuflecting, kneeling, raising of the hands; as a matter of fact, new ones are being presently introduced into liturgy (for instance, the ascensional movements of the dance).

25 Guzie, *The Book of Sacramental Basics*, 27.

26 Ibid., 62 and 71.

27 In *Jesus and the Eucharist* (New York: Paulist Press, 1974), Guzie mentions Langer's book *Philosophy in a New Key*: "My treatment of the 'two questions about reality' relies heavily on the philosophy of sign and symbol developed by Mrs. Langer" (158, note 2). In the Preface to her

book, Langer acknowledges her indebtedness to several authors, among them Ernst Cassirer, who was a resolute neo-Kantian (xiv–xv).

28 As Lonergan writes in *Method* (335), "For Kant understanding (*Verstand*) was the faculty of judgment."

29 In *Eucharist as Meaning: Critical Metaphysics and Contemporary Sacramental Theology* (Collegeville, MN: Liturgical Press, 2014), chap. 1 and *passim*, Joseph C. Mudd offers a balanced representation and assessment of Chauvet's thought. He also shows how Lonergan's philosophy can contribute to the understanding of the liturgical experience.

30 See Liam G. Walsh, "The Divine and the Human in St. Thomas's Theology of the Sacraments," in *Ordo Sapientiae et Amoris: Hommage au Professor Jean-Pierre Torrell OP*, ed. Carlos-Josaphat Pinto de Oliveira (Fribourg: Éditions Universitaires, 1993), 321–52.

31 See Louis-Marie Chauvet, *Symbol and Sacrament: A Sacramental Reinterpretation of Christian Existence*, trans. Patrick Madigan and Madeleine Beaumont (Collegeville, MN: The Liturgical Press, 1995), esp. chaps. 1–2.

32 See Oliva Blanchette's "Are There Two Questions of Being?" *The Review of Metaphysics* 45 (1991): 259–87; "Suárez and the Latent Essentialism of Heidegger's Fundamental Ontology," *The Review of Metaphysics* 53 (1999): 3–19; and *Philosophy of Being A Reconstructive Essay in Metaphysics* (Washington, DC: The Catholic University of America Press, 2003), esp. 13–26, 41–2, 108–9, 335, and 362.

33 See Walsh, "The Divine and the Human," 325.

34 Severe as I am here about Heidegger's immanentism, I nevertheless welcomed some of his intuitions in my book, *Mystical Consciousness: Western Perspectives and Dialogue with Japanese Thinkers* (Albany, NY: SUNY Press, 2003), 146–58 and 162–3.

35 See Chauvet, *The Sacraments: The Word of God at the Mercy of the Body*, trans. Madeleine Beaumont (Collegeville, MN: The Liturgical Press, 2001), 9–14.

36 See Bernard Cooke, *Sacraments and Sacramentality* (Mystic, CT: Twenty-Third Publications, 1983), chaps. 1–4.

37 Joseph Martos, *Doors to the Sacred: A Historical Introduction to Sacraments in the Catholic Church*, rev. ed. (Liguori, MO: Liguori/Triumph, 2001), 116.

38 On mediacy and immediacy, see Louis Roy, *Transcendent Experiences: Phenomenology and Critique* (Toronto: University of Toronto Press, 2001), chap. 10, section entitled "Directness and Mediation."

39 See "The Subject," in *A Second Collection: Papers by Bernard J.F. Lonergan, S.J.*, ed. William F.J. Ryan and Bernard J. Tyrrell (Toronto: University of Toronto Press, 1996), 69–86, at 78–9.

40 Robert M. Doran, *Psychic Conversion and Theological Foundations* (Chico, CA: Scholars Press, 1981), 200.

41 Lonergan, "The Mediation of Christ in Prayer," in *Philosophical and Theological Papers 1958–1964*, ed. Robert C. Croken, Frederick E. Crowe, and Robert M. Doran, volume 6 of *Collected Works of Bernard Lonergan* (Toronto: University of Toronto Press, 1996), 160–82, at 174–82.

42 See Joseph Flanagan's "Transcendental Dialectic of Desire and Fear," in *Lonergan Workshop*, ed. Fred Lawrence, vol. 1 (Chico, CA: Scholars Press, 1978), 69–91, esp. 76–9 and "Literary Criticism of the Bible," in *Trinification of the World*, ed. Thomas A. Dunne and Jean-Marc Laporte (Toronto: Regis College Press, 1978), 210–40, esp. 228–40.

43 Although Frye writes at times in a manner that seems typical of philosophical idealism, I understand that, as a literary critic, he wants to be uncommitted to any ontology. For our purposes, we may note that the mere presence of anagogic symbols does not guarantee a critical-realist interpretation; even vertical symbols can be lived in an idealist frame of mind. See Northrop Frye, *Anatomy of Criticism* (Princeton: Princeton University Press, 1957), 119 and 125.

Study 11
Implications for Education

"Lonergan's whole career was dedicated to the university ideal in Catholic studies."[1] This judgment made by Frederick Crowe, a leading expert on the thought of Bernard Lonergan, does not come as a surprise to those who know how close Lonergan was to North American higher education. He would give a summer workshop on a Catholic college campus every year throughout the 1950s and 60s and he taught at Harvard University and at Boston College during the 1970s.

In this Study I would like to show how Lonergan's philosophical and theological ideas suggest a definite orientation for Catholic education. I will begin each part of this essay by briefly referring to a particular educational problem, and then I will select aspects of Lonergan's thought that can help to address the problem. I shall thus speak, first of the learning activities in the humanities, science, and philosophy; second of moral development and its religious underpinnings; and third of the renewal of Christian faith in a college setting.

LEARNING IN SECULAR FIELDS OF KNOWLEDGE

A good deal of current educational literature bemoans such phenomena as students' ignorance, premature specialization, inadequate use of textbooks, etc. Thus Fred Lawrence, a distinguished Lonergan scholar, writes: "In universities today education for specialized professionals (technocrats or bureaucrats) has all but supplanted genuinely liberal education; and education for careers has practically displaced education for citizenship. Anyone who knows what goes on in universities today cannot but agree that they have become seminaries for what Max Weber called "specialists without spirit or vision and voluptuaries without heart."[2]

One part of the problem seems to be that teachers focus too much on concepts and formulas to the detriment of the students' intellectual activities. One concentrates on contents to be learned rather than on learning wits. The implicit philosophy of the classroom is often conceptualism (accentuating information instead of understanding) and pragmatism (accentuating practical rules instead of quest for meaning and truth).

It is extremely difficult for young learners, inundated with data and innumerable hypotheses and theories, to achieve integration. On the one hand, we can no longer have recourse to the narrow and static synthesis provided, until the 1960s, by the classicism of Catholic schools, which had been shaped by Greco-Roman humanism and modern scholasticism. On the other hand, we cannot remain content with the prevailing relativism which, as Allan Bloom has argued, stultifies the minds of American students.[3]

What we need is a modest, partial, ongoing synthesis that is revisable over time. Such revisions best occur not through sudden, inexplicable shifts in incommensurable paradigms,[4] but, as Lonergan proposed in *Method in Theology* (28–9), according to a methodical control of meaning that must be based on transcultural foundations. One may wonder whether such foundations are attainable. But before stating how they can be reached, we ought to stress the necessity for intellectual foundations. The human mind spontaneously seeks unity. The complexities of contemporary natural and human sciences, however, preclude any rounded system. But if the educational emphasis on objects to be studied is matched by an equally strong emphasis on the knowing subjects, students will get a sense of what it concretely means to be involved in a process of integration. Their efforts at elaborating a provisional synthesis will be situated in a context where the quest for truth is apprehended as a worthwhile journey.

Among the steps leading to a personal integration, Lonergan commends active methods in education. At first, these must involve bodily and external activity. But as the child gives way to the teenager and subsequently to the college student, active methods more properly consist of investigating the relevant data and images, raising the right questions, and counting on the human intellect's natural wonder so that the learner will dynamically facilitate the occurrence of insights.[5]

Again, to train young minds for the task of integrating, Lonergan makes a second recommendation. After pondering Piaget's distinction between assimilation and adjustment, he highlights the chronological priority of the former over the latter. General education amounts to developing one's assimilative power. This habit is acquired, first by learning the use of spoken and written language and by reading literature, and second by "the study of mathematics rather than natural science, and of philosophy and history rather than the human sciences."[6] This preference does not entail any disparagement of the sciences, especially by someone like Lonergan who spent so much time understanding their methods and paying attention to their results. In contrast to any intellectual conformity, he praises the versatility of scholars such as Jean Piaget himself, the economist Colin Clark, the sociologist Talcott Parsons, the orientalist William Foxwell Albright, who could all excel in more than one field of study because they had acquired a fundamental creative ability.[7]

Lonergan was aware that when youth are introduced to the sciences only, they run the danger of being satisfied with simply memorizing what the most important thinkers of the last decades have said, and then with just keeping abreast. As a commentator aptly puts it:

> Lonergan's overhaul of the understanding of the cognitional process and his claim that human authenticity is achieved in self-transcendence strike at the roots of some current cultural assumptions about education: that coming to knows means collecting data out there and storing concepts formulated by other people, or that the goal of education has little to do with knowing what is real or true or valuable and everything to do with credentials and financial security.[8]

So far, what I have said may give the impression that Lonergan was a rationalist with an exaggerated stress on the intellect. This misrepresentation, however, would fail to take into consideration his appreciation for practical common sense (see *Insight*, chapters 6 and 7), an appreciation for not just the intellectual pattern of experience but also for the other patterns of experience – biological, aesthetic, and dramatic (see *Insight*, chapter 6, section 2). All these orientations towards reality can facilitate learning.

Lonergan also draws attention to the importance of philosophy in reinforcing the students' selective integration. He remarks that not all products of human imaginings should be integrated.[9] Besides sense, truth, and value, there are aberrations in the realm of action, in historiography, in the human studies, and in philosophy. The symbolic animal which is the human person naturally looks for meaning. It seeks understanding, asks about the truth-value of what it has grasped, and deliberates regarding its commitments. When adverted to, this basic quest constitutes the dynamic fourfold transcendental structure. It is normative because it enables the knowing and acting person to discriminate between sense and nonsense. Students need to acquire this normative self-knowledge which is the core of philosophy. Thus they will get in touch with the part of themselves that is the source of genuine creativity and responsibility, and that is open to the Mystery.

Although greatly aided by secular learning and by philosophy, full intellectual integration, since it is never purely cognitional, lies beyond the ken of secular disciplines. This should become progressively clear in the course of the following discussion of moral and religious aspects of education.[10]

MORAL DEVELOPMENT AND RELIGION

The cultural ambiance in which students live raises problems of ethical formation. The German sociologists Max Weber's separation between facts (considered by the sciences) and values (left to individual preferences) has generated what Alasdair MacIntyre called "emotivism."[11] To the Western individualistic conscience, values are a matter of personal choice and cannot be rationally discussed. This stance entails a mixture of unfocused moral idealism, indifference with regard to relevant information, unexamined principles of conduct, and hidden agendas in the minds of many students, especially with respect to their goal of quickly becoming successful and wealthy.

To face these issues, Lonergan's approach can be helpful. It begins with the human subject in action. Most young people feel a need for personal authenticity. Full development as a human being can become one's "most prized achievement" (*Method*, 254). In all ages and cultures, good educators have spotted their best ally: the desire to excel which is so prominent in a healthy youth. Writing about the "good choices and actions" thanks to which a person does develop, Lonergan uses a suggestive metaphor when he characterizes such achievement as "the work of the free and responsible subject producing the first and only edition of himself."[12]

Moreover, as Walter Conn points out, Lonergan offers guidelines for authenticity. In his introduction to the theme of self-realization, Conn observes that "authenticity itself is not a criterion ... but rather an ideal which stands in need of a criterion."[13] And he explains: "the *criterion* of human authenticity, of the responsible person, is the self-transcendence that is effected through sensitive and creative understanding, critical judgment, responsible decision, loyal commitment, and genuine love."[14]

This is a typical Lonerganian listing of the cognitional and affective acts that make for authenticity. As we saw earlier, Lonergan characterizes the movement of human progress as going "from below upwards."[15] It starts with experiencing the data, then asks questions for understanding, which are followed by the need to determine the truth of one's hypotheses, after which there emerge questions for deliberation concerning one's values and courses of action. However, being a self that continually grows in the right direction proves to be extremely difficult.

Important as this upward movement surely is in Lonergan's eyes, he nonetheless considers it to be hindered by four kinds of bias: the dramatic bias, which results from a malfunctioning of the psyche; the individual bias of egotism; the group bias of social and economic self-interest; and finally the general bias typical of the short-term pragmatism of common sense (see *Insight*, 214–31 and 244–67). In the light of such threats to its ideal development, Lonergan concludes that the upward movement to human maturity encounters a radical "moral impotence" (see *Insight*, 643–56). This moral impotence makes it is impossible to find in oneself the motivation required in order to implement fully the transcendental precepts: be attentive, be intelligent, be rational, be reasonable, be in love. Not only are the psyche and the will inadequate to the task, but the intellect, having absorbed a lot of false ideas during the process of its socialization, easily falls prey to a wrong estimation (or sometimes even denial) of ethical issues, of sin, and of moral impotence.

Given the ambiguities that mark the upward movement of self-realization and self-transcendence, a second movement is needed, which can rescue the first. It is the movement "from above downwards."[16] Both movements were described at length in Study 3. Suffice it to repeat, very succinctly here, that the second movement does not go, as the first movement does, from data through acts of understanding, judgments of fact, and judgments of value to decisions; instead, this second movement proceeds from a basic state of religious love, which makes it possible to accept the judgements of value and of fact handed on by tradition, to try to understand the meaning of these judgments, and eventually to arrive at expressing them in new words, symbols, and artefacts, which is to say, data.

Such is the movement of grace; such is the general way Christian salvation is granted. Now it remains for us to see what this theological vision entails as corollaries for Christian education.

EDUCATION FOR CHRISTIAN FAITH

Faith seems to be very difficult to communicate. Even sons and daughters of Catholic parents often show little understanding of the core doctrines professed by the Church. They tend to be selective: they choose the beliefs they find interesting and discard the others. Emotional or practical relevance rather than truth has become the criterion for one's religious ideas. How, then, is it possible, in an age of individualism, to share the traditional doctrines with members of the younger generation?

The movement from above downwards, which has just been portrayed, can help us to understand how such sharing takes place. Although faith can be shared, strictly speaking it cannot be communicated by humans. Only God can communicate faith and he does so by pouring an unrestricted lovingness into people's hearts. Anthropologically, Lonergan situates this God-given love at the top of human conscious intentionality. Faith is the awareness that accompanies such being-in-love. It is defined as "the knowledge born of religious love" (*Method*, 115).

He also distinguishes between faith and belief. He sees faith as an inner word, as the conscious and yet unformulated knowledge derived from unrestricted loving. He sees belief as an outer word, as the explicit knowledge handed on by a religious tradition. The link between faith and belief is the following: "Among the values that faith discerns is the value of believing the word of religion, of accepting the judgments of fact and the judgments of value that the religion proposes" (118).

So far as the downward movement is concerned, there is a dynamic that operates as follows. It all begins with religious experience, in which God grants love and faith. Then, on the fourth level, the eye of faith discriminates between the values and disvalues that are apprehended in feelings, and greets the judgments of value that are offered by an authentic tradition. On the third level, the heart invites reason to accept the judgments of fact that the Bible presents as words of God and that are passed on by the Church, acknowledged as trustworthy. On the second level, the heart challenges the intellect to appropriate, as much as it can, the meanings transmitted by Christianity, which, on the first level, the believer wishes to communicate.

This vision entails four consequences for the education of faith. In the first place, students must be offered the possibility of experiencing living communities of faith. In a propitious environment, they should be able to single out individual believers or groups of believers whose personalities and ways of life are what Lonergan calls "incarnate meaning" (*Method*, 73). It is not necessary that, on a Catholic campus, everyone be a professed Christian. But one must find a sufficient number of significant believers in order to be challenged by a forceful context of meaning. Such a context consists of credible persons, proposed activities, shared values, faith-symbols that are relevant to our culture, and classes in which the contents of Christianity are presented in a coherent manner. Students will have access to their own experience of transcendent love, provided this experience is activated by witnesses who are themselves loving, committed, dedicated, in solidarity, and cooperating with others.

In the second place, the distinction between meaning and truth, which was employed in Study 6, may help to differentiate two sides of Christian pedagogy. Meaning is on the level of understanding, whereas truth is on the level of judgment. On the one hand, when people ask about the meaning of Christian texts, narratives, beliefs, practices, rituals, forms of art, etc., their questions, which arise when they seek to understand these data, will propel them from the first level to the upper levels, where they will eventually verify and appraise their ideas. So there must be ample room in Catholic catechesis and theology for this upward movement in which sound information is offered and relevant questions are posed regarding Christian teachings in relation to the students' life-experience.

On the other hand, it is incumbent upon religious educators to make it clear that such apprehension of meaning cannot settle the question of whether Christian doctrines are true or not. Students should be guided towards raising this question for themselves and should consider the option of responding affirmatively. Assuredly nothing in this intricate and engaging process can be automatic or easy. What is at stake is the most important option in a person's life: the decision to believe or not to believe in the God of Jesus Christ.

And this difficulty brings us to the third educational aspect to be underlined. Catholic pedagogues must foster the cultivation of questions. According to Lonergan, questions constitute the dynamism of the upward ascent from experiencing to understanding and to judging. In mathematics, in the various sciences, in literature, history, philosophy, and theology, the right questions must be hit upon in connection with the appropriate information. Questions matter more than answers, norms, and rules, because without the questions, the latter do not make much sense. Only by starting with questions can students develop their minds. And if they possess a well-trained mind, they will be more likely to greet the illuminating power of Christian teachings.

However – and this is our fourth educational component – if their heart is to develop as well, a tutoring of feelings is required. According to Lonergan, values are apprehended in "intentional feelings" (*Method*, 30–1), namely in feelings that are related to represented objects. Since both values and disvalues are apprehended, he is insistent that one should both foster sound feelings and correct aberrant feelings (see *Method*, 32–4). Charles Davis, a thinker who received much from Lonergan, lucidly expressed the need for discernment concerning feelings:

> Human feelings, by their dynamism, point beyond themselves; they are an expression of self-transcendence; they take us, as we say, out of ourselves; that is, into truth, goodness, and beauty. The discernment of spirits, the education and purification of feelings are fundamentally matters of uncovering and releasing that dynamic self-transcendence, of allowing it its full range, so that it overcomes the self-centeredness, the unobjectivity of a retreat out of reality into an unreal, egotistic world characteristic of immaturity and corruption.[17]

Educators can have recourse to psychological techniques, either in class or in private conversation, in order to help students take fuller cognizance of their feelings. As a consequence, young learners will be in a better position to appreciate their transcendent experiences, in which a stable feeling of being in love is offered to them. Furthermore, cultivating the feelings that open them up to values will allow them to discover the necessity of a moral conversion and to engage in it.

CONCLUSION

Lonergan's philosophy and theology suggest a definite way of tackling three sets of recurrent problems in Catholic education: the integration of learning, moral development, and the sharing of Christian faith.

NOTES

1 Frederick E. Crowe, "'The Role of a Catholic University in the Modern World' – An Update," in *Communicating a Dangerous Memory*, ed. Fred Lawrence, Supplementary Issue of the *Lonergan Workshop* Journal (Atlanta, GA: Scholars Press, 1987), 1.
2 Frederick G. Lawrence, "Lonergan as Political Theologian," in *Religion in Context: Recent Studies in Lonergan*, ed. Timothy P. Fallon and Philip Boo Riley (Lanham, MD: University Press of America, 1988), 1–21, at 19, quoting Max Weber, *The Protestant Ethic and the Spirit of Capitalism*, trans. Talcott Parsons (New York: Charles Scribner & Sons, 1958), 182.
3 See Allan Bloom, *The Closing of the American Mind* (New York: Simon and Schuster, 1987). On classicism and relativism, see Study 7.
4 See Thomas Kuhn, *The Structure of Scientific Revolutions* (Chicago: University of Chicago Press, 2nd ed., 1970).
5 See Lonergan, *Topics in Education*, ed. Robert M. Doran and Frederick E. Crowe, volume 10 of *Collected Works of Bernard Lonergan* (Toronto: University of Toronto Press, 1993), 104–5. This emphasis on the learner's insights, in contrast to concepts, characterizes his book *Insight*.
6 Lonergan, *Topics in Education*, 205.
7 Ibid., 206–7.
8 Moira Carley, "Religious Education in a World of Shifting Horizons: The Contribution of Bernard J.F. Lonergan, S.J. (1904–1984)," *Theoforum* 41 (2010): 77–91, at 82.
9 Lonergan, "The Role of a Catholic University in the Modern World," in *Collection*, ed. Frederick E. Crowe and Robert M. Doran, volume 4 of *Collected Works of Bernard Lonergan* (Toronto: University of Toronto Press, 1988), 108–13, at 113.

10 A helpful discussion of the current challenges of Catholic education is provided by Cyril Orji, *The Catholic University and the Search for Truth* (Winona, MN: Anselm Academic, 2013). Part Two is entitled "Bernard Lonergan's Thought as a Possible Way Forward"; chapter 6 shows the complementarity between Lonergan's views and Howard Gardner's "groundbreaking work on Multiple Intelligence" in student learning.

11 Alasdair MacIntyre, *After Virtue*, 2nd ed., (Notre Dame, IN: University of Notre Dame Press, 1984).

12 Lonergan, "The Subject," in *A Second Collection: Papers by Bernard J.F. Lonergan, S.J.*, ed. William F.J. Ryan and Bernard J. Tyrrell (Toronto: University of Toronto Press, 1996, reprint), 69–86, at 83.

13 Walter E. Conn, *Conscience: Development and Self-Transcendence* (Birmingham, AL: Religious Education Press, 1981), 5.

14 Conn, *Conscience*, 6.

15 Lonergan, "Natural Right and Historical Mindedness," in *A Third Collection: Papers by Bernard J.F. Lonergan, S.J.*, ed. Frederick E. Crowe (New York: Paulist Press, 1985), 169–83, at 180.

16 Ibid., 181. In *Old Things and New: A Strategy for Education*, Supplementary Issue of the *Lonergan Workshop*, ed. Fred Lawrence (Atlanta, GA: Scholars Press, 1985), Frederick E. Crowe developed the implications for education of these two vector forces, which he calls "the way of achievement" and "the way of heritage."

17 Charles Davis, *Body as Spirit* (New York: Seabury Press, 1976), 16.

Part Four

Ethics

Study 12

A Comparison with Macmurray

Contemporary phenomenological, existential, and theological thinking conspicuously insists on "the experiential." In its legitimate reaction against modern conceptualism, positivism, and instrumental rationality, the postmodern emphasis on personal experience has brought to the fore a theme that is of central import for present-day philosophers: relatedness. Moreover, in the writings of several authors, the emphasis on interpersonal relationships has been tied to what they consider to be the true nature of religion. This Study aims at comparing the respective vision of the human person and religion held by two thinkers whose lives by and large overlapped in time: the Scot John Macmurray (1891–1976)[1] and the Canadian Bernard Lonergan (1904–1984).

Macmurray's principal concern had to do with the quality of human relationships in society. He wondered about the relations between science and ethics, the first representing the realm of means and the second representing the realm of values. In the first half of the twentieth century, as scientific discoveries and technological know-how were accumulating tools for making things, the pressing question became for him and for many others in the industrialized countries: How are these tools being employed? Whom is technology benefiting? Furthermore, with a sharp Marxist eye and an equally sharp psychological eye, Macmurray spotted a dissociation between the professed values and the actual values of Western civilization.[2] He was convinced that the means were not put at the service of the values that were praised in churchmen's and politicians' speeches, namely freedom, equality, community. He realized that the means were used in such a way as to perpetuate domination, inequality, and social divisions.[3]

As regards Lonergan's interests, it must be noted that during the decades between the two World Wars, he devoted considerable time to studying economics and political theory.[4] During that period, in response to current issues, he launched into an in-depth critique of the contemporary scene and he undertook to sketch a whole theology of history.[5] Like Macmurray, Lonergan's thinking was very much marked by the economic and political crisis of the 1930s. He took very seriously, and commented on, concrete social problems in Canada.

Having taken into consideration such preoccupations, expressed by our two authors, I will successively delineate Macmurray's and Lonergan's philosophy of the person. We shall discover Macmurray's tenets concerning the primacy of action and of the personal, the individual's modes of apperception, and the task of religion. Thereafter, we shall contrast Macmurray's and Lonergan's conception of intersubjectivity. And in the last section I will amplify what has been said about relatedness in Study 4.

THE PRIMACY OF ACTION AND OF THE PERSONAL

Macmurray's philosophy of "the form of the personal," as expounded in his Gifford Lectures of 1953 and 1954, is a twofold endeavour to respond to the problem of the dissociation between means and values. The first volume of these lectures, entitled *The Self as Agent*, proposes the doctrine of the primacy of action,[6] while the second volume, entitled *Persons in Relation*, asserts the primacy of the personal and explicates the deeper meaning of the first doctrine.[7] The primacy of action is directed against the idealism of those who content themselves with ideals and principles, without accurately checking whether they work in practice. And the primacy of the personal is directed against the static materialism of those who place their trust and hope in economic and political structures – the structures either of the so-called free market or of communist countries.

Several threads can be discerned in the thesis of the primacy of action. On the one hand, the weakest thread is the epistemological justification he sets out to provide. In order to break through the confinement of what he considers to be the idealist standpoint, which extols pure theory, he implements the mistaken strategy of impoverishing "thought" and of overestimating the cognitional properties both of the "experience" that precedes it and of the "action" that follows it. For him, "the 'purer' our thought becomes, the more it excludes not merely perception, but all sensuous elements, and moves in a shadowy world of abstract and general ideas." As a consequence of this conceptualist account of thinking, Macmurray pictures it as "exclusive" of many intellectual acts and, in this sense, as "negative," whereas he represents action as "inclusive" and "positive," in the sense that in action "all the capacities of the Self are in full and unrestricted employment."[8] As we observed in Study 8, Lonergan often criticized conceptualism, albeit not in Macmurray himself, on whose views he did not comment.

On the other hand, the best thread in Macmurray's tapestry is what he has learned from Marx, namely the principle of "the interplay, in all human activities, between theory and practice."[9] According to this principle, society, which is a continuing process, conditions and is conditioned by human thinking. Macmurray is quite clear that those who do not pay sufficient attention to the social determinations as well as to the social function of their ideas are liable to overlook the negative effects they produce, whereas those who are aware of the two-way relation between ideology and decision are likely to offer a better contribution.

His doctrine of the primacy of the personal emphasizes the priority of "community" over "society," or of "personal life" over "social life."[10] In society we inexorably treat others as objects and as means; in community we consider them as subjects and as ends. The intersubjective attitude arises from the fundamental experience of encountering someone as a person – *la rencontre de l'autre*, as has been phrased in French personalist circles. It consists in discovering someone who responds to me in a way that no material element, no plant, and no animal can. "It is the consciousness of mutual relationship, of the meeting of like with like, for in it we find a response from the object at our own level."[11] This interpersonal experience rules out the suggestion that an individual could exist by itself, as a self-sufficient substance. On the contrary, because he saw relationships as constitutive of human existence, Macmurray could write: "there can be no man until there are at least two men in communication."[12]

Furthermore, this quality of consciousness – both the consciousness of the other person and the consciousness of oneself – has ontological implications for Macmurray. "Personality is mutual in its very being. The self is one term in a relation between two selves. It cannot be prior to that relation and equally, of course, the relation cannot be prior to it. '*I*' exists only as one member of the '*you and I*'. The self only exists in the communion of selves."[13] As is evident in this quotation, Macmurray's personalism unfolds into an ontology: he contends that only persons in relation properly exist and that the lower levels of the mechanical (inanimate) and of the organic (biotic) are only "abstract" or "negative" aspects of this "positive" reality whose core is personal.

CATEGORIES OF APPERCEPTION

It is Macmurray's profound conviction that the greatest threat to fellowship is fear. He construes the dialectic of fear and love as the contrast between building defences round oneself and taking the risk of forgoing some advantages for the sake of friendship and for the sake of the common good. His approach to this dialectic uncovers its roots in childhood. A repetition of acts whereby the mother is successively absent and present to her child sets up a pattern of withdrawal and return which constitutes a basic two-phase rhythm in human relationships. Whereas the beginning of love can be visible in the enjoyment by the baby of the mother's care, fear arises from the danger to personal security which deprivation brings forth.[14]

During the early formative years of life, somebody can adopt one of three basic dispositions, called "categories of apperception, which apply both to individuals and to societies."[15] In the first one, called the "communal," love is predominant and there is a firm intention of upholding community. The second and third modes are marked by fear. In the second one, called the "contemplative," people make up for their frustration by withdrawing into a world of their own, in which they can entertain their favorite ideas and feelings. This is the world of the idealists, who do not pay close attention to the exact relation between ideals and actual behaviour. In the third mode, called the "pragmatic," individuals make up for their frustration by withdrawing from the interpersonal reality into the exercise of strength, force, or cunning.

In the second type, one can recognize the "good" or "submissive" child, and in the third, the "bad" or "aggressive" child. On one side stands the "contemplative," who cherishes, in an idealist and illusory manner, a set of ideals divorced from practice; on the other side stands the "pragmatic," who strives to bring about or to keep in place a presumably realistic state of affairs in society, by having recourse to power and manipulation.

Inspired by Marx, Macmurray denounces religious idealism as entertaining noble beliefs despite their lack of impact on society, and as ignoring the role that other ideas, very different from the noble beliefs, do play within the nexus of economic, political, legal, and social relations. To the extent that we succumb to idealism, he argues, our underground motive is tantamount to the desire to protect interests incompatible with our ideals. Our conduct then gives the lie to our pretense. He would concur with Lonergan, who points out: "When knowledge is deficient, then fine feelings are apt to be expressed in what is called moral idealism, i.e. lovely proposals that don't work and often do more harm than good" (*Method*, 38).

Still, Macmurray equally condemned the ruthless realism of the pragmatic people, as he observed it among the capitalists of his day. Whereas the idealists deceive themselves, the pragmatics deceive others. The former make believe that ideals by themselves can make a difference; the latter make believe that their policies benefit the majority of the population. Fear makes both the idealists and the pragmatics lose sight of the profound worth of concrete persons and focus either on their inner world of ideas and feelings (in the case of the idealists) or on their achievements in the outer, material world (in the case of the pragmatics).

Only in the first type, the communal, is love predominant. Macmurray views love as the apex of the quest for objectivity, as full self-transcendence, on the grounds that it reaches out to people as they are. In love, the centre of interest and attention resides in the other. This conviction of Macmurray's derives from a positive assessment of emotion. In *Reason and Emotion* he brilliantly demonstrates that, far from being necessarily subjectivistic, that is, far from inevitably perceiving reality in a distorted fashion, emotion possesses the capacity to correspond adequately to reality.

In his Preface to the second edition of that book, he begins by stating that it is a typically Western mistake to imagine that reason is opposed to emotion; instead, he teaches that reason comprises both intellect and emotion, and he speaks of "emotional reason" and of "emotional rationality."[16] Rather than being "just feeling," emotion is part and parcel of reason's "capacity to behave consciously in terms of the nature of what is not ourselves." He adds that "reason is the capacity to behave in terms of the nature of the object, that is to say, to behave objectively."[17] In order to act realistically, we have to subordinate our beliefs, wishes, and desires to matter-of-fact situations.

In this continuing process, emotions exercise a crucial function, for they put us in contact with values, which attract us: "For the determination of values we are dependent on our emotions."[18] This is a point that Lonergan will stress, thirty years after Macmurray. The latter goes on to suggest that emotions contribute to the rationality or irrationality of our conduct. "Feelings can be rational or irrational in precisely the same way as thoughts, through the correctness or incorrectness of their reference to reality. In thinking thoughts we think the things to which the thoughts refer. In feeling emotions we feel the things to which the emotions refer. And, therefore, we can feel rightly or wrongly."[19]

This being the case, "the real problem of the development of emotional reason is to shift the centre of feeling from the self to the world outside."[20] However, Macmurray claims that in order to accomplish this demanding adjustment, we must achieve the kind of self-knowledge that psychoanalysts recommend. Indeed, "we can suppress our feelings so that they work in us without our knowing that they are there ... Obviously, if we are to be real in our feeling we must know what we really feel."[21] And since idealistic thoughts and over-romantic feelings fail to conform to reality, Macmurray regrets that oftentimes "thought becomes abstract and formal, while feeling becomes sentimental."[22] Hence the importance of increasing one's ability both to recognize one's ineffective thoughts and to detect one's inappropriate feelings.

THE TASK OF RELIGION

In the face of the problem of fear, Macmurray envisages religion as offering a possible reconciliation. He asserts that the core of religion is faith overcoming fear through the belief in the victory of interpersonal existence over what jeopardizes it, and through the intention to sustain this interpersonal existence.

Religion's ultimate value amounts to intending community. Macmurray defines "the religious attitude" as "that attitude of mind for which our relations to other people are central."[23] Therefore, in its rituals, that attitude expresses forgiveness and a renewed faith in communal existence.[24] On the one hand, it is incumbent upon human freedom to elicit shared intentions. On the other hand, love – without which genuinely shared intentions are impossible – needs religious support. Macmurray ascribes to the churches the task of actively encouraging the practice of love. He sees Jesus as prioritizing human relationships and as achieving a social revolution by peaceful means.[25]

In his view, religion is a human activity whereby people celebrate their mutuality and affirm their intention of community. It conveys the spontaneous joy of living together and it renews the purposefulness of enhancing fellowship.[26] Fellowship is the quality of interpersonal bond that is revealed in human encounter. Macmurray spells it out in terms of freedom and equality. He remarks that in an intimate relationship pervaded by trust and friendship, each of the partners feel free to express the whole of himself or herself and that each treats the other as an equal. In front of obstacles to relationship, be it in the family or in society, religion plays the part of allowing people to reiterate their intention of fellowship or community. For Macmurray, religion fulfils a social function by exercising a positive and vital influence for the sake of the personal.

In recent centuries, the development of science has fostered many kinds of dissociations: between spirit and body, mind and heart, means and values, no less than between higher and lower classes and between rich and poor nations. To counter all suchlike divisions, Macmurray envisages the role of religion as integrating the disconnected aspects of human life and as unifying humankind in bonds of fellowship. By developing this viewpoint, he has enriched the unitary, religious understanding of society previously offered by Rousseau and Durkheim.

He expounds at great lengths the difference between false and valid religion – a difference that parallels the contrast between defensiveness and risk-taking. In his categories, both the contemplative and the pragmatic people are defensive and consequently very likely to court divine favours instead of actually engaging in the human community with all the risks involved. Thus false religion says, "If you believe in God and perform your religious duties, God will protect you from the things you are afraid of." By contrast, valid religion does not attempt to shun the cross. Rather, it is inspired by Jesus' words, "In the world ye shall have tribulation, but fear not."[27]

For Macmurray, Judaism is authentic religiousness because it does not make a dichotomy between the sacred and the secular, the spiritual and the temporal, this world and the next. With this non-dualistic view of human life in mind, Macmurray situates Jesus in the context of the Old Testament by stressing that his mission consisted in beginning to establish the kingdom of God *on earth*.[28] Furthermore, at the time of Jesus, Israel had passed from monolatry to monotheism and, by doing so, had moved forward in the direction of universalism, since God was recognized as the Lord of all the earth. Indeed, in Macmurray's outlook, religious progress equates with "universalization."

Whereas Old Testament religion, even at the end of its evolution, was still bound to one particular nation, Jesus was "the religious genius" whose task consisted in raising the level of spiritual awareness by communicating "the universal meaning of religion for all time and all people."[29] In Macmurray's philosophy, however, there are no redemptive features associated with the death and the resurrection of Jesus. He portrays him as a perfect man, as an individual in whom there was no fear. He sees him as a model and as a prophet who preached faith in love.

Unfortunately, this faith, which corresponds to a fundamental trust, is not grounded in a divine agency; instead, it derives from a belief in some historical necessity. Macmurray holds a secularized version of the doctrine of providence and uses the label "Christianity" to designate the force of progress at work within the dialectic of history. For him, there is no isolated, super-personal, transcendent Reality; God does not exist independently of creation, since if he did, he would be understood as standing apart from persons in relation. This possibility is foreclosed by Macmurray's monism, namely by the doctrine that only the universe exists. He states: "God, if He is so conceived as the one individual, cannot be personal, since a person cannot exist apart from other persons. The stuff of personality consist of social relations."[30] Only *human* social relations exist. Thus Macmurray quotes Blake approvingly, "God only exists and is in existing beings or men."[31] How? As "infinite personality," not as infinite Person. God is projected as "universal personality," that is, as an idea that universalizes human interpersonal relationships taken together.

INTERSUBJECTIVITY

In his reflections on common sense as practicality in human dealings, Lonergan's point of departure is close to Macmurray's. As stated above, this Scottish philosopher's thesis consists in affirming an unequivocal priority of "personal life" over "social life." Macmurray wants to ameliorate society by transferring the properties of small-scale community to large-scale society. For his part, Lonergan does not think that the latter could operate as the former. Rather, he retains the distinct functioning of each. So he characterizes "intersubjectivity" as a natural, elemental "sense of belonging together" obtained in the family and in the circle of relatives and friends (*Insight*, 237). By contrast, practical intelligence sets up "vast structures of interdependence" as it pursues an all-embracing "good of order." "It consists in an intelligible pattern of relationships" that organizes individual desires so that they can integrate the desires of large groups of citizens (238). In Lonergan's judgment, both intersubjectivity and the good of order are indispensable: human beings need the former, with its intimate relationships, and the latter, with its potential to bring about innovations in science, technology, written law, the economy, and so forth.

He highlights an inevitable tension between intersubjectivity and the good of order, owing to their disparate manners of tackling human problems: "Besides the detached and disinterested stand of intelligence, there is the more spontaneous viewpoint of the individual subjected to needs and wants, pleasures and pains, labor and leisure, enjoyment and privation" (240). And he details this "radical tension of community" as follows:

> Intersubjective spontaneity and intelligently devised social order possess different properties and different tendencies. Yet to both by his very nature man is committed. Intelligence cannot but devise general solutions and general rules. The individual is intelligent, and so he cannot enjoy peace of mind unless he subsumes his own feelings and actions under the general rules that he regards as intelligent. Yet feeling and spontaneous action have their home in the intersubjective group, and it is only with an effort and then only in favored times that the intersubjective groups fit harmoniously within the larger pattern of social order (241).

Obviously, as he contrasts "intersubjective spontaneity" with "intelligently devised social order," Lonergan is making a case in favour of the latter, and his intention is understandable in such a book as *Insight*, which praises human intelligence mostly in its scientific and philosophical manifestations.

However, in other writings he rectifies the balance by paying more attention to the affective aspect of human relationships. In *Method in Theology* he highlights the significance of feelings in a manner that parallels Macmurray's points about them. A great number of feelings are "intentional responses" to values; as such, they are intrinsic to intentionality's movement towards appreciating reality, especially at the fourth level. Like Macmurray, Lonergan also offers thoughtful considerations on the development of feelings as well as on their aberrations (see 30–4).

In *Method* he returns to the topic of intersubjectivity as he points to the very early formation of a "we," which remains throughout human life and which amounts to an unplanned, vital, and functional solidarity in emotions and in reactions to events. "It is as if 'we' were members of one another prior to our distinctions of each from the others" (57). This "we" manifests itself in some of the ways in which feelings are communicated: community of feeling, fellow-feeling, psychic contagion, and emotional identification (see 57–9). It culminates in love: "Mutual love is the intertwining of two lives. It transforms an 'I' and a 'thou' into a 'we' so intimate, so secure, so permanent, that each attends, imagines, thinks, plans, feels, speaks, acts in concern for both" (33).

In addition to emotions and reactions, meaning is carried in intersubjective situations, for example the various meanings that different kinds of smiles may express (see 59–61), or the incarnate meaning found in a singular personality or a group (see 73). Lonergan observes: "The bodily presence of another is the presence of the incarnate spirit of the other; and that incarnate spirit reveals itself to me by every shift of eyes, countenance, color, lips, voice, tone, fingers, hands, arms, stance."[32]

So, interpersonal communication originates in intersubjectivity: "On the elementary level this process [of communication] has been described as arising between the self and the other when, on the basis of already existing intersubjectivity, the self makes a gesture, the other makes an interpretative response, and the self discovers in the response the effective meaning of his gesture" (*Method*, 357). Such is the wealth of mutual self-expression displayed in bodily and spoken language, which Lonergan also calls "the co-presence of persons."[33]

INTENTIONALITY FOR THE SAKE OF RELATEDNESS

As noted in the last section, Lonergan said much about human relationships. He saw them as the goal of a universally operative human agency. This basic agency spontaneously aims at relatedness as it consciously heads towards what is other than itself. Moreover, given that intentionality is aware of itself intending otherness, Lonergan could objectify it. He did so by taking recourse to the spatial picture of four levels, each typified by a principal activity: experiencing, understanding, judging, and deciding.

Two fundamental assumptions underlie Lonergan's thought in this respect. The first one is epistemological. It consists in rejecting the subject/object dichotomy that mars Kantianism, and in subscribing to the Aristotelian doctrine of the intentional identity between the knower and the known. The second assumption regards ethics. It amounts to repudiating the voluntarism that connects the lover and the beloved in an extrinsic way and that generates the individualistic portrayal of conscience as an independent, self-reliant centre whose decisions amount to arbitrary choices. On the contrary, mature love consists in delight, affection, and care for those who have been recognized as good.

This approach to knowledge and love presupposes the realization that knowing is not for the most part a looking, perceiving, imagining, or reasoning (although it subsumes such activities), but a judging based on evidence and understanding. It also presupposes the discovery that loving cannot be reduced to a physical taking, or giving, or hugging (although it expresses itself in such gestures), but is a disposition propped up by value-judgments. These two convictions are mutually supportive, since correct representations of knowing and of loving help clarify each other. On the one hand, there is a "being-in" insofar as the knowing subject becomes one with the known reality; on the other hand, there is a reciprocal "being-for" insofar as the lover affectively and rationally acknowledges the worth of the loved one.

Such a philosophy of the person, founded on adequately formulated psychological experience, has a significant advantage. Like

Macmurray, Lonergan helps us realize that relatedness lies at the very core of ontology. In both authors' writings, human cognition and human affectivity, far from being subjectivistic and ego-centred, *naturally* stretch out towards the real. As demonstrated in Study 2 and in Study 3, for Lonergan genuine objectivity is the offspring of authentic subjectivity. In interpersonal relationships as in other areas of human activity, truth is reached when the human subjects apply all their potential: psyche, intelligence, affectivity, free will. Intentionality congenitally attempts to go beyond itself in openness to persons, things, and situations that it observes, understands, verifies, and appreciates.

In Lonergan's view, the intentional dynamism in quest of truth is accompanied by an affective pull. Human actions are the result both of cognitive enquiries and of emotional movements. In particular, the momentum of our operations comes in large measure from symbols, that is, from those combinations of images and feelings that propel us as we develop and as we ascend into superior ways of relating and being. At the highest level of intentionality, self-love based on self-esteem gives a person the inner security that is required for right judgments of value and courageous decisions.[34]

CONCLUSION

Macmurray and Lonergan are one in repudiating several modern tenets: a dualistic conception of the person, divided into mind and body; the primacy of thought over praxis; a neglect of interpersonal relationships; a mechanical and individualistic conception of society, or an organic and gregarious conception of society; a disparagement of affectivity; and a disconnection between religion and the rest of human life. And they are agreed on the following convictions: the unity of the person; the subordination of thought to praxis; intersubjectivity as fundamental; a society that exists for the sake of the interpersonal relationships; the valuing of intentionality, including emotion, in reaching out towards reality; the positive role of religion.

The philosophical vision provided by Macmurray is surely at one and the same time grand and vulnerable. It has the merit of establishing links between the numerous areas that make up human experience: science, art, and religion; action and thought; impersonal and personal relations; the social and the psychic; politics and ethics. He locates religion at the crossroads where all these avenues intersect. However, his awkward fashion of trying to establish the complementarity of transcendence and immanence in God entails the impossibility of positing the existence of a Creator distinct from the universe. In view of the fact that Macmurray does not consider God as a living reality, distinct from the universe, religion is confined within the limits of a sort of cosmic interpersonal. His concept of religion can best be interpreted in the context of his personalist ontology, itself influenced by the monism of British idealism.

Like Macmurray, Lonergan revels in connecting all the realms of human experience, among which religion stands out as foundational. Nevertheless, his conception of religion is not immanentist, as is the case for Macmurray. He represents religion as an autonomous realm of meaning, whose worth cannot be reduced to symbolizing and improving social relationships. Finally, although not unimportant, his account of the domain of the interpersonal is less central than his Scottish contemporary's account, undoubtedly because he considers science, technology and highly organized societies as great assets for humankind, whereas Macmurray is more critical of their predominance.

NOTES

1 See John E. Costello, *John Macmurray: A Biography* (Edinburgh: Floris Books, 2002) and Esther McIntosh, *John Macmurray's Religious Philosophy: What it Means to be a Person* (Farnham, UK : Ashgate, 2011), both with an extensive bibliography. See my review of McIntosh's book in *New Blackfriars* 94 (2013): 380–1.

2 On Marx's insights regarding religion, see Louis Roy, "Why Are Most Christians on the Defensive with respect to Marxism?" *New Blackfriars* 64 (1983): 29–34; on Freud's (and Feuerbach's) insights regarding religion, see Louis Roy, *Le sentiment de transcendance, expérience de Dieu?* (Paris: Cerf: 2000), chap. 4.

3 For a full treatment of this position, see Louis Roy's doctoral dissertation, "The Form of the Personal": A Study of the Philosophy of John Macmurray with Particular Reference to his Critique of Religious "Idealism," Dissertation Abstracts International, 45, no. 12A (1984): 3667, available at Ann Arbor, MI: University Microfilms International, order no. DA8501107.

4 See Lonergan's *For a New Political Economy*, ed. Philip J. McShane, volume 21 of *Collected Works of Bernard Lonergan* (Toronto: University of Toronto Press, 1998) and *Macroeconomic Dynamics: An Essay in*

Circulation Analysis, ed. Frederick G. Lawrence, Patrick H. Byrne, and Charles Hefling, Jr., volume 15 of *Collected Works of Bernard Lonergan* (Toronto: University of Toronto Press, 1999).

5 See Lonergan's "*Pantôn Anakephalaiôsis* (The Restoration of All Things)" and "Analytic Concept of History," ed. Frederick E. Crowe and Robert M. Doran, *Method: Journal of Lonergan Studies* 9 (1991): 134–72, and 11 (1993): 1–35, respectively.

6 See Macmurray, *The Self as Agent* (London: Faber, 1957; reprint, 1995).

7 See Macmurray, *Persons in Relation* (London: Faber, 1961; reprint, 1995).

8 Macmurray, *The Self as Agent*, 86–8. For more on this topic, see Louis Roy's doctoral dissertation, *The Form of the Personal*, chap. 3.

9 Macmurray, *The Self as Agent*, 21.

10 See Macmurray, *Reason and Emotion* (London: Faber, 1935; 2nd ed., 1962; reprint, 1995), chapter entitled "The Personal Life." On this topic, see also Louis Roy, "Interpersonal Knowledge according to John Macmurray," *Modern Theology* 5 (1989): 349–65.

11 Macmurray, *Interpreting the Universe* (London: Faber, 1933), 126.

12 Macmurray, *Persons in Relation*, 12.

13 Macmurray, *Interpreting the Universe,* 137.

14 Macmurray, *Persons in Relation*, 45–63.

15 Ibid., 103–46.

16 Ibid., 5 and 15.

17 Ibid., 16 and 18.

18 Ibid., 36.

19 Ibid., 25.

20 Ibid., 30.

21 Macmurray, *Freedom in the Modern World* (London: Faber, 1932; reprint 1974), 150.

22 Ibid., 163.

23 Macmurray, *The Structure of Religious Experience* (London: Faber, 1936), 33.

24 Ibid., 48–9.

25 Macmurray, *The Philosophy of Jesus* (London: Friends Home Service Committee, 1973; reprint 1977).

26 Macmurray, *The Structure of Religious Experience*, 44–6.

27 Macmurray, "To Save from Fear," in *Ye Are my Friends and To Save from Fear* (London: Quaker Home Service, 1979), 7–8.

28 See Macmurray, *Reason and Emotion*, 248–9.

29 Ibid., 240 and 242.

30 Macmurray, "Objectivity in Religion," in *Adventure: The Faith of Science and the Science of Faith*, ed. Burnett H. Streeter (London: Macmillan, 1927), 177–215, at 189.

31 Macmurray, *Reason and Emotion*, 210.

32 "Dimensions of Meaning," in *Collection*, ed. Frederick E. Crowe and Robert M. Doran, volume 4 of *Collected Works of Bernard Lonergan* (Toronto: University of Toronto Press, 1988), 232–45, at 242.

33 "The Analogy of Meaning," in *Philosophical and Theological Papers 1958–1964*, ed. Robert C. Croken, Frederick E. Crowe, and Robert M. Doran, volume 6 of *Collected Works of Bernard Lonergan* (Toronto: University of Toronto Press, 1996), 183–13, at 187.

34 Based on Lonergan and many other thinkers, Steven Wentworth Arndt provides a wealth of phenomenological observations in "The Structures of Interpersonal Relationships," *Method: Journal of Lonergan Studies* 7 (1989): 51–70.

Study 13

A Comparison with Gandhi

In the history of the human race, several philosophers set themselves a twofold task: to challenge the institutions of their time and to propound an ideal of human achievement. We find instances of such endeavour in Plato's masterwork *The Republic*, in Rousseau's passionate *Discours sur les sciences et les arts*, and in Kierkegaard's famous contrast between the aesthetic and the ethical. These authors vividly picture the dramatic conflict that exists, within the human soul and in society at large, between authentic and inauthentic existence.

The purpose of this Study is to meditate on some aspects of Gandhi's extraordinary wisdom and to compare his thoughts with those of Lonergan on the issue of human authenticity. Although both of them – one being an Indian and the other a Canadian of Irish descent – were critical of British policies, they differ enormously. Mohandas Karamchand Gandhi (1869–1948) was a religious ethicist and activist whose writings, speeches, and symbolic gestures aimed at addressing the masses. Lonergan was a Jesuit who chose the scholarly lecture, article, or book as the privileged medium to convey his views. For all their dissimilarity, these two thinkers offer a diagnosis and a prescription regarding our time that are worth pondering. Accordingly, this Study will compare Gandhi's and Lonergan's critiques of Western civilization and their distinctive models of human excellence.

GANDHI'S DIAGNOSIS AND PRESCRIPTION

In the document entitled "Hind Swaraj," written in 1909,[1] Gandhi voices his critique of Western civilization, especially of its deleterious effects on the Indian mind. He uncovers the mediocrity of Western politicians, newsmen, lawyers, physicians. He traces the malaise in civilization back to several factors: lack of morality and religion; the belief that there is no intrinsic connection between an end and the means chosen to pursue it; the great importance ascribed to physical comfort and bodily adornment; the indulging of one's passions, which leads to personal dissatisfaction and to life-corroding competition; the desire to acquire riches at the cost of degrading the masses through industrialization and urbanization.

He also stresses the limitations of the sciences, which cannot by themselves help us make good use of the education we have received. He condemns "machinery" as representing a great sin, because it encourages greed on the part of the owners, turns the mill workers into slaves and hampers the prosperity of India. He argues that the well-being of his country ought to be based on handicraft.

His stance, which he slightly softened after "Hind Swaraj," derived from his awareness that British manufacturers were destroying thriving village crafts in India. Such rural de-industrialization was bringing about widespread unemployment and massive poverty. As a specialist of Gandhi's thought explains, "mechanization was acceptable to him only if it did not displace useful labour, and did not lead to the concentration of production and distribution in a few hands. Where machinery was essential, he was all for establishment of factories in which workers were assured not only of a living wage, but of a task which was not mere drudgery.[2]" We shall see shortly that only a few years later (in the 1930s) Lonergan also became very concerned about the ills of capitalism.

In kindred essays, Gandhi denounces colonization, bureaucratic arrogance, oppression, and humiliation, the exercise of violence, and rationalism (that is, the stance of reason which claims omnipotence for itself without realizing that faith and prayer can sanctify reason itself).[3] He recommends a holistic education:

> Useful manual labour, intelligently performed, is the means *par excellence* for developing the intellect ... A balanced intellect presupposes a harmonious growth of body, mind and soul. That is why we give to manual labour the central place in our curriculum of training here. An intellect that is developed through the medium of socially useful labour will be an instrument for service and will not easily be led astray or fall into devious paths.[4]

Gandhi's response to ruptures in the social fabric begins when he identifies himself with the Indian masses and "with starved humanity." In 1919 he avows: "I have been travelling throughout India. I cannot bear the heart-rending cry of the poor … They heave a sigh of despair. It is my duty to give these men a satisfactory reply. It is the duty of every servant of the country, but I am unable to give a satisfactory reply."[5]

His total commitment to the relief of the poor undercuts any dichotomy between private religiousness and politics.[6] In the "Farewell" chapter of his *Autobiography*, he states that, if an individual wants "to love the meanest of creation as oneself," one "cannot afford to keep out of any field of life." He explains: "my devotion to Truth has drawn me into the field of politics." And he firmly concludes: "Those who say that religion has nothing to do with politics do not know what religion means."[7]

His solution involves "Satyagraha," which literally means "firmness in truth" or "Truth-Force."[8] It cannot be dissociated from its twin concept of "Ahimsa," non-violence,[9] which should not be confused with sheer passivity: "This power is not 'passive' resistance; indeed it calls for intense activity." It is this practice that spiritualizes political life. "Passive resistance seeks to rejoin politics and religion and to test every one of our actions in the light of ethical principles."[10] Gandhi's originality consists in translating Hindu spirituality into action.

Passive resistance ought neither to be construed as a weapon of the weak nor associated with hatred and violence.[11] Time and time again Gandhi insists that it requires "an indomitable will," "fearlessness," "great spiritual force."[12] Thomas Merton remarks that this "holding on to truth" is in no way reducible to "a useful technique for attaining a pragmatic end," but on the contrary comes about as "the fruit of inner freedom."[13] Acting on truth is very demanding: "This path has always been for the brave because a much greater effort is required to go up the steep slope of truth than to climb the Himalayas."[14]

At the end of "Satyagraha in South Africa," Gandhi highlights the fragility of acting on truth, as he points out that if people abandon this basic attitude, all that has been gained through it is lost. His stance is grounded in the inseparability of end and means. "There is a law of nature that a thing can be retained by the same means by which it had been acquired. A thing acquired by violence can be retained by violence alone, while one acquired by truth can be retained only by truth."[15]

Such a deep conviction cannot be the outcome of mere reasoning: "non-violence, which is a quality of the heart, cannot come by an appeal to the brain" (27).[16] It is a matter of love (25). "Hatred can be overcome only by love" (32). Since ill will may eventually melt, one should always hope to convert one's opponent by love. Such love, however, is not naïve; oftentimes it will coexist with a distrust based on the evidence of experience. "The real love is to love them that hate you, to love your neighbour even though you distrust him. I have sound reasons for distrusting the English official world" (58).

The satyagrahi goes as far as "to lay down one's life" (29). He or she must practise no less than "the art of sacrificing self" (31). Therefore it will come as no surprise to hear Gandhi assert that it requires "a living faith in God" as well as "God's grace" (31). Among his models, Gandhi places Jesus, whom he describes as "a man who was completely innocent, [who] offered himself as a sacrifice for the good of others, including his enemies" (34).

What is the source of Gandhi's extraordinary convictions? His religious experience. He tells us that thanks to English friends, he became acquainted with the *Bhagavad-Gita* in 1889 and that this classic of Asian spirituality was a permanent influence on his view of life. There he "learnt the principle of winning over even an enemy with love."[17] He was impressed by the convergence of the teachings of Krishna in the *Gita* and of Christ in the Sermon on the Mount.[18] For Gandhi the *Gita* is not a mere text for historical or literary criticism: "it is a record of the concrete experience of its author … And if it is a record of anybody's experience, it must not be beyond us to be able to test the truth of it by repeating the experience."[19]

In 1926, at the ashram of Ahmedabad, he gave daily talks on the *Gita*. What stands out for Gandhi in the *Gita* is detachment. It encompasses "freedom from bondage to the body" (289), for example, control of the senses (54), chastity (26), and mastery over emotions such as anger (13) and fear (14), including fear of death (32).

But it goes deeper since it means, more importantly, detachment vis-à-vis the ego: the attention given to the ego is drastically reduced as the individual forgets itself in the Brahman (49), particularly during the course of action: "he who does everything without thinking that he himself does it can say that not he but the Lord does everything" (210). Moreover, without ruling out the vigour that

Sri Krishna expects of valiant combatants, Arjuna – the hero of the *Gita* – must be "unconcerned with defeat or victory" (37). Throughout his commentary, Gandhi repeats that detachment is required in regard to the fruits of one's actions (46).

This attitude is based on a sense of purposefulness despite all appearances to the contrary: "once we accept God the ways of the world cease to bother us. Then we have to accept that no creation of God can be purposeless." Stating that "optimism indicates faith," he adds: "The optimist lives in fear of God, listens with humility to the inner voice, obeys its promptings and believes that God ordains everything for the best."[20]

Thanks to interiorization, far from being self-enforced, detachment becomes positive and profoundly free. Hence Gandhi's advice: "Only give up a thing when you want some other condition, so much that the thing no longer has any attraction for you, or when it seems to interfere with that which is more greatly desired."[21] Hence giving-up is accompanied with joy: "no renunciation is truly such unless it gives us joy."[22]

In Gandhi, religion is experiential through and through. Newman (whom Gandhi occasionally quotes approvingly) would have recognized his distinction between notional and real apprehension in this sentence: "it is one thing to believe in God and quite another to realize God emotionally and act accordingly." He would have concurred with Gandhi's pronouncement that "there cannot be real non-attachment without spiritual knowledge." He and Lonergan would have nodded at the following passage: "The process through which the soul has been passing is an effort of the heart. The intellect has been hooked to its service by prayer, meditation and constant watchfulness which are essentially matters of the heart and which have been the predominant factors that have contributed to the growing revelation of truth."[23]

LONERGAN'S DIAGNOSIS AND PRESCRIPTION

In the 1930s, Lonergan was very concerned about the economic crisis which affected the Western world, including Canada. Like Gandhi, he exposed economic, social, and moral factors that contributed to the disorder. Like Gandhi, he thought that religion could make a difference in society. In typescripts that were written in 1935 and in 1937–38, we find Lonergan's twofold attempt at elaborating an in-depth critique of the contemporary scene and at drawing out a whole theology of history.[24]

From 1940 until 1947, he taught theology in Montreal. Frederick Crowe tells us that Lonergan addressed very concrete issues, as he commented "on such topics as Quebec's opportunity (some years before Quebec's quiet revolution!), on the Antigonish movement to help depressed fishermen, on the needed rebirth of rural living." Gandhi would have resonated with a question that Lonergan asked, "Why is the control of industry in the hands of fewer and fewer?" He would have cheered at Lonergan's avowal, "Unless the masses achieve economic independence, then … [democracy] will be a noble experiment that failed."[25]

Furthermore, by about 1944, theologian-philosopher though he was by training, Lonergan went as far as diving into economics and working successively on two manuscripts, the second of which was revised in the 1970s. In these essays, an understanding of economic mechanisms is proposed as a prerequisite to establishing relations between the market and ethics. In sum, it is clear that Lonergan's mind was driven to a penetrating diagnosis of Western culture. This diagnosis was later furthered in chapters 7, 18, and 20 of *Insight* and in some sections of *Method in Theology*.[26]

Lonergan's solution is not the same as Gandhi's and yet one can see a considerable amount of agreement between them. On the one hand, the difference resides in Lonergan's high esteem for the theoretical life; on the other hand, his views turn out to be as significantly religious and ethical as Gandhi's.

Gandhi and Lonergan differ in their respective assessment of human intellectual curiosity. The former disparages knowledge of the mere material as he contrasts it with knowledge of the soul. In his commentary on the *Gita*, he declares: "The laws of physical nature pale into insignificance when compared with those of the *atman*, for the former concern only the world of name and form. It is wise not to have too much curiosity regarding them" (88).

Gandhi opposes mere learning and religious knowledge, as he mentions "persons who are learned and yet devoid of knowledge" (42). For him, the most essential requirement is religious illumination (128). Moreover, in regard to mystical texts, he rules out any speculative interest in order not to lose sight of the everyday struggle for self-purification. Thus he counsels: "We should understand the meaning of the words of the *Gita* not merely to satisfy our curiosity but with the aim of putting its teaching into practice. In my case, the constant reading of the *Gita* has filled my life with prayer. We should leave alone what we cannot put into practice. It is a misuse of our intellectual energy and a waste of time to go on reading what we cannot put into practice" (154; see 240).

As an expert on the *Gita* observes, Gandhi the lawyer reads this great classic with a view to disclosing its practical intent.[27] For example, it is not the meditative performance that matters, but the attitude of detachment within action: "renunciation of the fruit of action is said to be better even than such meditation" (231). The accent does not fall on introspective inwardness: "If anyone asks us whether we have attained spiritual knowledge, our reply should be 'Only God knows; I do not know'" (239).

By contrast, while exposing its aberrations, Lonergan analyzes the intellectual life in a systematic fashion. For him, the desire to know must be fathomed in its diverse manifestations because it constitutes our very relating to all the facets of what exists. It is the basic dynamism that makes us pay attention to the data, try to understand them, determine the truth of what we have understood, ask questions about values and potentially worthwhile actions, and search for an ultimacy. Coupled with an affective thrust, the desire to know shows itself to be naturally open to reality. It honours the real in its five aspects: as datum, meaning, truth, value, and infinity.

The self-knowledge Lonergan wants to foster consists in grasping and correlating the acts we have just enumerated. Those acts are consciously performed in mathematics, in the arts and sciences, in intersubjective living, in technology and business, in politics and the media, in philosophy and theology, as well as in religion. Differentiated though they are, all these spheres of human activity are *one* because similar conscious acts are done by the same embodied spirit. Lonergan's method, with its philosophical, psychological, and theological ramifications, provides us with guidelines in order to move towards a full cognitional integration.

Lonergan recommends a twofold approach to solving twentieth-century problems: creativity and healing. Creativity arises from the desire to know, which has just been described. Because of the respect for reality that the human desire to know entails, the arts, sciences, and technology can have numerous beneficial effects. However, because of the many forms of bias – dramatic, individual, group, and general bias – that affect society, humans stand in need of healing.[28]

In his views on healing, which equates with the implanting of a new heart (Ezek 36:26), Lonergan comes very close to Gandhi. To my knowledge, Lonergan never studied the latter's writings,[29] and yet the similarities are striking. For instance, Gandhi talks about the knowledge that springs up from the heart. Referring to the kinship among all living beings, to the conviction that "the universe is the same as ourselves," he asserts: "Only that person in whom this idea has sunk from the intellect to the heart ... can feel its truth in direct experience."[30] Referencing one of Pascal's *Pensées* ("the heart has reasons which reason does not know"), Lonergan comments: "By the heart's reasons I would understand feelings that are intentional responses to values." And he adds: "besides the factual knowledge reached by experiencing, understanding, and verifying, there is another kind of knowledge reached through the discernment of value and the judgments of value of a person in love" (*Method*, 115).

Like Gandhi, Lonergan highlights the supreme importance of love. This love amounts to a basic state, a "being in love in an unrestricted fashion" (105). From love faith derives. "Faith is the knowledge born of religious love" (115). Besides aiding "an apprehension of transcendent value" (115), faith fosters the discernment of relative values in concrete living and thus enhances progress (116–17). By observing possibilities of remedying moral illnesses, "faith has the power of undoing decline" (117). But if believers are to act upon their apprehension of the values that ought to be implemented, even at personal cost, they must be prepared to have recourse to "self-sacrificing love" (117). Again, this self-sacrificing love is a central piece in Gandhi's ethics, as already pointed out in the previous section.

Interestingly both use the word "law" as they stress the necessity and fruitfulness of sacrifice. Gandhi talks of "the law of suffering" and of "the ancient law of self-sacrifice."[31] Elsewhere, as he commends "the law of love," he ties it to his sense of the purposefulness of the universe, of which I spoke earlier: "The more I work at this law the more I feel the delight in life, the delight in the scheme of this universe. It gives me a peace and a meaning of the mysteries of nature that I have no power to describe."[32]

For his part, Lonergan puts forward "the law of the cross."[33] It is called "law" by reason of its appropriateness in the way it governs the economy of salvation. It consists in drawing good out of evil. According to God's wise design, Jesus, the just person par excellence, by freely accepting and enduring undeserved suffering, was victorious over competing violent strategies. Instead of wiping out the evils of this world through an exercise of sheer power, the divine solution concentrates on the root of the matter, namely sin, which is the radical defect in the human will. The law of the cross expresses the divine capacity to transform existing evils into real goods by means of a human cooperation first exemplified in Jesus. For all people of good will who consent to its significance, the law of the cross corresponds to a precept – return love for hatred – that contains the most effective and persuasive response to the plight of humankind.

Both Gandhi and Lonergan also underline the reward intrinsic to generosity. Gandhi writes: "He who has sacrificed everything for satyagraha has gained everything, for he lives in contentment. Contentment is happiness. Who has ever known any happiness other than this? Every other kind of happiness is but a mirage."[34] Such happiness derives from God, but by means of a heterocentric movement: "If we desire to end the suffering of others, our suffering, too, will end."[35] As the psychoanalyst Erikson remarks, "to take active charge of senseless suffering by deliberately choosing to court meaningful suffering can be experienced as an exhilarating mastery over fate with a new ritualization such as *Satyagraha*."[36] And as Lonergan states, "the drive to value rewards success in self-transcendence with a happy conscience and saddens failures with an unhappy conscience" (*Method*, 35).

Elsewhere Gandhi notes that the lack of numerous material possessions is "for enjoyment of personal service to your fellow beings; service to which you dedicate yourselves, body, soul and mind."[37] And Lonergan states: "being in love with God is the basic fulfilment of our conscious intentionality. That fulfilment brings a deep-set joy that can remain despite humiliation, failure, privation, pain, betrayal, desertion. That fulfilment brings a radical peace, the peace that the world cannot give" (*Method*, 105). Compare with Gandhi: "I have not a shadow of a doubt that this blessed state of inward joy and freedom from anxiety should last in the midst of the greatest trials conceivable."

For both of them, being-in-love is the fulfilment of our deepest desire. Gandhi declares: "Life to me would lose all its interest if I felt that I *could* not attain perfect love on earth. After all, what matters is that our capacity for loving ever expands."[38] As for Gandhi, religious experience for Lonergan is part of an overall process of self-transcendence; it is dependent on and exerts an influence upon moral conversion, where love for other human beings is primary (*Method*, 104–5, 240–3).

Another overlapping field is their common esteem for all religions. Gandhi holds "that it is the duty of every cultured man or woman to read sympathetically the scriptures of the world."[39] In *Method in Theology*, Lonergan proposes a theological method that is at the service of all authentic religious people.

AUTHENTICITY

Let us synthesize our reflections by noting that Gandhi's and Lonergan's diagnoses and prescriptions regarding the modern world assume the ideal of human authenticity, explicitly in the case of Lonergan, and implicitly in the case of Gandhi.

An analogy of authenticity can be found in a work of art. If given proper explanation, we readily understand the difference between an authentic painting by Rembrandt and a pseudo-Rembrandt. Likewise, we talk of genuine as opposed to false human beings. Authenticity is the quality, the excellence, the value of a *concrete* person or community; this quality can increase or decrease. By contrast, no increase or decrease attaches to the similar concept of human dignity because the latter has to do with the equal worth of human beings *in general*. According to Lonergan, self-transcendence is the opposite of subjectivistic self-enclosure. It is the movement whereby someone reaches out to the real world of persons and things, knows them as objectively as possible, and undertakes to respect and enhance them.

Lonergan distinguishes five commands that help establish a relation to the real. As mentioned earlier, he expresses them in the form of five transcendental precepts coming from our conscience: "be attentive, be intelligent, be reasonable, be responsible, be in love" (*Method*, 268). As the individual in quest of authenticity climbs various levels, self-transcendence becomes more and more demanding. Each of these successive precepts requires more than the preceding one because it takes over the demands of the preceding one and adds its own to them. Thus being in love is the most difficult since it includes being attentive, intelligent, reasonable, and responsible.

I have not come across passages in which Gandhi would tackle the issue of human authenticity. Yet he believed in the perfectibility of individual persons.[40] And surely his *Autobiography* reveals a man struggling for authenticity throughout what he calls his experiments with truth. His very achievement is attested by the fact that it became a redoubtable challenge for a woman who conducted a series of interviews with him. "Margaret Bourke-White, the correspondent of the *Life* magazine, who was in India during the years 1946–8, and whose last interview with Gandhi took place just a few hours before his assassination, confesses in her book, *Half-way to Freedom* that it took her 'the better part of two years to respond to the undeniable greatness of this man.'"[41]

In Gandhi's commentary on the *Gita*, his stress on going beyond the ego makes implausible an explicit treatment of authenticity as a theme. After all, authenticity begins with the ego, which is spontaneously desirous of excelling as an individual. It is only in religious experience that the ego loses itself by entering – as Lonergan puts it with reference to the title of a Western classic of mysticism – into "the cloud of unknowing" (*Method*, 29, 266, 278, 342). When Gandhi talks about "self-realization," far from building on the ego, he points to "our higher self" which is essentially in touch with the divine and which merges with it.[42]

CONCLUSION

Gandhi was a lawyer turned religious activist; Lonergan was a scholar. Let us sum up what we can learn from both.

Lonergan offers us a systematic view of human authenticity in all its manifestations, whereas Gandhi's reflections focus on the most important conditions of authenticity, that is to say, the religious, moral, and practical ones. Gandhi frequently illustrates the outstanding ethical quality that derives from genuine mystical awareness.

Therefore, bringing Gandhi and Lonergan together can help prevent imbalance, insofar as disciples might be tempted either by the one-sidedness of secular learning and intellectual self-appropriation, or by the one-sidedness of religious-ethical conviction. Gandhi draws our attention to the complete detachment without which no resolution of the social disorder can take place, while also underlining the kind of practice that this detachment entails. Lonergan emphasizes the need to appropriate ourselves as knowers and doers if we are to research and act responsibly, while also situating the importance of moral and religious conversion for human authenticity.

NOTES

1 See *Collected Works of Mahatma Gandhi*, 90 vols. (Ahmedabad: Navajivan Press, 1958–84), vol. X, 6–68. Henceforth CW.

2 B.R. Nanda, *Gandhi and his Critics* (Delhi: Oxford University Press, 1985), 124; see the whole chapter 14, "Man versus Machine."

3 Gandhi, "Tyranny of Words," in CW, vol. XXXI, 498.

4 Raghavan Iyer, ed., *The Essential Writings of Mahatma Gandhi* (Delhi: Oxford University Press, 1993), 392.

5 Iyer, *Essential Writings*, 365; see 418.

6 Thomas Merton, ed., *Gandhi on Non-Violence: Selected Texts from Mohandas K. Gandhi's Non-Violence in Peace and War* (New York: A New Directions Paperbook, 1964), 5, 7 and 48.

7 M.K. Gandhi, *An Autobiography or The Story of My Experiments with Truth*, trans. Mahadev Desai (London: Penguin Books, 1982), 453.

8 Gandhi, *Autobiography*, 292; *Essential Writings*, 301.

9 See John T. Traynor, "The Moral Bases of Gandhi's Transformational Leadership: *Satyagraha and Ahimsa*," (a doctoral dissertation, Gonzaga University, 1996). I am grateful to Robert Croken and Michael Shields of the Lonergan Research Institute, Toronto, for allowing me to read their copy of this thesis.

10 Iyer, *Essential Writings*, 308 and 90.

11 Gandhi, *Autobiography*, 291.

12 Iyer, *Essential Writings*, 237, 289, 301.

13 Merton, *Gandhi on Non-Violence*, 4, note, and 6.

14 Iyer, *Essential Writings*, 223.

15 Gandhi, *Satyagraha in South Africa*, (Ahmedabad: Navajivan Publishing House, 1950), 338. My attention was drawn to this important statement by Gandhi by an article that documents some of the innovative tactics he designed in his attempts to elicit good-will from his adversaries and to achieve justice and agreement with people of other faiths. See Francis X. Clooney, "Experimenting with Gandhi: The Harmony of Religions as Deed and Memory," *Journal of the Indological Society of Southern Africa* 1 (1993): 55–67.

16 References are to Merton's *Gandhi on Non-Violence.*

17 Mahatma Gandhi, *The Bhagvadgita* (*sic*) (Delhi: Orient Paperbacks, no date), 9. Other references in this paragraph come from this book.

18 Iyer, *Essential Writings*, 65–9.

19 Ibid., 172; see 204.

20 Ibid., 158, 167.

21 Reported by Richard Gregg and quoted by Nanda, *Gandhi and His Critics*, 150.
22 Gandhi, *Bhagvadgita*, 284.
23 Iyer, *Essential Writings*, 156, 180, 230.
24 Lonergan, "*Pantôn Anakephalaiôsis* (The Restoration of All Things)" and "Analytic Concept of History," ed. Frederick E. Crowe and Robert M. Doran, *Method: Journal of Lonergan Studies* 9 (1991): 134–72, and 11 (1993): 1–35.
25 Frederick E. Crowe, "Bernard Lonergan and Liberation Theology," in *Appropriating the Lonergan Idea*, ed. Michael Vertin (Washington, DC: The Catholic University of America Press, 1989), 116–26, at 118; see also 117. On the Antigonish Movement, see Jim Lotz and Michael R. Welton, *Father Jimmy: The Life and Times of Father Jimmy Tompkins* (Wreck Cove, Cape Breton Island: Breton Books, 1997).
26 See Crowe, *Appropriating the Lonergan Idea*, 118–23.
27 J.T.F. Jordens, "Gandhi and the *Bhagavadgita*," in *Modern Indian Interpreters of the Bhagavadgita*, ed. Robert N. Minor (Albany, NY: SUNY Press, 1986), 88–109.
28 "Healing and Creating in History," in *A Third Collection: Papers by Bernard J.F. Lonergan, S.J.*, ed. Frederick E. Crowe (New York: Paulist Press, 1985), 100–9.
29 There is no "Gandhi" entry in the *Combined Lonergan Indices* of the Lonergan Center at Santa Clara University.
30 Gandhi, *Bhagvadgita*, 142.
31 Gandhi, "Speech on Capital and Labour and Rowlatt Bills," in *CW*, vol. XV, 165; Iyer, *Essential Writings*, 238
32 Iyer, *Essential Writings*, 243.
33 Lonergan, *De Verbo Incarnato* (Rome: Gregorian University Press, 1964), pt. V, thesis 17, and Supplement, articles 22–3. Forthcoming as *The Incarnate Word*, volume 8 of *Collected Works of Bernard Lonergan.*
34 Gandhi, "Who Can Offer Satyagraha?" in *CW*, vol. IX, 227.
35 Gandhi, *Bhagvadgita*, 183.
36 Erik H. Erikson, *Gandhi's Truth: On the Origins of Militant Nonviolence* (New York: Norton, 1969), 335.
37 Iyer, *Essential Writings*, 118; see 381: "For human beings renunciation itself is enjoyment."
38 Iyer, *Essential Writings*, 171, 167.
39 "Crime of Reading Bible," in *CW*, vol. XXXI, 350. Bharatan Kumarappa has collected and edited Gandhi's essential texts on Hinduism and world religions in *Hindu Dharma* (Ahmedabad: Navajivan Press, 1950. See also

A. Pushparajan, *From Conversion to Fellowship: The Hindu-Christian Encounter in the Gandhian Perspective* (Allahabad: St Paul Publication, 1990).

40 See Traynor, "The Moral Bases," 75 and 78.

41 Nanda, *Gandhi and His Critics*, 142.

42 Gandhi, *Bhagvadgita*, 28, 125, 140, 144, 151–2, 226.

Study 14

Foundations for Human Rights

Far from being cerebral and aloof, Bernard Lonergan was concerned with world events. Early in his life he was assailed by the kind of worries that Latin-American liberation theologians were eventually to embrace. His intellectual evolution was influenced by the economic crisis of the 1930s. As mentioned in the preceding Study, in the 1940s he became interested in the Antigonish Movement, whose aims included helping depressed fishermen in Nova Scotia, encouraging the needed rebirth of rural living, and working on problems as concrete as the hungry children evacuated from the bombed cities of England. In 1944 he completed two manuscripts on the economy, a theme to which he returned in the 1970s, with an emphasis on its ethical dimension.

And yet Lonergan never wrote about human rights. One of the reasons is that throughout his career as a professor of dogmatic theology, he never taught that subject. Another factor, according to John Haughey, was that he never liked the static conceptualism that mars the usual understanding of the notion of right, as it is restricted to a classicist and prescriptivist code of behaviour.[1] Therefore, expounding "the characteristics of an ethics using categories derived from Lonergan," Frederick Crowe states that "it will focus sharply on responsibility rather than on rights."[2] He explains: "Rights are sacred, but they are not fundamental. What is fundamental is responsibility, and to recognize that is to change the whole course of ethical thinking ... There is a world of difference between the question, What are my rights here? and the question, What should I do in this situation?"[3]

In fact, the question, "What should I do in this situation?" takes into consideration the rights of others as well as my rights. It includes the question, "What are *their* rights here?" Most importantly, it suggests that Lonergan's emphasis bears on questioning. For that reason, the first two sections of this Study will present human nature as dynamic and intentional. Thereafter, humanity will be diagnosed as wounded and Lonergan's solution will be introduced. At the end, we shall be able to conclude that notwithstanding his silence on the topic, he offers a significant contribution to the founding and strengthening of the legitimacy and practice of human rights.[4]

HUMAN NATURE AS DYNAMIC

We can say that implicitly in Lonergan's works, the rights that people possess are grounded in human nature. Based on Aristotle, he views nature as a *physis*, namely a principle of movement (in the questions) and of rest (in the answers).[5] His concept of nature is inspired not only by Aristotle but also by Thomas Aquinas. The latter's approach is in no way static, since he begins his explication of natural law with a listing of three human tendencies. He puts forward the principle that "the order of the precepts of the natural law is according to the order of the natural inclinations." Then he briefly describes the three essential human inclinations:

> In man there is first of all an inclination to good in accordance with the nature which he has in common with all substances: inasmuch as every substance seeks the preservation of its own being, according to its nature. And by reason of this inclination, whatever is a means of preserving human life, and of warding off its obstacles, belongs to the natural law. Secondly, there is in man an inclination to things that pertain to him more specially, according to that nature which he has in common with other animals. And in virtue of this inclination, those things are said to belong to the natural law, which nature has taught to all animals, such as sexual intercourse, education of offspring and so forth. Thirdly, there is in man an inclination to good according to the nature of his reason, which nature is proper to him; thus man has a natural inclination to know the truth about God, and to live in society. And in this respect, whatever pertains to this inclination belongs to the natural law, for instance, to shun ignorance, to avoid offending those among whom one has to live, and other such things regarding the above inclination.[6]

Lonergan accentuates the anthropological aspect of St Thomas's thought.[7] Following in the steps of the medieval master, he sees human nature from a dynamic viewpoint.[8] We can notice an important difference from the modern perspective that, initiated by Descartes, finds its base in logic. Let us look, for instance, at Kant's categorical imperative; "Act only according to that maxim whereby you can at the same time will that it should become a universal law."[9] This imperative does not cover much ground. Consequently, on the one hand, Kant's fundamental commands, primary though they are, are very few: Respect for one's life (no suicide), faithfulness to one's promises (no lying), development of one's talents (no laziness), and assistance to people in need (no indifference). On the other hand, he has the twofold merit of grounding the dignity of the human person as an end and not a means and of recognizing its autonomy.[10]

By contrast, Lonergan finds universality in human nature and its expression as natural law, not in self-evident propositions or in innate certitudes, but in that nature as operating concretely, that is, as historicity.[11] For him, the way human nature functions can be empirically known by all, as our next section will demonstrate.

GROUNDING BASIC RIGHTS IN HUMAN INTENTIONALITY

Despite his disagreement with Descartes and Kant, Lonergan accepts the turn to the subject, which characterizes modern philosophy. Under the influence of Brentano and Husserl, he focuses on intentionality, but in his own terms, namely as human subjectivity in quest of objectivity, dynamically open and orientated towards reality. The discovery of its inalienable operations grounds and safeguards human rights.

In his description of the constitutive elements of intentionality, Lonergan utilizes the metaphor of four levels, as was expounded in Study 4. Here is a short reminder. First, on the level of experience, intentionality receives sense data. Second, on the level of understanding, one asks, "What is it?" "Why?" "How?" and the outcome is an idea, a concept, a hypothesis. Third, on the level of judgment, one asks, "Does what I have understood match the data it is meant to explain?" which results in an intellectual commitment, expressed as a yes or a no. Fourth, on the level of behaviour, one asks, "Is this prospect really what I want?" which leads to the final steps of making a decision and taking action (see *Method*, 9, 14–20, 120–1).

Corresponding to those four levels of intentionality are four transcendental precepts: be attentive, be intelligent, be reasonable, be responsible (see *Method*, 231). Each of those precepts demands a respect for reality – a reality that includes at once nature (the infrahuman beings) and the human race (the persons). Basic human rights, that is, those that are inherent and inalienable, derive from an obedience to the transcendental precepts. It is thanks to the normative operations of intentionality that they are endowed with an objective validity.

Human rights, which are not all basic, are myriad; there exists no definitive list of them. Nevertheless, the implementation of the transcendental precepts triggers four procedures: attention to information from events and documents; acts of understanding; verifications; and value-judgments. All those activities are purposeful and generate responsible actions. For example, whenever one particular human right conflicts with another, the four levels of intentionality facilitate an enquiry, which terminates in a comparative evaluation, with a given degree of probability attached to it.

Furthermore, we may ask, "Are all legally adopted rights morally valid?" Once more, intentionality plays the role of the critical referent. The judgments that people utter must be considered. Alongside popular judgments, those of the jurists and the intellectuals may criticize the ideological framework spontaneously employed. Laws are meant to concretize prior, underlying exigencies, namely those of natural right. Lonergan's philosophy is incompatible with the voluntarism of juridical positivism, according to which specific rights derive from legal decisions (which at times are but expressions of the arbitrary will of those who exercise power).

If rights are to be more than mere legal decisions, what is needed is that a whole society – or the majority of it – create and partake of cherished values in a way that is as harmonious as possible. Thus Lonergan delineates a scale of values:

> We may distinguish vital, social, cultural, personal, and religious values in an ascending order. Vital values, such as health and strength, grace and vigor, normally are preferred to avoiding the work, privations, pains involved in acquiring, maintaining, restoring them. Social values, such as the good of order which

> conditions the vital values of the whole community, have to be preferred to the vital values of individual members of the community. Cultural values do not exist without the underpinning of vital and social values, but none the less they rank higher. Not on bread alone doth man live. Over and above mere living and operating, men have to find a meaning and value in their living and operating. It is the function of culture to discover, express, validate, criticize, correct, develop, improve such meaning and value. Personal value is the person in his self-transcendence, as loving and being loved, as originator of values in himself and in his milieu, as an inspiration and invitation to others to do likewise. Religious values, finally, are at the heart of the meaning and value of man's living and man's world. (*Method*, 31–2)

Thanks to appropriating one's four levels of intentionality and one's participation in the five kinds of value just mentioned in the scale, a person develops a philosophic consciousness that is no longer indiscriminate, but rather more differentiated. Moreover, values may interact in a very beneficial, mutually corrective fashion, as Joseph Ogbonnaya points out: "By the principle of sublation (which means the successive levels retain, preserve and go beyond and complete the previous levels), the various values relate to one another, lead to one another and give rise to the other. Thus religious values guide personal values, personal values guide cultural values that equally guide social values, and social values in turn guide vital values."[12]

A WOUNDED HUMANITY

By ignoring higher values, namely cultural, personal, and religious values, we bring about distortions in society and in ourselves. However, it is not an easy task to respect even lower values, namely vital and social values. For instance, oppression and misery are the "price" to pay for monetary gains. So we are confronted with injustices, either occasional or structural.

As briefly noted in Study 11, Lonergan describes four types of bias: dramatic, individual, group, and general (see *Insight*, 214–31 and 239–61). Let us highlight the first and the fourth, since his contribution on these two types is more original than on the other two. The second and the third will simply be adumbrated here.

Dramatic bias lodges between the psyche and the understanding. It consists in what Lonergan calls a "scotosis" (from the Greek *skotōsis*, darkening) and a "scotoma," the resultant blind spot. It is at the same time unconscious and conscious, hidden and visible. So it is comprised of two aspects: "Fundamentally, the scotosis is an unconscious process. It arises, not in conscious acts, but in the censorship that governs the emergence of psychic contents. Nonetheless, the whole process is not hidden from us" (*Insight*, 215). We shall see later that there are possibilities of overcoming the scotosis.

Lonergan thinks that scotosis is a way of blocking the emergence of insights and the formulating of questions that might lead to insights. This exclusion of relevant questions and pertinent insights goes along with the malfunctioning of our inner censorship:

> The scotosis is an aberration, not only of the understanding, but also of the censorship. Just as wanting an insight penetrates below the surface to bring forth schematic images that give rise to the insight, so not wanting an insight has the opposite effect of repressing from consciousness a scheme that would suggest the insight … The aberration of the censorship is primarily repressive; its positive activity is to prevent the emergence into consciousness of perspectives that would give rise to unwanted insights; it introduces, so to speak, the exclusion of arrangements into the field of the unconscious. (*Insight*, 215–16)

As a result, images and affects that could have been helpful are inhibited:

> The effect of the repression is an inhibition imposed upon neural demand functions. However, if we distinguish between demands for images and demands for affects, it becomes clear that the inhibition will not block both in the same fashion. For insights arise, not from the experience of affects, but rather from imaginative presentations. Hence, to prevent insights, repression will have to inhibit demands for images. On the other hand, it need inhibit demands for affects only if they are coupled with the undesired images. (*Insight*, 216)

However, the censor may become less and less repressive, so as to cooperate with the emergence of images that are the materials of insight. It is in this transformation that psychological conversion consists, as was noted in Study 2.[13]

Individual bias and group bias do not need long explanations: individual and group egoisms are biased in favour of merely subjective interests over the truly good. I will describe each of them compendiously (see *Insight*, 244–50). By individual bias, Lonergan means the egoism that consists in not recognizing the limits of one's self-interest. The individual self is hampered because of an incomplete development of its intelligence, since it negates its orientation towards the common good. It thus precludes questions and insights that might have thrown light on the needs of others.

Group bias is the same phenomenon, except on a much broader plane. It takes place whenever the interests of two or more antagonistic groups clash, each group having recourse to offensive and defensive mechanisms. A particular group or social class employs its practical reason and its power to exploit, manipulate, dominate, coerce, or marginalize other groups or classes. As Lonergan points out, social tension arises between, on one side, people's subjective desires, pleasures, privations, and sufferings and, on the other side, their intelligence sensitive to the practical requirements of an objective situation. Then a transition may take place from the tension to the dialectic (a term which in the book *Insight* has a negative sense). That which could have been simply natural degenerates into a dialectic: the natural and inevitable tension culminates in a social dialectic, which is unnatural, avoidable, and prejudicial.

The fourth bias is the general bias (see *Insight*, 250–61). It is rooted in a spontaneous tendency of common sense. Each culture or subculture possesses its common sense, namely its horizon of knowledge and interest. For all their enormous differences, all the species of common sense suffer from a crucial deficiency: common sense is essentially concerned with practical affairs and not in theoretical issues, even when the latter have to do with practical affairs. Accordingly, as Plato discovered, it almost unavoidably brushes aside the questions or ideas that contradict its favourite opinions. In addition to this blindness, with regard to social facts that actually are absurd, common sense considers them as normal. Being enclosed in its pragmatic horizon and lacking an ability to criticize collective situations in a somewhat objective manner, common sense envisages only immediate results and overlooks long-term consequences. Because it sustains a long cycle of decadence, it produces harmful effects that are no less considerable than those brought about by group bias. Finally, without the light of Christian revelation, common sense cannot take account of the limitations intrinsic to its short-sighted practicality.

A COMPLEX SOLUTION

Acutely aware of these types of bias, Lonergan rejects the solution proposed by political liberalism. Speaking of "enlightened self-interest," the editors of his essay on economics deplore its average construal: "This has tended to mean calculating how looking out for someone else's interest might be to one's advantage. According to Lonergan, it has not meant the surmounting of biases that is required for overcoming social and cultural decline."[14]

Another stratagem that he rules out is "the relentless modern drift to social engineering and totalitarian controls" (*Insight*, 767). Speaking of "depersonalization," he states: "Wherever the demon of organization invades and tyrannizes his [man's] spirit, there are at once revealed the signs of a false and abnormal orientation of society."[15] He denounces manipulations worked out by technocrats: "Managing people is not treating them as persons. To treat them as persons one must know and one must invite them to know."[16] Owing to the emphasis that he places on the desire to know, he views human beings not as passive subjects, who ought to receive without any discussion the decisions taken in their absence by those who keep power in their own hands. On the contrary, being subjects who know or who strive to know, they are participants and agents in their own history and, as such, they have the right to have a say in their own destiny. The acknowledgment of the active and free character of persons and groups is the first step towards an overcoming of the biases. The sphere of human rights is not a restricted enclave, a zone of concessions granted in order to mitigate the rigours of the economy and of politics.

Concretely, this entails that, beyond the physical respect owed to human beings, we must cultivate a more profound one: respect for the culture of the communities that are in a position of political weakness (without overlooking their lacunas). It also requires an attentiveness to family life, intersubjective links, neighbourhood relationships, work conditions, skills, values, customs, commitments. Such respect presupposes means and structures of communication, as well as freedom to elect one's leaders, to make decisions, and to listen to the voice of victims.

In this way, the practical reason of a community can be exercised by a good number of agents. Lonergan's philosophy is inimical to a tendency of the international market that intensifies consumerist individualism. In contrast to this dehumanizing current, his philosophy may be said to be "communitarian," provided it is not understood as favouring only small-scale communities.[17] Indeed he puts forward a definite communitarianism, tempered by an accent on each person's relation with the Transcendent. Moreover, his version of equality is not abstract, as in Kant, but enriched by his sense of community with its stress on concrete relationships.

In *Insight* the religious solution that Lonergan delineates consists in the influence of "conjugate forms," namely faith, hope, and charity (see *Insight*, 718–51) engaged in the combat for the common good and against evil. In *Method in Theology* he generally shies away from the Thomist vocabulary of faith, hope, and charity, and he speaks of "conversions." His three conversions – intellectual, moral, and religious – were described before (in Study 2). The fourth conversion, called psychic conversion, which addresses the dramatic bias and which was briefly defined in Study 2, will not be re-introduced here, since it was explicated, not by Lonergan, but by Doran. Let us now rehearse the three conversions, in order to see how they endeavour to offset the lacunas of the biases.

Intellectual conversion consists in appropriating one's cognitional processes, which take place on the first three levels of intentionality. The intellectually converted have found out that objectivity is not a matter of taking a good look at what is "already out there now real" (see "Real," in the Index of *Insight*, 859). On the contrary, they have gone beyond the imagination – while sublating it – to the higher sorts of operations: insights and judgments. From this epistemological discovery a correct metaphysics of being proceeds.[18]

The two other conversions result in an all-important modification of attitudes on the fourth level of intentionality. Moral conversion demands not only horizontal developments, which require no basic changes in one's preferences, but also a vertical exercise of liberty, a leap upwards, so to speak, thanks to which a person begins to consistently promote an option for true values, even when they are not compatible with pleasures or satisfactions. Thus one can respect not only individual values but the scale of values (introduced above) and can reach personal authenticity.

The third type of conversion, the religious one, is the fruit of a very special experience: a conscious and dynamic state of being in love unrestrictedly with the mystery. This experience generates faith, which Lonergan defines as "the knowledge born of religious love" (*Method*, 115). This faith is of the greatest profit for our world, for it recognizes values more clearly and, in the face of evil, is willing to sacrifice much in order to undo it. Faith is a source of wise and courageous decisions, which make up for the decadence caused by sin. Groups inspired by faith, hope, and charity see their motivation enhanced so that they readily promote the common good, bring about progress, and counter social decline (see *Method*, 117–18). However, before the last day of history, we shall never experience a perfect society. Since the dialectic of conflictive positions is permanent, it will always be necessary to make a valiant effort as we study situations and problems, analyze them, and search for remedies and improvements.

To this religious solution, Lonergan adds several more down-to-earth and yet not ineffective solutions: education (as reported in Study 11); psychotherapy (see *Insight*, 223–7); having recourse to humour, irony, and satire (already practised by Kierkegaard)[19] in the arts, literature, and mass media, so as to expose aberrations (see *Insight*, 647–9); the fact that any pronounced aberrant process is hardly bearable and thus creates the principles for its own reversal, thanks to sound responses on the part of critical reason and of culture (see *Insight*, 249–50 and 259–61); and the interdisciplinary collaboration of competent scholars in the examination and revision of political projects and in the implementation of a "cosmopolis," namely a free and reforming cooperation on a global scale (see *Insight*, 263–7; *Method*, 359–61 and 365–7).

CONCLUSION

The conception that Lonergan has developed of the human being and its life in society helps situate the issues, problems, tools, and remedies for a praxis of the essential rights. He offers an epistemological-anthropological basis that favours an acknowledgment and a flowering of human rights. In effect, the epistemological ground is human nature, as observable in its invariable dynamisms, namely the four levels of intentionality along with their transcendental precepts. Furthermore, the anthropological ground explains the distortions that affect those dynamisms. Lastly, his solution also includes a vision of human persons in relation with others, a threefold conversion, and several, more ordinary means having to do with education, psychotherapy, the arts, literature, mass media, and philosophy-enlightened political cooperation.

Thus a professor of jurisprudence in Washington correctly opined: "Although Lonergan was not directly concerned with the specifics of ethical or legal rules, some moralists have found inspiration and guidance in his paradigm for their own rethinking of natural law and the moral teachings associated with it."[20]

NOTES

1 See John C. Haughey, "Responsibility for Human Rights: Contributions from Bernard Lonergan," *Theological Studies* 63 (2002): 764–85, at 774.

2 Frederick E. Crowe, "Rethinking Moral Judgments: Categories from Lonergan," in *Science et Esprit* 40 (1988): 137–52, at 144. This passage (144–6) is missing in Frederick E. Crowe, *Lonergan and the Level of Our Time*, ed. Michael Vertin (Toronto: University of Toronto Press, 2010), 315–31.

3 Crowe, "Rethinking Moral Judgments," at 145.

4 I do not have the space here to compare Lonergan's thought on human rights with Maritain's. See Jacques Maritain, *Man and State* (Washington, DC: The Catholic University of America Press, 1951); see also Meghan J. Clark, "Reasoned Agreement versus Practical Reasonableness: Grounding Human Rights in Maritain and Rawls," *The Heythrop Journal* 53 (2012): 637–48.

5 See Lonergan's "Natural Right and Historical Mindedness," in *A Third Collection: Papers by Bernard Lonergan*, ed. Frederick E. Crowe (New York, Paulist Press, 1985), 169–83, at 172.

6 Thomas Aquinas, *Summa Theologiae*, I-II, q. 94, a. 2.

7 See Johannes Baptist Metz, *Christliche Anthropozentrik: Über die Denkform des Thomas von Aquin* (Munich: Kösel Verlag, 1962).

8 Mauricio Beuchot Puente also proposes an option for a renewed Thomist "iusnaturalismo," in *Los derechos humanos y su fundamentación filosófica* (México, D.F.: Universidad Iberoamericana, 1997).

9 Immanuel Kant, *Grounding for the Metaphysics of Morals*, trans. James W. Ellington, volume 4 of the Akademie edition (Indianapolis, IN: Hackett Publishing Company, 1981), 421 and, for the rest of my paragraph, 422–3, 429, 431.

10 See Louis Roy, "Does Christian Faith Rule out Human Autonomy?" *The Heythrop Journal* 53 (2012): 606–23.

11 See Lonergan, "Natural Right and Historical Mindedness," 172–5.

12 Joseph Ogbonnaya, *Lonergan, Social Transformation, and Sustainable Human Development* (Eugene, OR: Pickwick Publications, 2013), 96; for the sake of clarity, I have modified the punctuation. On pages 93–108, Ogbonnaya helpfully reports Robert M. Doran's elaboration of Lonergan's scale of values.

13 See Elizabeth A. Murray, "Unmasking the Censor," in *Meaning and History in Systematic Theology: Essays in Honor of Robert M. Doran, SJ*, ed. John D. Dadosky (Milwaukee: Marquette University Press, 2009), 423–47.

14 "Editors' Introduction" to *Macroeconomic Dynamics: An Essay in Circulation Analysis*, ed. Frederick G. Lawrence, Patrick H. Byrne, and Charles C. Hefling, volume 15 of *Collected Works of Bernard Lonergan* (Toronto, University of Toronto Press, 1999), lxx.

15 Lonergan, "Respect for Human Dignity," in *Shorter Papers*, ed. Robert C. Croken, Robert M. Doran, and H. Daniel Monsour, volume 20 of *Collected Works of Bernard Lonergan* (Toronto, University of Toronto Press, 2007), 121–7, at 126.

16 Lonergan, "Cognitional Structure," in *Collection*, ed. Frederick E. Crowe and Robert M. Doran, volume 4 of *Collected Works of Bernard Lonergan* (Toronto, University of Toronto Press, 1988), 205–21, at 220–1.

17 See Francisco Sierra Gutiérrez, "La comunidad como sujeto," *Universitas Philosophica* (Bogota), No. 39 (December 2002): 79–118.

18 See *Insight*, chaps. 12–16, and Oliva Blanchette, *Philosophy of Being: A Reconstructive Essay in Metaphysics* (Washington, DC: The Catholic University of America Press, 2003).

19 See Amy Pauley, "The Significance of Satire and Humour in Lonergan's Ethical Framework," *Theoforum* 43 (2012): 269–90.

20 David Granfield, *The Inner Experience of Law: A Jurisprudence of Subjectivity* (Washington, DC: The Catholic University of America Press, 1988), 209. This work is much indebted to Lonergan's thought.

Study 15

God's Providence: For What Kind of World?

Although belief in providence is very strong in popular religion, non-believers generally find the notion of providence unacceptable. Even some believers have difficulty with it when trying to be clear-minded and honest. One facet of this problem is the challenge of developing an overall worldview that flows from reflections on the universe as presented by the contemporary sciences and that takes into consideration lived experience, particularly in its painful aspects. In this Study, based on Lonergan's *Grace and Freedom* and *Insight*, I will propose a conception of divine providence that takes into account the sciences as well as the search for meaning within both personal and collective history. I will situate this position halfway between two inadequate visions of the universe: as pure chance or as inflexible necessity. The thesis to be submitted consists in envisioning a complete intelligibility, which to a great extent lies beyond our comprehension, although our personal and collective experience allows us to discover partial meanings marked by contingency and chance.

NEITHER PURE CHANCE NOR NECESSITY

Our world is not a world of pure chance. Many signs invite us to believe that there is a certain intelligibility to the universe. While fully aware of suffering, numerous writers belonging to the great religions such as Hinduism, Judaism, Christianity, and Islam have described the order and beauty of the world, and they have detected in this a divine intention. Further, since the epoch of Socrates, almost all philosophers have presented the human entity as a person in search of meaning. On their side, the scientists always assume that it is possible to organize data in terms of hypotheses that shed light on that data.

Can one move from intelligibility pertaining to a certain domain – which has just been adumbrated – to comprehensive, all-encompassing intelligibility? Without comprehensive intelligibility, the limited, partial meanings, which characterize people's day-to-day living or even their highly significant events, would never find their complete justification;[1] the "why" of their origins and the nature of their final destination would remain obscure. This would leave the human spirit unsatisfied in its desire to understand. Partial meanings nevertheless do provide sufficient explanation at the level of scientific intelligibility. Methodologically, the intelligibility of each scientific field restricts itself to one aspect of reality.

In addition, total intelligibility evokes the spectre of strict necessity, which must be dispelled immediately. Our world is not a world of necessity, even if some quasi-necessary regularities can be detected (sometimes improperly labelled "determinisms"). There is no encompassing determinism, no chain of predetermined events, no vast machine in which each piece must be exactly as it is and not otherwise. The deterministic mechanism of modern science was a philosophical error that scientists got rid of in the early twentieth century. Beings and events are contingent in the sense that they could be otherwise and they might even not have happened at all. And in a contingent universe without determinism, it is possible to construe the human person as truly free.

Because beings and events are contingent, there is chance in the world. Chance presupposes contingency, namely the fact that something happens and yet might have not happened. However, the "chance" that I am repudiating and that will be defined further on is the "pure chance" as the Nobel laureate in physiology and medicine Jacques Monod defines it, namely total randomness, mere coincidence, basic absence of intelligibility in the non-human world. Of course, Monod recognizes ordered systems in biological processes; for him it is their emergence that is a matter of pure chance.[2]

SCIENCE AND CONCRETE EVENTS

Having created beings placed in multiform spatial and temporal interactions, God makes use of them, and even their shortcomings, in order to bring about new events, things, and individuals. According to Thomas Aquinas, providence consists in an "application," that is, in putting agents in relation to each other, in assigning each being to the proper effect that it can exercise on another.[3] The totality of these relations constitutes an overall order that Aquinas attributes to the eternal mind of God, which lies beyond our capacity to *understand* exhaustively.[4] Nevertheless, even though this overall order is beyond us, we can still *affirm* it philosophically, within or outside an experience of religious faith, basing ourselves on the incomplete meanings that are within our grasp. Every time we are struck by a sequence of events producing a meaningful result, we glimpse a fragment of this comprehensive intelligibility.

When scientific laws explain series of causes and effects, they provide an account of *how* things happen, but they do not give the reason *why* this being or this circumstance influences that other being at such-and-such a time and place. The natural sciences are especially limited in this regard, because they do not address the meanings inherent in human action. And even the human sciences, which endeavour to spot meanings inherent in human action, postulate only a partial intelligibility, because each of them (such as economics, sociology, psychology, etc.) has its restricted area of application.

While we can detect certain orderly arrangements and certain developments over time, the excessive quantity of facts to be noted and the presence of evil keep us from having access to the comprehensive intelligibility of the world. The "why" of concrete events lies beyond the grasp of the sciences. It remains incomprehensible insofar as we are unaware of many dimensions of what happens. And yet it is not totally incomprehensible; for example, in history and in our reflection on the events that surround us, we can identify sequences that have meaning.

SCIENTIFIC LAWS AND CHANCE

As has already been pointed out, although the sciences explain *how* things happen, they nevertheless do not give the reason *why* this being or this circumstance influences that other being at such-and-such a time and place. They do not explain all the temporal and spatial relations that beings have with one another. Consequently, the sciences admit to being methodologically incomplete and therefore not always refractory to a philosophical or religious affirmation of providence.

What do the sciences really explain? Two kinds of intelligibility pertain to phenomena. Motions or events in the world are explained first by abstract, classical laws, such as those of Newtonian physics. But these classical laws only help to understand schemes of recurrence within which interacting entities are located. The second type of intelligibility is provided by statistical frequencies, which are abstract like the classical laws, and yet are closer to reality since they measure the actual occurrences of events. Hence the statistical frequencies must be situated halfway between the classical laws and what is going on concretely (see Lonergan, *Insight*, chapters 3 and 4). (A third type of intelligibility, which regards concrete events, will be introduced later.)

Let us briefly illustrate the statistical intelligibility. For example, subatomic particles, as much as atmospheric phenomena or economic transactions, can be understood by means of mathematical curves from which the corresponding concrete events do not diverge systematically. As Joseph Flanagan remarks, "a probability is an ideal frequency which expects exceptions but does not expect 'systematic' exceptions."[5] If the divergence is systematic, it gives rise to a revision of the statistics by taking account of factors that so far have not been closely examined; such a reconsideration brings about the elaboration of new curves that more adequately fit a larger number of data.

This means that, as mentioned before, there are two sorts of scientific intelligibility, classical and statistical, as well as chance in the world. Lonergan defines chance as "the nonsystematic divergence of actual frequencies from the ideal frequencies named probabilities" (*Insight*, 137).[6] There is almost always a certain distance between statistical ideality and de facto actuality. Chance consists in any random – that is, non-systematic – divergence from statistical probabilities.[7] Chance is any concrete event which results from a coincidence of conditions or factors of varying probability – for instance, the lottery or accidents.

Flipping heads or tails is an example of chance where the probability of each outcome is equal, namely 50 per cent. In effect, chance is at play when it is not possible to foretell with certainty which outcome will occur. Chance can be defined as a haphazard result that cannot be predicted by classical and even by statistical laws. Thus, the mathematical probability in a lottery is clear; it depends on the number of tickets purchased and the number of winners to be picked. Chance is something else, namely the fact that just *this* person is the winner. Or again, in the case of an accident, chance is the fact that *this* person or *this* group is the victim. The sciences do not explain chance in its particularity. They can tell us a lot about a child's illness and its causes but have nothing to offer as to why *this* child has been affected. They can make us understand *how* this happened but not *why* it happened to this child.

The intelligibilities studied by the sciences can be integrated into the philosophic notion of providence. But human beings wonder about the concrete and wonder especially about chance. For instance, faced with evil, people often ask why it has happened to them – to this individual, to that group. So belief in providence also rests as much on the experience of uniform order as on the experience of chance, because both these experiences give rise to a search for meaning. In theology, which reflects this dual search for meaning, it is equally vital to integrate both scientific regularities and concrete encounters with chance.

Only if we knew all the anterior conditions – which is virtually impossible – could we understand, post factum, how a chance event occurred. So no event whatsoever can be entirely explained. Hence religiosity tends to deny chance and to replace it with a pseudo-explanation, namely providentialism, which does not agree with the sound doctrine of providence that is presented in this Study. The phenomenon of astonishing coincidences leads scores of people to believe that God's providence controls all particular events one by one as they unfold in time. This providentialist explanation often arises spontaneously in happy circumstances where people feel protected or favoured. But the same interpretation is scandalous in the case of ill-fated events that burden those unfortunates without resources, without help, crushed by what happens to them. This is why, faced by events such as Hitler's systematic extermination of the Jews, some resort to the presence of Satan. The erroneous interpretive approach emphasizes direct action by God or Satan or some non-scientific source, while downplaying contingency in the world as well as human freedom.

PROGRESSIVE INTEGRATION OF CONDITIONS IN A HIERARCHICAL WORLD

In this universe made up of more or less probable events, lower phenomena condition but do not determine the higher phenomena. For instance, chemical phenomena have a physical base, biological phenomena have a chemical base, etc. Conditions that are inferior and yet sufficient (in terms of number and of temporal and physical proximity) are thus required for superior phenomena to appear and last. God's providence ordains these conditions, not in a predetermined manner for each individual, but according to probabilities that are high enough for the things to occur according to an overall plan for groups of individuals. For example, in a specific cultural situation all the conditions are in place for the possibility that A, B, C, D, E will marry; it is statistically probable that a certain number of these persons will marry; no particular one of them is predestined to marry; A could marry B, or could marry C, or could remain unmarried.

As one goes higher in the scale of beings, one becomes aware that various levels of functioning apply together. The chemical conditions of the brain do not exclude the physical conditions; the neurological conditions of living do not exclude the chemical conditions; the psychical conditions do not exclude the neurological conditions; the conditions arising from reflection and from freedom do not exclude the psychical conditions; supernatural conditions do not exclude conditions that arise from reflection and from freedom.

One feature of order in the universe is the fact that there are cycles, i.e. schemes of recurrence, whose elements – concrete, dynamic, interactive – repeat. The water cycle is an example. Then there are sets of cycles such as the integration in animals of the neurological, respiratory, vascular, digestive, muscular, and motor systems; or the economic, social, cultural, and religious cycles of humanity. When we move from examining physical cycles to examining physiological ones or human ones, we notice a greater complexity.

EVIL AND LIBERATION

These cycles can be disturbed when one element breaks down. Thus, *physical* evil is the loss of a good that is proper to a being (for example, the absence of wings for a bird). In a finite world, it seems that, contrary to what most Fathers of the Church thought, physical (not moral) evil affecting some individuals would have been wished by the Creator in view of the greater good of a species or of the universe as a whole. Thus, for example, the fact that carnivores naturally devour other animals – which they must do in order to feed themselves and survive, and which is nevertheless an instance of physical evil – is not the result of original sin; it antecedes it.

In the same way, God does not prevent *moral* evil and does not punish all individuals directly in proportion to their faults during their life on earth. The Creator establishes a world structured in such a fashion that human beings, endowed with freedom, do wrong to themselves when they wrong others. In fact, across the ages, humans have become incapable of acting harmoniously. This corresponds to the doctrine of original sin, that dreadful solidarity in the consequences of moral evil.

What is worse is that these consequences are distributed unevenly. This unequal and unjust distribution is explained by a long series of sins and of errors resulting from sins. God does not mend this distribution artificially, but gives human beings the possibility of making corrections. Thus he remains present to humanity by maintaining the resources of creation, by sending his Son among us, and by giving his Holy Spirit who acts within persons to help them love and see clearly. As a result, with human collaboration, God begins to rectify the defective cycles of recurrence (see *Insight*, chapters 7 and 20). And if he does not transform these situations in an instant, it is in order to involve human freedom actively in its process of restoration. Only at time's end will at once physical and moral evil be eliminated (see Isa 11:6–9 and Rev 21:3–5).

GOD'S POWER, CONTINGENCY, AND FREEDOM

The contingency of events (the fact that they could be different or could fail to occur at all) and human freedom take nothing away from the almighty power of God. The power of God is manifested in the fact that he desires and establishes contingency and freedom in our world.[8] Human freedom can accomplish great things thanks to various resources, the most important of which is hope. The Creator sets up a zone of action for human and sub-human agents. He is the master of history, but not like an absolute monarch. He allows the playing-out of probabilities for groups of events. He accepts the risk of human freedom, sin, and salvation. Indeed, he shares his creativity with human beings. Thus, as bringing about novelties together, God and finite agents are co-creators.

We may compare this with parents who encourage their children to do things for themselves that the parents could do in their place. This is the better approach in that the children develop through their own efforts, successes, and failures. But this freedom of children does not entail self-sufficiency. Adults too derive motivation and energy from the friendships that sustain them. Parents encourage their children, and friends support other adults, and yet they do not act in their place. This is an analogy for God's presence in human lives.

God's mastery is not diminished at all by the fact that it is mysterious and mediated. On the contrary, we could think of God's presence like that of an enormous spring of water, a source of life; the water flows through the mountains in accordance with natural and statistical laws, shaped by interacting conditions that reflect an overall design. In his eternal present, God knows all the details, he knows that this stream takes that detour around this rock, etc. God is the first cause, hence is not one of the secondary causes that operate within time; the original spring does not cease its immediate influence upon the stream, and the current that is the stream is no different from the spring. The cooperation between God and the world constitute a single, identical action.

CONCLUSION

In this Study I have endeavoured to avoid a naïve providentialism and to show how the notion of divine providence can go along with a scientific approach. However, in addition to this intellectual grounding, the acceptance of God's active presence in the world also has affective roots, which were not examined here. So the reflections I have elaborated, while hopefully useful, are far from encompassing all facets of the belief in divine providence.[9] Indeed, the limited philosophical and theological remarks offered do not detract from the need for an extremely challenging personal struggle with the fact of evil, which *seems* to give the lie to trust in God.

NOTES

1 On partial meanings, see Louis Roy, *Coherent Christianity* (Ottawa: Novalis, 2005), chap. 2, section 3: "The discovery of comprehensive meaning."

2 See Jacques Monod, *Chance and Necessity*, trans. A. Wainhouse (New York: Random House, Vintage Books, 1972); see also Kenneth R. Melchin, *History, Ethics and Emergent Probability: Ethics, Society and History in the Work of Bernard Lonergan* (Lanham, MD: University Press of America, 1987), chap. 2.

3 On "application" in Aristotle and Aquinas, see *Grace and Freedom: Operative Grace in the Thought of Thomas Aquinas*, ed. Frederick E. Crowe and Robert M. Doran, volume 1 of *Collected Works of Bernard Lonergan* (Toronto: University of Toronto Press, 2000). See also "Application" in the Index of Concepts and Names.

4 See Thomas Aquinas, *Summa Theologiae*, I, q. 14, q. 22, a. 1, and I-II, q. 93.

5 Joseph Flanagan, *Quest for Self-Knowledge: An Essay in Lonergan's Philosophy* (Toronto: University of Toronto Press, 1997), 67; see 65–8 and 96–100.

6 See Lonergan's "Mission and the Spirit," section 2: "Probability and Providence," in *A Third Collection: Papers by Bernard J.F. Lonergan, S.J.*, ed. Frederick E. Crowe (New York: Paulist Press, 1985).

7 See Philip McShane, *Randomness, Statistics and Emergence* (Notre Dame, IN: University of Notre Dame Press, 1970), esp. chap. 6.

8 See Lonergan, *Grace and Freedom*, chaps. I-4, I-5, II-3, and II-4.

9 See Louis Roy's essay, "Evil, Miracles, and Science," to be published soon.

General Conclusion

What were the few recurrent *Leitmotive* of this book? There are three, already adumbrated in the Introduction, to which readers may want to go back. The first is Lonergan's basic standpoint, stemming from a self-knowledge that is explicated in an accurate description of the fourfold human intentionality as cross-cultural. This self-knowledge issues forth as a cognitional theory that gives rise to a critical realism and to a "generalized empirical method," which is integrative and, at times, evaluative.

The second *Leitmotiv* is his nuanced assessment of human historicity; by means of its insights, judgments, and decisions, historicity fashions culture. This sense of history allows scholars to appreciate both the particular and the permanent in works that convey meanings. Hence, for instance, Lonergan's redefining of belief and faith (the former being more specific and the latter being more universal). Hence also his warning about classicism as a shortcoming which has blighted Roman Catholic thinking for a long time, and about current relativism as ultimately impeding human commitment to truth.

The third *Leitmotiv* is his frequent situating of the God-question and religious experience within the life of the human spirit in general, while honouring their cognitive aspects as much as their affective aspects. Hence the locating of religion amid the various cognitive operations and affective states in the realms of meaning.

In addition to theology, philosophy of religion, and epistemology, Lonergan applied these three *Leitmotive* to several fields: ethics, politics, human rights, the economy, and the natural and social sciences, with implications for theology, mysticism, liturgy, education, psychology, and more than a few branches of philosophy. To get a sense of that variety as well as of the overlapping and the coherence of the themes presented in this book, I recommend the perusal of the Conclusion offered in each of the Studies.

Besides Lonergan's complex treatments of individual issues, we find in his writings numerous seminal reflections that invite further elaboration. Thus I have developed some of his ideas and I have compared his thoughts with those of other thinkers, with a view to continuing the conversation.

Index